THE SCHOLAR'S LIBRARY
General Editor:—GUY BOAS, M.A.

EIGHT ESSAYISTS

EIGHT ESSAYISTS

Edited by
A. S. CAIRNCROSS
M.A., D.LITT.

LONDON
MACMILLAN & CO LTD
NEW YORK · ST MARTIN'S PRESS
1965

MACMILLAN AND COMPANY LIMITED
Little Essex Street London WC 2
also Bombay Calcutta Madras Melbourne

THE MACMILLAN COMPANY OF CANADA LIMITED
70 Bond Street Toronto 2

ST MARTIN'S PRESS INC
175 Fifth Avenue New York 10100 NY

PRINTED IN GREAT BRITAIN

ACKNOWLEDGMENTS

THANKS are due to Mrs. G. K. Chesterton and Messrs. Methuen & Co., Ltd., for permission to reprint the five essays by the late G. K. Chesterton included in this volume .

FOREWORD

It was the Renaissance that produced the first essayists—Montaigne and Bacon, and taught them to know their own ignorance. While the men of the Middle Ages offered a ready-made explanation of the universe, these men of the Renaissance were content to make an attempt at one aspect of experience and write a little about something. They wrote essays.

But for full efflorescence the essay had to wait for the further advance of tolerance and practical wisdom in " our indispensable eighteenth century "—the end of religious wars, the Bill of Rights, and the beginnings of liberal thought. Sir Roger de Coverley's famous phrase " that much might be said on both sides "—which could well serve as the essayist's motto—was no empty commonplace, but the expression of an historical advance of the greatest importance, bought with a century of bitter political experience. It is true that in the age of Anne the essay, like every other form of literature, often did service as a weapon in the party struggle ; yet its main development, in Steele and Addison, was devoted to the cultivation of good sense, moderation, tolerance—in short, civilization.

At the same period, the rise of the newspaper furnished its opportunity, and the coffee-house developed its form and style. With its initial advantage of brevity, the essay has appeared almost entirely in periodical form. It has continued faithfully to reproduce the good sense and good conversation, the wit, and ridicule of eccentricity, that were first perfected in the coffee-house clubs of Queen Anne's London. In general, therefore, it has been more closely related to ordinary life, and less narrow, pedantic, or artificial, than almost any other form of literature.

From the eighteenth century may be dated the intimate tone of the essay. This intimacy, now one of his most cherished privileges, gives the essayist the inestimable advantage of taking his reader completely into his confidence, as if for a short friendly talk, between equals, on any subject under the sun. Such confidence is flattering. The reader is won over from the very beginning. An essay of Steele's, for example, opening with the casual mention of some incident he has met with, wins the attention at once ; retains it as he goes on to develop off-handedly his thoughts and applications ; and satisfies it in good time as he rounds off with a sound and sensible conclusion. Bacon, of course, is not intimate. But no essayist since Steele has quite closed the door of personal revelation. Some, indeed, like Lamb or Chesterton, have thrown it wide open, revealing themselves, their lives, habits, and eccentricities, down to the most trivial detail.

The essay thus ranges over the whole field of human activity. Bacon uses it for philosophical observations ; Steele, Addison, and Goldsmith, for social criticism ; Lamb throws into its mould everything from dramatic criticism to denunciation of bad manners ; Hazlitt speaks of painting, the Lake poets, the Ministers of the day, fives, moral philosophy, and psychology ; Stevenson writes of men and books ; Chesterton tilts at all things " that creep, or swim, or fly, or run." And their style is as various and elastic as their matter.

The essay must be not only intimate and varied, but also simple. The simplicity of the finished essay, however, is the deceptive simplicity of great art. Its very ease and natural tone are the high level of prose form and style. Dr. Johnson, advising on the formation of a good prose style, demanded the giving of one's days and nights to the study of Addison. The great essayists have also been great prose-writers.

This anthology introduces eight authors of high quality, many of whom have also excelled in other branches of literature. The first seven are usually regarded as the outstanding familiar essayists of the last three centuries. To this company the late G. K. Chesterton has been added as a representative of that number of great twentieth century essayists whom the scope and limits of this volume unfortunately exclude. The selection thus illustrates the main trend of a form of personal and individual expression in which English literature and the great English authors have peculiarly excelled.

A. S. C.

CONTENTS

FRANCIS BACON

RICHARD STEELE

JOSEPH ADDISON

CONTENTS

OLIVER GOLDSMITH

CHARLES LAMB

WILLIAM HAZLITT

R. L. STEVENSON

G. K. CHESTERTON

FRANCIS BACON

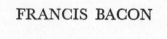

OF STUDIES

STUDIES serve for Delight, for Ornament, and for Ability. Their Chiefe Use for Delight, is in Private-nesse and Retiring ; For Ornament, is in Discourse ; And for Ability, is in the Judgement and Disposition of Businesse. For Expert Men can Execute, and perhaps Judge of particulars, one by one ; But the generall Counsels, and the Plots, and Marshalling of Affaires, come best from those that are *Learned.* To spend too much Time in *Studies*, is Sloth ; To use them too much for Ornament, is Affectation ; To make Judgement wholly by their Rules is the Humour of a Scholler. They perfect Nature, and are per-fected by Experience : For Naturall Abilities, are like Naturall Plants, that need Proyning by *Study :* And *Studies* themselves, doe give forth Directions too much at Large, except they be bounded in by experience. Crafty Men Contemne *Studies* ; Simple Men Admire them ; And Wise Men Use them : For they teach not their owne Use ; But that is a Wisdome without them, and above them, won by Observation. Reade not to Contradict, and Confute ; Nor to Beleeve and Take for granted ; Nor to Finde Talke and Discourse ; But to weigh and Consider. Some *Bookes* are to be Tasted, Others to be Swallowed, and some Few to be Chewed and Digested : That is, some *Bookes* are to be read onely in Parts ; Others to be read but not Curiously ; And some Few to be read wholly, and with Diligence and Attention. Some *Bookes* also may be read by Deputy, and Extracts made of them by Others : But that would be, onely in the lesse important Arguments, and the Meaner Sort of *Bookes :* else distilled *Bookes*, are like Common distilled Waters, Flashy Things. Reading maketh a Full Man ; Conference a Ready Man ; And Writing an Exact Man. And therefore, If a Man Write little, he had need have a Great memory ; If he Conferre little, he had need have a Present Wit ; And if he Reade little, he had need have much Cunning, to seeme to know that, he doth not. *Histories* make Men Wise ; *Poets* Witty ; The *Mathematicks* Subtill ; *Naturall Philosophy* deepe ; *Morall* Grave ; *Logick* and *Rhetorick* Able to Contend. *Abeunt studia in Mores.* Nay there is no Stond or Impediment in the Wit, but may be wrought out by Fit *Studies :* Like as Diseases of the Body, may have Appropriate Exercises. Bowling is good for the Stone and Reines ; Shooting for the Lungs and Breast ; Gentle Walking for the Stomacke ; Riding for the Head ; And the like. So if a Mans Wit be Wandring, let him *Study* the *Mathematicks* ; For in Demonstrations, if his Wit be called away never so little, he must begin again : If his Wit be not Apt to distinguish or find differences, let him *Study* the *Schoole-men* ; For they are *Cymini sectores.* If he be not Apt to beat over Matters, and to call up one Thing, to Prove and Illustrate another, let him *Study* the *Lawyers Cases* : So every Defect of the Minde, may have a Speciall Receit.

OF TRAVAILE

TRAVAILE, in the younger Sort, is a Part of Education ; In the Elder, a Part of Experience. He that *travaileth* into a Country, before he hath some Entrance into the Language, goeth to *Schoole*, and not to *Travaile*. That Young Men travaile under some Tutor, or grave Servant, I allow well ; So that he be such a one, that hath the Language, and hath been in the Country before ; whereby he may be able to tell them, what Things are worthy to be seene in the Country where they goe ; what Acquaintances they are to seeke ; What Exercises or discipline the Place yeeldeth. For else young Men shall goe hooded, and looke abroad little. It is a strange Thing, that in Sea voyages, where there is nothing to be seene, but Sky and Sea, Men should make Diaries ; but in *Land-Travaile*, wherein so much is to be observed, for the most part, they omit it ; As if Chance, were fitter to be registred, then Observation. Let Diaries, therefore, be brought in use. The Things to be seene and observed are : The Courts of Princes, specially when they give Audience to Ambassadours : The Courts of Justice, while they sit and heare Causes ; And so of Consistories Ecclesiasticke : The Churches, and Monasteries, with the Monuments which are therein extant : The Wals and Fortifications of Cities and Townes ; And so the Havens & Harbours : Antiquities, and Ruines : Libraries ; Colledges, Disputations, and Lectures, where any are : Shipping and Navies : Houses, and Gardens of State, and Pleasure, neare great Cities : Armories : Arsenals : Magazens : Exchanges : Burses ; Ware-houses : Exercises of Horsemanship ; Fencing ; Trayning of Souldiers ; and the like : Comedies ; Such whereunto the better Sort of persons doe resort ; Treasuries of Jewels, and Robes ; Cabinets, and Rarities : And to conclude, whatsoever is memorable in the Places ; where they goe. After all which, the Tutors or Servants, ought to make diligent Enquirie. As for Triumphs ; Masques ; Feasts ; Weddings ; Funeralls ; Capitall Executions ; and such Shewes ; Men

5

need not to be put in mind of them ; Yet are they
not to be neglected. If you will have a Young Man,
to put his *Travaile*, into a little Roome, and in short
time, to gather much, this you must doe. First, as
was said, he must have some Entrance into the
Language, before he goeth. Then he must have such
a Servant, or Tutor, as knoweth the Country, as was
likewise said. Let him carry with him also some
Card or Booke describing the Country, where he
travelleth ; which will be a good Key to his Enquiry.
Let him keepe also a Diary. Let him not stay long
in one Citty, or Towne ; More or lesse as the place
deserveth, but not long : Nay, when he stayeth in one
City or Towne, let him change his Lodging, from one
End and Part of the Towne, to another ; which is a
great Adamant of Acquaintance. Let him sequester
himselfe from the Company of his Country men, and
diet in such Places, where there is good Company of
the Nation, where he travaileth. Let him upon his
Removes, from one place to another, procure Re-
commendation, to some person of Quality, residing
in the Place, whither he removeth ; that he may use
his Favour, in those things, he desireth to see or know.
Thus he may abridge his *Travaile*, with much profit.
As for the acquaintance, which is to be sought in
Travaile ; That which is most of all profitable, is
Acquaintance with the Secretaries, and Employd
Men of Ambassadours ; For so in *Travailing* in one
Country he shall sucke the Experience of many. Let
him also see and visit, Eminent Persons, in all Kindes,
which are of great Name abroad ; That he may be
able to tell, how the Life agreeth with the Fame.
For Quarels, they are with Care and Discretion to be
avoided : They are, commonly, for Mistresses ;
Healths ; Place ; and Words. And let a Man be-
ware, how he keepeth Company, with Cholerick and
Quarelsome Persons ; for they will engage him into

their owne Quarels. When a *Travailer* returneth home, let him not leave the Countries, where he hath *Travailed*, altogether behinde him ; But maintaine a Correspondence, by letters, with those of his Acquaintance, which are of most Worth. And let his *Travaile* appeare rather in his Discourse, then in his Apparrell, or Gesture : And in his Discourse, let him be rather advised in his Answers, then forwards to tell Stories : And let it appeare, that he doth not change his Country Manners, for those of Forraigne Parts ; But onely, prick in some Flowers, of that he hath Learned abroad, into the Customes of his owne Country.

OF MASQUES AND TRIUMPHS

THESE Things are but Toyes, to come amongst such Serious Observations. But yet, since Princes will have such Things, it is better, they should be Graced with Elegancy, then Daubed with Cost. *Dancing to Song*, is a Thing of great State, and Pleasure. I understand it, that the Song be in Quire, placed aloft, and accompanied with some broken Musicke : And the Ditty fitted to the Device. *Acting in Song*, especially in *Dialogues*, hath an extreme Good Grace : I say *Acting*, not *Dancing*, (For that is a Meane and Vulgar Thing ;) And the *Voices* of the *Dialogue*, would be Strong and Manly, (A Base, and a Tenour ; No Treble ;) And the *Ditty* High and Tragicall ; Not nice or Dainty. *Severall Quires*, placed one over against another, and taking the Voice by Catches, *Antheme* wise, give great pleasure. *Turning Dances* into *Figure*, is a childish Curiosity. And generally, let it be noted, that those Things, which I here set downe, are such, as doe naturally take the Sense, and not

7

respect Petty Wonderments. It is true, the *Altera-tions of Scenes*, so it be quietly, and without Noise, are Things of great Beauty, and Pleasure : For they feed and relieve the Eye, before it be full of the same Object. Let the *Scenes* abound with *Light*, specially *Coloured* and *Varied* : And let the Masquers, or any other, that are to come down from the *Scene*, have some Motions, upon the *Scene* it selfe, before their Comming down : For it drawes the Eye strangely, & makes it with great pleasure, to desire to see that, it cannot perfectly discerne. Let the *Songs* be *Loud*, and *Cheerefull*, and not *Chirpings*, or *Pulings*. Let the *Musicke* likewise, be *Sharpe*, and *Loud*, and *Well Placed*. *The Colours*, that shew best by Candlelight, are ; White, Carnation, and a Kinde of Sea-Water-Greene ; And *Oes*, or *Spangs*, as they are of no great Cost, so they are of most Glory. As for *Rich Em-broidery*, it is lost, and not Discerned. Let the *Sutes* of the *Masquers*, be Gracefull, and such as become the Person, when the Vizars are off : Not after Examples of Knowne Attires ; Turks, Soldiers, Mariners, and the like. Let *Antimasques* not be long ; They have been commonly of Fooles, Satyres, Baboons, Wilde-Men, Antiques, Beasts, Sprites, Witches, Ethiopes, Pigmies, Turquets, Nimphs, Rusticks, Cupids, Statua's Moving, and the like. As for *Angels*, it is not Comicall enough, to put them in *Anti-Masques* ; And any Thing that is hideous, as Devils, Giants, is on the other side as unfit. But chiefly, let the *Musicke* of them, be Recreative, and with some strange Changes. Some *Sweet Odours*, suddenly comming forth, without any drops falling, are, in such a Company, as there is Steame and Heate, Things of great Pleasure ; & Refreshment. *Double Masques*, one of Men, another of Ladies, addeth State, and Variety. But All is Nothing, except the *Roome* be kept Cleare, and Neat.

For *Justs*, and *Tourneys*, and *Barriers* ; The Glories of them, are chiefly in the Chariots, wherein the Challengers make their Entry ; Especially if they be drawne with Strange Beasts ; As Lions, Beares, Cammels, and the like : Or in the Devices of their Entrance ; Or in the Bravery of their Liveries ; Or in the Goodly Furniture of their Horses, and Armour. But enough of these Toyes.

OF DISCOURSE

SOME in their *Discourse*, desire rather Commendation of Wit, in being able to hold all Arguments, then of Judgment, in discerning what is True : As if it were a Praise, to know what might be Said, and not what should be Thought. Some have certaine Common Places, and Theames, wherein they are good, and want Variety : Which kinde of Poverty is for the most part Tedious, and when it is once perceived Ridiculous. The Honourablest Part of Talke, is to give the Occasion ; And againe to Moderate and passe to somewhat else ; For then a Man leads the Daunce. It is good, in *Discourse*, and Speech of Conversation, to vary, and entermingle Speech, of the present Occasion with Arguments ; Tales with Reasons ; Asking of Questions, with telling of Opinions ; and Jest with Earnest : For it is a dull Thing to Tire, and, as we say now, to Jade, any Thing too farre. As for Jest, there be certaine Things, which ought to be priviledged from it ; Namely Religion, Matters of State, Great Persons, Any Mans present Businesse of Importance, And any Case that deserveth Pitty. Yet there be some, that thinke their Wits have been asleepe ; Except they

9

dart out somewhat, that is Piquant, and to the Quicke : That is a Vaine, which would be brideled ;

Parce Puer stimulis, & fortius utere Loris.

And generally, Men ought to finde the difference, between Saltnesse and Bitternesse. Certainly, he that hath a Satyricall vaine, as he maketh others afraid of his Wit, so he had need be afraid of others Memory. He that questioneth much, shall learne much, and content much ; But especially, if he apply his Questions, to the Skill of the Persons, whom he asketh : For he shall give them occasion, to please themselves in Speaking, and himselfe shall continually gather Knowledge. But let his Questions, not be troublesome ; For that is fit for a Poser. And let him be sure, to leave other Men their Turnes to speak. Nay, if there be any, that would raigne, and take up all the time, let him finde meanes to take them off, and to bring Others on ; As Musicians use to doe, with those, that dance too long Galliards. If you dissemble sometimes your knowledge, of that you are thought to know ; you shall be thought another time, to know that, you know not. Speach of a Mans Selfe ought to be seldome, and well chosen. I knew One, was wont to say, in Scorne ; *He must needs be a Wise Man, he speakes so much of Himselfe* : And there is but one Case wherein a Man may Commend Himselfe, with good Grace ; And that is in commending Vertue in Another ; Especially, if it be such a Vertue, whereunto Himself pretendeth. Speech of Touch towards Others, should be sparingly used : For *Discourse* ought to be as a Field, without comming home to any Man. I knew two *Noblemen*, of the West Part of *England ;* Whereof the one was given to Scoffe, but kept ever Royal Cheere in his House : The other, would aske of those, that had beene at the Others Table ; *Tell truely, was there never*

a Flout or drie Blow given ; To which the Guest would
answer ; *Such and such a Thing passed* : The Lord
would say ; *I thought he would marre a good Dinner*.
Discretion of *Speech*, is more then *Eloquence* ; And to
speak agreeably to him, with whom we deale, is more
then to speake in good Words, or in good Order. A
good continued Speech, without a good Speech of
Interlocution, shews Slownesse : And a Good Reply,
or Second Speech, without a good Setled Speech,
sheweth Shallownesse and Weaknesse. As we see in
Beasts, that those that are Weakest in the Course, are
yet nimblest in the Turne : As it is betwixt the Grey-
hound, & the Hare. To use too many Circumstances,
ere one come to the Matter, is Wearisome ; To use
none at all, is Blunt.

OF YOUTH AND AGE

A MAN that is *Young in yeares*, may be Old in Houres,
if he have lost no Time. But that happeneth rarely.
Generally, *youth* is like the first Cogitations, not so
Wise as the Second. For there is a *youth* in thoughts
as well as in Ages. And yet the Invention of *Young
Men*, is more lively, then that of Old : And Imaginations streame into their Mindes better, and, as it were,
more Divinely. Natures that have much Heat, and
great and violent desires and Perturbations, are not
ripe for Action, till they have passed the Meridian of
their yeares : As it was with *Julius Cæsar, & Septimius
Severus*. Of the latter of whom, it is said ; *Iuventutem
egit, Erroribus, imò Furoribus, plenam*. And yet he was
the Ablest Emperour, almost, of all the List. But
Reposed Natures may doe well in *Youth*. As it is
seene, in *Augustus Cæsar, Cosmus* Duke of *Florence*,

Gaston de Fois, and others. On the other side, Heate and Vivacity in *Age*, is an Excellent Composition for Businesse. *Young Men*, are Fitter to Invent, then to Judge ; Fitter for Execution, then for Counsell ; And Fitter for New Projects, then for Setled Businesse. For the Experience of *Age*, in Things that fall within the compasse of it, directeth them ; But in New Things, abuseth them. The Errours of *Young Men* are the Ruine of Businesse ; But the Errours of *Aged Men* amount but to this ; That more might have beene done, or sooner. *Young Men*, in the Conduct, and Mannage of Actions, Embrace more then they can Hold, Stirre more then they can Quiet ; Fly to the End, without Consideration of the Meanes, and Degrees ; Pursue some few Principles, which they have chanced upon absurdly ; Care not to Innovate, which draws unknowne Inconveniences ; Use extreme Remedies at first ; And, that which doubleth all Errours, will not acknowledge or retract them ; Like an unready Horse, that will neither Stop, nor Turne. *Men of Age*, Object too much, Consult too long, Adventure too little, Repent too soone, and seldome drive Businesse home to the full Period ; But content themselves with a Mediocrity of Successe. Certainly, it is good to compound Employments of both ; For that will be Good for the *Present*, because the Vertues of either *Age*, may correct the defects of both : And good for Succession, that *Young Men* may be Learners, while *Men* in *Age* are Actours : And lastly, Good for *Externe Accidents*, because Authority followeth *Old Men*, And Favour and Popularity *Youth*. But for the Morall Part, perhaps *Youth* will have the preheminence, as *Age* hath for the Politique. A certaine *Rabbine*, upon the Text ; *Your Young Men shall see visions, and your Old Men shall dreame dreames* ; Inferreth, that *Young Men* are admitted nearer to God then *Old* ; Because *Vision* is a clearer Revelation, then a *Dreame*. And certainly, the more a Man drinketh of the World, the more it intoxicateth ; And *Age* doth profit rather in the Powers of Understanding, then in the Vertues of the Will and Affections. There be some have an Over-early Ripenesse in their yeares, which fadeth betimes ; These are first, Such as have Brittle Wits, the Edge whereof is soone turned ; Such as was *Hermogenes* the *Rhetorician*, whose Books are exceeding Subtill ; Who after-wards waxed Stupid. A Second Sort is of those, that have some naturall Dispositions, which have better Grace in *Youth*, then in *Age* : Such as is a fluent and Luxuriant Speech ; which becomes *Youth* well, but not *Age* : So *Tully* saith of *Hortensius ; Idem manebat, neque idem decebat*. The third is of such, as take too high a Straine at the First ; And are Mag-nanimous, more then Tract of yeares can uphold. As was *Scipio Affricanus*, of whom *Livy* saith in effect ; *Ultima primis cedebant*.

RICHARD STEELE

MR. BICKERSTAFF ON HIMSELF

I HAVE received this short epistle from an unknown hand.

" SIR,
" I have no more to trouble you with than to desire you would in your next help me to some answer to the enclosed concerning yourself. In the meantime I congratulate you upon the increase of your fame, which you see has extended itself beyond the bills of mortality."

" SIR,
" That the country is barren of news has been the excuse, time out of mind, for dropping a correspondence with our friends in London ; as if it were impossible out of a coffee-house to write an agreeable letter. I am too ingenuous to endeavour at the covering of my negligence with so common an excuse. Doubtless, amongst friends, bred, as we have been, to the better knowledge of books as well as men, a letter dated from a garden, a grotto, a fountain, a wood, a meadow, or the banks of a river, may be more entertaining than one from Tom's, Will's, White's, or St. James's. I promise, therefore, to be frequent for the future in my rural dates to you. But from fear you should, from what I have said, be induced to believe I shun the commerce of men, I must inform you, that there is a fresh topic of discourse lately arisen amongst the ingenious in our part of the world, and is become the more fashionable for the ladies giving in to it.

17

This we owe to Isaac Bickerstaff, who is very much
censured by some, and as much justified by others.
Some criticise his style, his humour, and his matter ;
others admire the whole man.   Some pretend, from
the informations of their friends in town, to decipher
the author ; and others confess they are lost in their
guesses.   For my part, I must own myself a professed
admirer of the paper, and desire you to send me a
complete set, together with your thoughts of the squire
and his lucubrations."

There is no pleasure like that of receiving praise
from the praiseworthy ; and I own it a very solid
happiness, that these my lucubrations are approved by
a person of so fine a taste as the author of this letter,
who is capable of enjoying the world in the simplicity
of its natural beauties.   This pastoral letter, if I may
so call it, must be written by a man who carries his
entertainment wherever he goes, and is undoubtedly
one of those happy men who appear far otherwise to
the vulgar.   I dare say, he is not envied by the vicious,
the vain, the frolic, and the loud ; but is continually
blessed with that strong and serious delight, which
flows from a well-taught and liberal mind.   With great
respect to country sports, I may say, this gentleman
could pass his time agreeably, if there were not a hare
or a fox in his county.   That calm and elegant satisfaction which the vulgar call melancholy is the true
and proper delight of men of knowledge and virtue.
What we take for diversion, which is a kind of forgetting ourselves, is but a mean way of entertainment, in
comparison of that which is considering, knowing, and
enjoying ourselves.   The pleasures of ordinary people
are in their passions ; but the seat of this delight is in
the reason and understanding.   Such a frame of mind
raises that sweet enthusiasm, which warms the
imagination at the sight of every work of nature, and

turns all round you into a picture and landscape. I shall be ever proud of advices from this gentleman ; for I profess writing news from the learned, as well as the busy world.

As for my labours, which he is pleased to inquire after, if they can but wear one impertinence out of human life, destroy a single vice, or give a morning's cheerfulness to an honest mind—in short, if the world can be but one virtue the better, or in any degree less vicious, or receive from them the smallest addition to their innocent diversions—I shall not think my pains, or indeed my life, to have been spent in vain.

Thus far as to my studies. It will be expected I should in the next place give some account of my life. I shall therefore, for the satisfaction of the present age, and the benefit of posterity, present the world with the following abridgment of it.

It is remarkable, that I was bred by hand, and ate nothing but milk until I was a twelvemonth old ; from which time, to the eighth year of my age, I was observed to delight in pudding and potatoes ; and indeed I retain a benevolence for that sort of food to this day. I do not remember that I distinguished myself in anything at those years, but by my great skill at taw, for which I was so barbarously used, that it has ever since given me an aversion to gaming. In my twelfth year, I suffered very much for two or three false concords. At fifteen I was sent to the University, and stayed there for some time ; but a drum passing by, being a lover of music, I enlisted myself for a soldier. As years came on, I began to examine things, and grew discontented at the times. This made me quit the sword, and take to the study of the occult sciences, in which I was so wrapped up, that Oliver Cromwell had been buried, and taken up again, five years before I heard he was dead. This gave me first the reputation of a conjurer, which has been of great disadvantage to me ever since, and kept me out of all public employments. The greater part of my later years has been divided between Dick's coffee-house, the Trumpet in Sheer Lane, and my own lodgings.

FASHIONABLE AFFECTATIONS

As bad as the world is, I find by very strict observation upon virtue and vice, that if men appeared no worse than they really are, I should have less work than at present I am obliged to undertake for their reformation. They have generally taken up a kind of inverted ambition, and affect even faults and imperfections of which they are innocent. The other day in a coffee-house I stood by a young heir, with a fresh, sanguine, and healthy look, who entertained us with an account of his diet-drink ; though, to my knowledge, he is as sound as any of his tenants.

This worthy youth put me into reflections upon that subject ; and I observed the fantastical humour to be so general, that there is hardly a man who is not more or less tainted with it. The first of this order of men are the valetudinarians, who are never in health ; but complain of want of stomach or rest every day until noon, and then devour all which comes before them. Lady Dainty is convinced, that it is necessary for a gentlewoman to be out of order ; and, to preserve that character, she dines every day in her closet at twelve, that she may become her table at two, and be unable to eat in public. About five years ago, I remember, it was the fashion to be short-sighted. A man would not own an acquaintance until he had first examined him with his glass. At a lady's entrance into the playhouse, you might see tubes immediately levelled at her from every quarter of the pit and side-boxes. However, that mode of infirmity is out, and the age has recovered its sight : but the blind seemed to be succeeded by the lame, and a jaunty limp is the present beauty. I think I have formerly observed, a cane is part of the dress of a prig, and always worn upon a button, for fear he should be thought to have an occasion for it, or be esteemed really, and not genteelly, a cripple. I have considered, but could never find out the bottom of this vanity. I indeed have heard of a Gascon general, who, by the lucky grazing of a bullet on the roll of his stocking, took occasion to halt all his life after. But as for our peaceable cripples, I know no foundation for their behaviour, without it may be supposed that, in this warlike age, some think a cane the next honour to a wooden leg. This sort of affectation I have known run from one limb or member to another. Before the limpers came in, I remember a race of lispers, fine persons, who took an aversion to particular letters in our language. Some never uttered the letter H ; and others had as mortal an aversion to S. Others have had their fashionable defect in their ears, and would make you repeat all you said twice over. I know an ancient friend of mine, whose table is every day surrounded with flatterers, that makes use of this, sometimes as a piece of grandeur, and at others as an art, to make them repeat their commendations. Such affectations have indeed been in the world in ancient times ; but they fell into them out of politic ends. Alexander the Great had a wry neck, which made it the fashion in his court to carry their heads on one side when they came into the presence. One who thought to outshine the whole court, carried his head so over complaisantly, that this martial prince gave him so great a box on the ear, as set all the heads of the court upright.

This humour takes place in our minds as well as bodies. I know at this time a young gentleman, who talks atheistically all day in coffee-houses, and in his degrees of understanding sets up for a free-thinker ; though it can be proved upon him, he says his prayers every morning and evening. But this class of modern wits I shall reserve for a chapter by itself.

Of the like turn are all your marriage-haters, who rail at the noose, at the words, " for ever and aye," and at the same time are secretly pining for some young thing or other that makes their hearts ache by her refusal. The next to these are such as pretend to govern their wives, and boast how ill they use them, when, at the same time, go to their houses and you shall see them step as if they feared making a noise, and are as fond as an alderman. I do not know but sometimes these pretences may arise from a desire to conceal a contrary defect than they set up for. I remember, when I was a young fellow, we had a companion of a very fearful complexion, who, when we sat in to drink, would desire us to take his sword from him when he grew fuddled, for it was his misfortune to be quarrelsome.

There are many, many of these evils, which demand my observation ; but because I have of late been thought somewhat too satirical, I shall give them warning, and declare to the whole world, that they are not true, but false hypocrites ; and make it out that they are good men in their hearts. The motive of this monstrous affectation, in the above-mentioned and the like particulars, I take to proceed from that noble thirst of fame and reputation which is planted in the hearts of all men. As this produces elegant writings and gallant actions in men of great abilities, it also brings forth spurious productions in men who are not capable of distinguishing themselves by things which are really praiseworthy. As the desire of fame in men of true wit and gallantry shows itself in proper instances, the same desire in men who have the ambition without proper faculties, runs wild and discovers itself in a thousand extravagances, by which they would signalise themselves from others, and gain a set of admirers. When I was a middle-aged man, they were many societies of ambitious young men in England, who, in their pursuits after fame, were every night employed in roasting porters, smoking cobblers, knocking down watchmen, overturning constables, breaking windows, blackening signposts, and the like immortal enterprises, that dispersed their reputation throughout the whole kingdom. One could hardly find a knocker at a door in a whole street after a midnight expedition of these *beaux esprits*. I was lately very much surprised by an account of my maid, who entered my bed-chamber this morning in a very great fright, and told me, she was afraid my parlour was haunted ; for that she had found several panes of my windows broken, and the floor strewed with halfpence. I have not yet a full light into this new way, but am apt to think, that it is a generous piece of wit that some of my contemporaries make use of, to break windows, and leave money to pay for them.

ON LONG-WINDED PEOPLE

BOCCALINI, in his *Parnassus*, indicts a laconic writer for speaking that in three words which he might have said in two, and sentences him for his punishment to read over all the works of Guicciardini. This Guicciardini is so very prolix and circumstantial in his writings, that I remember our countryman, Doctor Donne, speaking of that majestic and concise manner in which Moses has described the creation of the world, adds, " that if such an author as Guicciardini were to have written on such a subject, the world itself would not have been able to have contained the books that gave the history of its creation."

I look upon a tedious talker, or what is generally known by the name of a story-teller, to be much more insufferable than even a prolix writer. An author may be tossed out of your hand, and thrown aside when he grows dull and tiresome ; but such liberties are so far from being allowed towards your orators in common conversation, that I have known a challenge sent a person for going out of the room abruptly, and leaving a man of honour in the midst of a dissertation. This evil is at present so very common and epidemical, that there is scarce a coffee-house in town that has not some speakers belonging to it, who utter their political essays, and draw parallels out of Baker's *Chronicle*, to almost every part of her Majesty's reign. It was said of two ancient authors, who had very different beauties in their style, " that if you took a word from one of them, you only spoiled his eloquence ; but if you took a word from the other, you spoiled his sense." I have often applied the first part of this criticism to several of these coffee-house speakers whom I have at present in my thoughts, though the character that is given to the last of those authors, is what I would recommend to the imitation of my loving countrymen. But it is not only public places of resort, but private clubs and conversations over a bottle, that are infested with this loquacious kind of animal, especially with that species which I comprehend under the name of a story-teller. I would earnestly desire these gentlemen to consider, that no point of wit or mirth at the end of a story can atone for the half-hour that has been lost before they come at it. I would likewise lay it home to their serious consideration, whether they think that every man in the company has not a right to speak as well as themselves ? and whether they do not think they are invading another man's property, when they engross the time which should be divided equally among the company to their own private use ?

What makes this evil the much greater in conversation is, that these humdrum companions seldom endeavour to wind up their narrations into a point of mirth or instruction, which might make some amends for the tediousness of them ; but think they have a right to tell anything that has happened within their memory. They look upon matter of fact to be a sufficient foundation for a story, and give us a long account of things, not because they are entertaining or surprising, but because they are true.

My ingenious kinsman, Mr. Humphry Wagstaff, used to say, " the life of man is too short for a storyteller."

Methusalem might be half an hour in telling what o'clock it was : but as for us postdiluvians, we ought to do everything in haste ; and in our speeches, as well as actions, remember that our time is short. A man that talks for a quarter of an hour together in company, if I meet him frequently, takes up a great part of my span. A quarter of an hour may be reckoned the eight and fortieth part of a day, a day the three hundred and sixtieth part of a year, and a year the threescore and tenth part of life. By this moral arithmetic, supposing a man to be in the talking world one third part of the day, whoever gives another a quarter of an hour's hearing, makes him a sacrifice of more than the four hundred thousandth part of his conversable life.

I would establish but one great general rule to be observed in all conversation, which is this, " that men should not talk to please themselves, but those that hear them." This would make them consider, whether what they speak be worth hearing ; whether there be either wit or sense in what they are about to say ; and, whether it be adapted to the time when, the place where, and the person to whom, it is spoken.

For the utter extirpation of these orators and story-tellers, which I look upon as very great pests of society, I have invented a watch which divides the minute into twelve parts, after the same manner that the ordinary watches are divided into hours : and will endeavour to get a patent, which shall oblige every club or company to provide themselves with one of these watches, that shall lie upon the table, as an hour-glass is often placed near the pulpit, to measure out the length of a discourse.

I shall be willing to allow a man one round of my watch, that is, a whole minute, to speak in ; but if he exceeds that time, it shall be lawful for any of the company to look upon the watch, or to call him down to order.

Provided, however, that if any one can make it appear he is turned of threescore, he may take two, or, if he pleases, three rounds of the watch without giving offence. Provided, also, that this rule be not construed to extend to the fair sex, who shall still be at liberty to talk by the ordinary watch that is now in use. I would likewise earnestly recommend this little automaton, which may be easily carried in the pocket without any incumbrance, to all such as are troubled with this infirmity of speech, that upon pulling out their watches, they may have frequent occasion to consider what they are doing, and by that means cut the thread of the story short, and hurry to a conclusion. I shall only add, that this watch, with a paper of directions how to use it, is sold at Charles Lillie's.

I am afraid a *Tatler* will be thought a very im-proper paper to censure this humour of being talkative;

but I would have my readers know that there is a great difference between *tattle* and *loquacity*, as I shall show at large in a following lucubration ; it being my design to throw away a candle upon that subject, in order to explain the whole art of tattling in all its branches and subdivisions.

THE ART OF STORY-TELLING

Tom Lizard told us a story the other day, of some persons which our family know very well, with so much humour and life, that it caused a great deal of mirth at the tea-table. His brother Will, the Templar, was highly delighted with it, and the next day being with some of his Inns of Court acquaintance, resolved (whether out of the benevolence, or the pride of his heart, I will not determine) to entertain them with what he called " a pleasant humour enough." I was in great pain for him when I heard him begin, and was not at all surprised to find the company very little moved by it. Will blushed, looked round the room, and with a forced laugh, " Faith, gentlemen," said he, " I do not know what makes you look so grave, it was an admirable story when I heard it."

When I came home I fell into a profound contemplation upon story-telling, and as I have nothing so much at heart as the good of my country, I resolved to lay down some precautions upon this subject.

I have often thought that a story-teller is born, as well as a poet. It is, I think, certain, that some men have such a peculiar cast of mind, that they see things in another light, than men of grave dispositions. Men of a lively imagination, and a mirthful temper, will represent things to their hearers in the same manner

as they themselves were affected with them ; and
whereas serious spirits might perhaps have been dis-
gusted at the sight of some odd occurrences in life ;
yet the very same occurrences shall please them in a
well-told story, where the disagreeable parts of the
images are concealed, and those only which are
pleasing exhibited to the fancy. Story-telling is therefore not an art, but what we call a " knack " ; it doth
not so much subsist upon wit as upon humour ; and I
will add, that it is not perfect without proper gesticula-
tions of the body, which naturally attend such merry
emotions of the mind. I know very well, that a certain
gravity of countenance sets some stories off to advantage, where the hearer is to be surprised in the end ;
but this is by no means a general rule ; for it is frequently convenient to aid and assist by cheerful looks,
and whimsical agitations. I will go yet further, and
affirm that the success of a story very often depends
upon the make of the body, and formation of the
features, of him who relates it. I have been of this
opinion ever since I criticised upon the chin of Dick
Dewlap. I very often had the weakness to repine at
the prosperity of his conceits, which made him pass
for a wit with the widow at the coffee-house, and the
ordinary mechanics that frequent it ; nor could I myself forbear laughing at them most heartily, though
upon examination I thought most of them very flat
and insipid. I found after some time, that the merit
of his wit was founded upon the shaking of a fat
paunch, and the tossing up of a pair of rosy jowls.
Poor Dick had a fit of sickness, which robbed him of
his fat and his fame at once ; and it was full three
months before he regained his reputation, which rose
in proportion to his floridity. He is now very jolly
and ingenious, and hath a good constitution for wit.

Those who are thus adorned with the gifts of nature
are apt to show their parts with too much ostentation :

THE ART OF STORY-TELLING

I would therefore advise all the professors of this art never to tell stories but as they seem to grow out of the subject-matter of the conversation, or as they serve to illustrate, or enliven it. Stories, that are very common, are generally irksome; but may be aptly introduced, provided they be only hinted at, and mentioned by way of allusion. Those, that are altogether new, should never be ushered in, without a short and pertinent character of the chief persons concerned; because, by that means, you make the company acquainted with them; and it is a certain rule, that slight and trivial accounts of those who are familiar to us administer more mirth, than the brightest points of wit in unknown characters. A little circumstance, in the complexion or dress of the man you are talking of, sets his image before the hearer, if it be chosen aptly for the story. Thus, I remember Tom Lizard, after having made his sisters merry with an account of a formal old man's way of complimenting, owned very frankly, that his story would not have been worth one farthing, if he had made the hat of him whom he represented one inch narrower. Besides the marking distinct characters, and selecting pertinent circumstances, it is likewise necessary to leave off in time, and end smartly. So that there is a kind of drama in the forming of a story, and the manner of conducting and pointing it is the same as in an epigram. It is a miserable thing, after one hath raised the expectation of the company by humorous characters, and a pretty conceit, to pursue the matter too far. There is no retreating, and how poor is it for a story-teller to end his relation by saying " That's all " !

As the choosing of pertinent circumstances is the life of a story, and that wherein humour principally consists; so the collectors of impertinent particulars are the very bane and opiates of conversation. Old

men are great transgressors this way. Poor Ned
Poppy—he's gone—was a very honest man, but was
so excessively tedious over his pipe, that he was not
to be endured. He knew so exactly what they had for
dinner, when such a thing happened ; in what ditch
his bay stone-horse had his sprain at that time, and
how his man John,—no ! it was William, started a
hare in the common-field ; that he never got to the
end of his tale. Then he was extremely particular in
marriages and inter-marriages, and cousins twice or
thrice removed ; and whether such a thing happened
at the latter end of July, or the beginning of August.
He had a marvellous tendency likewise to digressions ;
insomuch that if a considerable person was mentioned
in his story, he would straightway launch out into an
episode on him ; and again, if in that person's story
he had occasion to remember a third man, he broke
off, and gave us his history, and so on. He always
put me in mind of what Sir William Temple informs
us of the tale-tellers in the north of Ireland, who are
hired to tell stories of giants and enchanters to lull
people asleep. These historians are obliged, by their
bargain, to go on without stopping ; so that after the
patient hath by this benefit enjoyed a long nap, he is
sure to find the operator proceeding in his work. Ned
procured the like effect in me the last time I was with
him. As he was in the third hour of his story, and
very thankful that his memory did not fail him, I
fairly nodded in the elbow-chair. He was much
affronted at this, till I told him, " Old friend, you
have your infirmity, and I have mine."

But of all evils in story-telling, the humour of telling
tales one after another, in great numbers, is the least
supportable. Sir Harry Pandolf and his son gave my
Lady Lizard great offence in this particular. Sir
Harry hath what they call a string of stories, which he
tells over every Christmas. When our family visits

there, we are constantly, after supper, entertained with
the Glastonbury Thorn. When we have wondered at
that a little, " Ay, but, father," saith the son, " let us
have the spirit in the wood." After that hath been
laughed at, " Ay, but, father," cries the booby again,
" tell us how you served the robber." " Alack-a-day,"
said Sir Harry, with a smile, and rubbing his forehead,
" I have almost forgot that : but it is a pleasant
conceit, to be sure." Accordingly he tells that and
twenty more in the same independent order ; and
without the least variation, at this day, as he hath
done, to my knowledge, ever since the Revolution. I
must not forget a very odd compliment that Sir Harry
always makes my lady when he dines here. After
dinner he strokes his belly, and says with a feigned
concern in his countenance, " Madam, I have lost
by you to-day." " How so, Sir Harry," replies my
lady. " Madam," says he, " I have lost an excellent
stomach." At this, his son and heir laughs im-
moderately, and winks upon Mrs. Annabella. This
is the thirty-third time that Sir Harry hath been thus
arch, and I can bear it no longer.

As the telling of stories is a great help and life to
conversation, I always encourage them, if they are
pertinent and innocent ; in opposition to those gloomy
mortals, who disdain everything but matter of fact.
Those grave fellows are my aversion, who sift everything with the utmost nicety, and find the malignity of
a lie in a piece of humour, pushed a little beyond exact
truth. I likewise have a poor opinion of those, who
have got a trick of keeping a steady countenance, that
cock their hats, and look glum when a pleasant thing
is said, and ask, " Well ! and what then ? " Men of
wit and parts should treat one another with benevolence : and I will lay it down as a maxim, that if
you seem to have a good opinion of another man's wit,
he will allow you to have judgment.

ON JUDICIOUS FLATTERY

An old acquaintance, who met me this morning, seemed overjoyed to see me, and told me I looked as well as he had known me do these forty years : " but," continued he, " not quite the man you were, when we visited together at Lady Brightly's. Oh! Isaac, those days are over. Do you think there are any such fine creatures now living, as we then conversed with ? " He went on with a thousand incoherent circumstances, which, in his imagination, must needs please me ; but they had quite the contrary effect. The flattery with which he began, in telling me how well I wore, was not disagreeable ; but his indiscreet mention of a set of acquaintance we had outlived, recalled ten thousand things to my memory, which made me reflect upon my present condition with regret. Had he indeed been so kind as, after a long absence, to felicitate me upon an indolent and easy old age ; and mentioned how much he and I had to thank for, who at our time of day could walk firmly, eat heartily, and converse cheerfully, he had kept up my pleasure in myself. But of all mankind, there are none so shocking as these injudicious civil people. They ordinarily begin upon something that they know must be a satisfaction ; but then, for fear of the imputation of flattery, they follow it with the last thing in the world of which you would be reminded. It is this that perplexes civil persons. The reason that there is such a general outcry among us against flatterers is, that there are so very few good ones. It is the nicest art in this life, and is a part of eloquence which does not want the preparation that is necessary to all other parts of it, that your audience should be your well-wishers ; for praise from an enemy is the most pleasing of all commendations.

It is generally to be observed, that the person most agreeable to a man for a constancy is he that has no shining qualities, but is a certain degree above great imperfections ; whom he can live with as his inferior, and who will either overlook, or not observe his little defects. Such an easy companion as this either now and then throws out a little flattery, or lets a man silently flatter himself in his superiority to him. If you take notice, there is hardly a rich man in the world, who has not such a led friend of small consideration, who is a darling for his insignificancy. It is a great ease to have one in our own shape a species below us, and who, without being listed in our service, is by nature of our retinue. These dependants are of excellent use on a rainy day, or when a man has not a mind to dress ; or to exclude solitude, when one has neither a mind to that or to company. There are of this good-natured order, who are so kind as to divide themselves, and do these good offices to many. Five or six of them visit a whole quarter of the town, and exclude the spleen, without fees, from the families they frequent. If they do not prescribe physic, they can be company when you take it. Very great benefactors to the rich, or those whom they call people at their ease, are your persons of no consequence. I have known some of them, by the help of a little cunning, make delicious flatterers. They know the course of the town, and the general characters of persons ; by this means they will sometimes tell the most agreeable falsehoods imaginable. They will acquaint you, that such a one of a quite contrary party said, " That though you were engaged in different interests, yet he had the greatest respect for your good sense and address." When one of these has a little cunning, he passes his time in the utmost satisfaction to himself and his friends ; for his position is never to report or speak a displeasing thing to his friend. As for letting him go on in an error, he knows advice against them is the office of persons of greater talents and less discretion.

The Latin word for a flatterer, *assentator*, implies no more than a person that barely consents ; and indeed such a one, if a man were able to purchase or maintain him, cannot be bought too dear. Such a one never contradicts you ; but gains upon you, not by a fulsome way of commending you in broad terms, but liking whatever you propose or utter ; at the same time, is ready to beg your pardon, and gainsay you, if you chance to speak ill of yourself. An old lady is very seldom without such a companion as this, who can recite the names of all her lovers, and the matches refused by her in the days when she minded such vanities, as she is pleased to call them, though she so much approves the mention of them. It is to be noted that a woman's flatterer is generally older than herself ; her years serving at once to recommend her patroness's age, and to add weight to her complaisance in all other particulars.

We gentlemen of small fortunes are extremely necessitous in this particular. I have indeed one who smokes with me often ; but his parts are so low, that all the incense he does me is to fill his pipe with me, and to be out at just as many whiffs as I take. This is all the praise or assent that he is capable of ; yet there are more hours when I would rather be in his company than in that of the brightest man I know. It would be a hard matter to give an account of this inclination to be flattered ; but if we go to the bottom of it, we shall find, that the pleasure in it is something like that of receiving money which we lay out. Every man thinks he has an estate of reputation, and is glad to see one that will bring any of it home to him. It is no matter how dirty a bag it is conveyed to him in, or by how clownish a messenger, so the money be good.

ON JUDICIOUS FLATTERY

All that we want, to be pleased with flattery, is to believe that the man is sincere who gives it us. It is by this one accident, that absurd creatures often outrun the most skilful in this art. Their want of ability is here an advantage ; and their bluntness, as it is the seeming effect of sincerity, is the best cover to artifice.

Terence introduces a flatterer talking to a coxcomb, whom he cheats out of a livelihood ; and a third person on the stage makes on him this pleasant remark, " This fellow has an art of making fools madmen." The love of flattery is, indeed, sometimes the weakness of a great mind ; but you see it also in persons, who otherwise discover no manner of relish of anything above mere sensuality. These latter it sometimes improves ; but always debases the former. A fool is in himself the object of pity, until he is flattered. By the force of that, his stupidity is raised into affectation, and he becomes of dignity enough to be ridiculous. I remember a droll, that upon one's saying, " The times are so ticklish, that there must great care be taken what one says in conversation " ; answered with an air of surliness and honesty, " If people will be free, let them be so in the manner that I am, who never abuse a man but to his face." He had no reputation for saying dangerous truths ; therefore when it was repeated, " You abuse a man but to his face ? " " Yes," says he, " I flatter him."

It is indeed the greatest of injuries to flatter any but the unhappy, or such as are displeased with themselves for some infirmity. In this latter case we have a member of our club, who, when Sir Jeffrey falls asleep, wakens him with snoring. This makes Sir Jeffrey hold up for some moments the longer, to see there are men younger than himself among us, who are more lethargic than he is.

When flattery is practised upon any other consideration, it is the most abject thing in nature ; nay, I cannot think of any character below the flatterer, except he that envies him. You meet with fellows prepared to be as mean as possible in their condescensions and expressions ; but they want persons and talents to rise up to such a baseness. As a coxcomb is a fool of parts, so is a flatterer a knave of parts.

The best of this order, that I know, is one who disguises it under a spirit of contradiction or reproof. He told an arrant driveller the other day, that he did not care for being in company with him, because he heard he turned his absent friends into ridicule. And upon Lady Autumn's disputing with him about something that happened at the Revolution, he replied with a very angry tone, " Pray, madam, give me leave to know more of a thing in which I was actually concerned, than you who were then in your nurse's arms."

A COFFEE-HOUSE AND ITS FREQUENTERS

It is very natural for a man who is not turned for mirthful meetings of men, or assemblies of the fair sex, to delight in that sort of conversation which we find in coffee-houses. Here a man of my temper is in his element ; for if he cannot talk, he can still be more agreeable to his company, as well as pleased in himself, in being only a hearer. It is a secret known but to few, yet of no small use in the conduct of life, that when you fall into a man's conversation, the first thing you should consider is, whether he has a great inclination to hear you, or that you should hear him. The latter is the more general desire, and I know very able flatterers that never speak a word in praise of the persons from whom they obtain daily favours, but still practise a skilful attention to whatever is uttered by those with whom they converse. We are very curious to observe the behaviour of great men and their clients ; but the same passions and interests move men in lower spheres ; and I, that have nothing else to do but make observations, see in every parish, street, lane, and alley, of this populous city, a little potentate that has his court and his flatterers, who lay snares for his affection and favour by the same arts that are practised upon men in higher stations.

In the place I most usually frequent, men differ rather in the time of day in which they make a figure, than in any real greatness above one another. I, who am at the coffee-house at six in the morning, know that my friend Beaver, the haberdasher, has a levee of more undissembled friends and admirers than most of the courtiers or generals of Great Britain. Every man about him has, perhaps, a newspaper in his hand ; but none can pretend to guess what step will be taken in any one court of Europe, till Mr. Beaver has thrown down his pipe, and declares what measures the allies must enter into upon this new posture of affairs. Our coffee-house is near one of the Inns of Court, and Beaver has the audience and admiration of his neighbours from six till within a quarter of eight, at which time he is interrupted by the students of the house ; some of whom are ready dressed for Westminster at eight in a morning, with faces as busy as if they were retained in every cause there ; and others come in their night-gowns to saunter away their time, as if they never designed to go thither. I do not know that I meet in any of my walks, objects which move both my spleen and laughter so effectually as those young fellows at the Grecian, Squire's, Searle's, and all other coffee-houses adjacent to the law, who rise early for no other purpose but to publish their laziness.

One would think these young virtuosos take a gay cap and slippers, with a scarf and party-coloured gown, to be ensigns of dignity ; for the vain things approach each other with an air, which shows they regard one another for their vestments. I have observed that the superiority among these proceeds from an opinion of gallantry and fashion. The gentleman in the strawberry sash, who presides so much over the rest, has, it seems, subscribed to every opera this last winter, and is supposed to receive favours from one of the actresses.

When the day grows too busy for these gentlemen to enjoy any longer the pleasures of their deshabille with any manner of confidence, they give place to men who have business or good sense in their faces, and come to the coffee-house either to transact affairs, or enjoy conversation. The persons to whose behaviour and discourse I have most regard, are such as are between these two sorts of men ; such as have not spirits too active to be happy and well pleased in a private condition, nor complexions too warm to make them neglect the duties and relations of life. Of these sort of men consist the worthier part of mankind ; of these are all good fathers, generous brothers, friends, and faithful subjects. Their entertainments are derived rather from reason than imagination ; which is the cause that there is no impatience or instability in their speech or action. You see in their countenances they are at home, and in quiet possession of their present instant as it passes, without desiring to quicken it by gratifying any passion, or prosecuting any new design. These are the men formed for society, and those little communities which we express by the word neighbourhoods.

The coffee-house is the place of rendezvous to all that live near it, who are thus turned to relish calm and ordinary life. Eubulus presides over the middle hours of the day, when this assembly of men meet together. He enjoys a great fortune handsomely, without launching into expense ; and exerts many noble and useful qualities, without appearing in any public employment. His wisdom and knowledge are serviceable to all that think fit to make use of them ; and he does the office of a counsel, a judge, an executor, and a friend, to all his acquaintance, not only without the profits which attend such offices, but also without the deference and homage which are usually paid to them. The giving of thanks is displeasing to him. The greatest gratitude you can show him is, to let him see that you are a better man for his services ; and that you are as ready to oblige others, as he is to oblige you.

In the private exigencies of his friends, he lends at legal value considerable sums which he might highly increase by rolling in the public stocks. He does not consider in whose hands his money will improve most, but where it will do most good.

Eubulus has so great an authority in his little diurnal audience, that when he shakes his head at any piece of public news, they all of them appear dejected ; and on the contrary, go home to their dinners with a good stomach and cheerful aspect when Eubulus seems to intimate that things go well. Nay, their veneration towards him is so great, that when they are in other company they speak and act after him ; are wise in his sentences, and are no sooner sat down at their own tables, but they hope or fear, rejoice or despond, as they saw him do at the coffee-house. In a word, every man is Eubulus as soon as his back is turned.

Having here given an account of the several reigns that succeed each other from daybreak till dinner-time, I shall mention the monarchs of the afternoon, on another occasion, and shut up the whole series of them with the history of Tom the Tyrant ; who, as the first minister of the coffee-house, takes the government upon him between the hours of eleven and twelve at night, and gives his orders in the most arbitrary manner to the servants below him, as to the disposition of liquors, coal, and cinders.

THE SPECTATOR CLUB

THE first of our society is a gentleman of Worcestershire, of ancient descent, a baronet, his name Sir Roger de Coverley. His great-grandfather was inventor of that famous country-dance which is called after him. All who know that shire are very well acquainted with the parts and merits of Sir Roger. He is a gentleman that is very singular in his behaviour, but his singularities proceed from his good sense, and are contradictions to the manners of the world only as he thinks the world is in the wrong. However, this humour creates him no enemies, for he does nothing with sourness or obstinacy ; and his being unconfined to modes and forms makes him but the readier and more capable to please and oblige all who know him. When he is in town, he lives in Soho-square. It is said, he keeps himself a bachelor by reason he was crossed in love by a perverse beautiful widow of the next county to him. Before this disappointment, Sir Roger was what you call a fine gentleman, had often supped with my Lord Rochester and Sir George Etherege, fought a duel upon his first coming to town, and kicked bully Dawson in a public coffee-house for calling him youngster. But being ill-used by the above-mentioned widow, he was very serious for a year and a half ; and though, his temper being naturally jovial, he at last got over it, he grew careless of himself, and never dressed afterward. He continues to wear a coat and doublet of the same cut that were in fashion at the time of his repulse, which, in his merry humours, he tells us, has been in and out twelve times since he first wore it. . . . He is now in his fifty-sixth year, cheerful, gay, and hearty ; keeps a good house both in town and country ; a great lover of mankind ; but there is such a mirthful cast in his behaviour, that he is rather beloved than esteemed.

His tenants grow rich, his servants look satisfied, all the young women profess love to him, and the young men are glad of his company. When he comes into a house he calls the servants by their names, and talks all the way upstairs to a visit. I must not omit, that Sir Roger is a justice of the quorum ; that he fills the chair at a quarter-session with great abilities, and three months ago gained universal applause, by explaining a passage in the game act.

The gentleman next in esteem and authority among us is another bachelor, who is a member of the Inner Temple, a man of great probity, wit, and understanding ; but he has chosen his place of residence rather to obey the direction of an old humorsome father, than in pursuit of his own inclinations. He was placed there to study the laws of the land, and is the most learned of any of the house in those of the stage. Aristotle and Longinus are much better understood by him than Littleton or Coke. The father sends up every post questions relating to marriage-articles, leases, and tenures in the neighbourhood ; all which questions he agrees with an attorney to answer and take care of in the lump. He is studying the passions themselves when he should be inquiring into the debates among men which arise from them. He knows the argument of each of the orations of Demosthenes and Tully, but not one case in the reports of our own courts. No one ever took him for a fool ; but none, except his intimate friends, know he has a great deal of wit. This turn makes him at once both disinterested and agreeable : as few of his thoughts are drawn from business, they are most of them fit for conversation. His taste of books is a little too just for the age he lives in ; he has read all, but approves of very few. His familiarity with the customs, manners, actions, and writings of the ancients, makes him a very delicate observer of what occurs to him in the present world. He is an excellent critic, and the time of the play is his hour of business ; exactly at five he passes through New-Inn, crosses through Russell-court, and takes a turn at Will's till the play begins ; he has his shoes rubbed and his periwig powdered at the barber's as you go into the Rose. It is for the good of the audience when he is at a play, for the actors have an ambition to please him.

The person of next consideration is Sir Andrew Freeport, a merchant of great eminence in the city of London ; a person of indefatigable industry, strong reason, and great experience. His notions of trade are noble and generous, and (as every rich man has usually some sly way of jesting, which would make no great figure were he not a rich man) he calls the sea the British Common. He is acquainted with commerce in all its parts, and will tell you that it is a stupid and barbarous way to extend dominion by arms : for true power is to be got by arts and industry. He will often argue, that if this part of our trade were well cultivated, we should gain from one nation ; and if another, from another. I have heard him prove, that diligence makes more lasting acquisitions than valour, and that sloth has ruined more nations than the sword. He abounds in several frugal maxims, amongst which the greatest favourite is, " A penny saved is a penny got." A general trader of good sense is pleasanter company than a general scholar ; and Sir Andrew having a natural unaffected eloquence, the perspicuity of his discourse gives the same pleasure that wit would in another man. He has made his fortunes himself ; and says that England may be richer than other kingdoms, by as plain methods as he himself is richer than other men ; though at the same time I can say this of him, that there is not a point in the compass, but blows home a ship in which he is an owner.

Next to Sir Andrew in the club-room sits Captain Sentry, a gentleman of great courage, good understanding, but invincible modesty. He is one of those that deserve very well, but are very awkward at putting their talents within the observation of such as should take notice of them. He was some years a captain, and behaved himself with great gallantry in several engagements and at several sieges ; but having a small estate of his own, and being next heir to Sir Roger, he has quitted a way of life in which no man can rise suitably to his merit, who is not something of a courtier as well as a soldier. I have heard him often lament, that in a profession where merit is placed in so conspicuous a view, impudence should get the better of modesty. When he had talked to this purpose, I never heard him make a sour expression, but frankly confess that he left the world, because he was not fit for it. A strict honesty, and an even regular behaviour, are in themselves obstacles to him that must press through crowds, who endeavour at the same end with himself, the favour of a commander. He will, however, in his way of talk excuse generals, for not disposing according to men's desert, or inquiring into it ; for, he says, that great man who has a mind to help me, has as many to break through to come at me, as I have to come at him ; therefore he will conclude, that the man who would make a figure, especially in a military way, must get over all false modesty, and assist his patron against the importunity of other pretenders, by a proper assurance in his own vindication. He says it is a civil cowardice to be backward in asserting what you ought to expect, as it is a military fear to be slow in attacking when it is your duty. With this candour does the gentleman speak of himself and others. The same frankness runs through all his conversation. The military part of his life has furnished him with many adventures, in the relation of which he is very agreeable to the company ; for he is never overbearing, though accustomed to command men in the utmost degree below him ; nor ever too obsequious, from a habit of obeying men highly above him.

But that our society may not appear a set of humorists, unacquainted with the gallantries and pleasures of the age, we have amongst us the gallant Will Honeycomb, a gentleman who, according to his years, should be in the decline of his life, but having been very careful of his person, and always had a very easy fortune, time has made but very little impression, either by wrinkles on his forehead, or traces on his brain. His person is well turned, and of a good height. He is very ready at that sort of discourse with which men usually entertain women. He has all his life dressed very well, and remembers habits as others do men. He can smile when one speaks to him, and laughs easily. He knows the history of every mode, and can inform you from which of the French king's wenches our wives and daughters had this manner of curling their hair, that way of placing their hoods ; . . . and whose vanity to show her foot made that part of the dress so short in such a year. In a word, all his conversation and knowledge has been in the female world. As other men of his age will take notice to you what such a minister said upon such an occasion, he will tell you, when the Duke of

44

Monmouth danced at court, such a woman was then smitten—another was taken with him at the head of his troop in the Park. In all these important relations, he has ever about the same time received a kind glance, or a blow of a fan from some celebrated beauty, mother of the present Lord Such-a-one. . . . This way of talking of his very much enlivens the conversation among us of a more sedate turn ; and I find there is not one of the company, but myself, who rarely speak at all, but speaks of him as of that sort of man who is usually called a well-bred fine gentleman. To conclude his character, where women are not concerned, he is an honest worthy man.

I cannot tell whether I am to account him whom I am next to speak of, as one of our company ; for he visits us but seldom ; but when he does, it adds to every man else a new enjoyment of himself. He is a clergyman, a very philosophic man, of general learning, great sanctity of life, and the most exact good breeding. He has the misfortune to be of a very weak constitution, and consequently, cannot accept of such cares and business as preferments in his function would oblige him to ; he is therefore among divines what a chamber-counsellor is among lawyers. The probity of his mind, and the integrity of his life, create him followers, as being eloquent or loud advances others. He seldom introduces the subject he speaks upon ; but we are so far gone in years, that he observes, when he is among us, an earnestness to have him fall on some divine topic, which he always treats with much authority, as one who has no interest in this world, as one who is hastening to the object of all his wishes, and conceives hope from his decays and infirmities. These are my ordinary companions.

JOSEPH ADDISON

SIR ROGER AT HOME

HAVING often received an invitation from my friend Sir Roger de Coverley to pass away a month with him in the country, I last week accompanied him thither, and am settled with him for some time at his country-house, where I intend to form several of my ensuing speculations. Sir Roger, who is very well acquainted with my humour, lets me rise and go to bed when I please ; dine at his own table or in my chamber as I think fit, sit still and say nothing without bidding me be merry. When the gentlemen of the country come to see him, he only shows me at a distance : as I have been walking in his fields I have observed them stealing a sight of me over a hedge, and have heard the knight desiring them not to let me see them, for that I hated to be stared at.

I am the more at ease in Sir Roger's family, because it consists of sober and staid persons : for as the knight is the best master in the world, he seldom changes his servants ; and as he is beloved by all about him, his servants never care for leaving him ; by this means his domestics are all in years, and grown old with their master. You would take his valet-de-chambre for his brother, his butler is grey-headed, his groom is one of the gravest men that I have ever seen, and his coachman has the looks of a privy-counsellor. You see the goodness of the master even in the old house-dog, and in a grey pad that is kept in the stable with great care and tenderness out of regard to his past services, though he has been useless for several years.

I could not but observe with a great deal of pleasure the joy that appeared in the countenance of these ancient domestics upon my friend's arrival at his country-seat. Some of them could not refrain from tears at the sight of their old master ; every one of them pressed forward to do something for him, and seemed discouraged if they were not employed. At the same time the good old knight, with a mixture of the father and the master of the family, tempered the inquiries after his own affairs with several kind questions relating to themselves. This humanity and good nature engages everybody to him, so that when he is pleasant upon any of them, all his family are in good humour, and none so much as the person whom he diverts himself with : on the contrary, if he coughs, or betrays any infirmity of old age, it is easy for a stander by to observe a secret concern in the looks of all his servants.

My worthy friend has put me under the particular care of his butler, who is a very prudent man, and, as well as the rest of his fellow-servants, wonderfully desirous of pleasing me, because they have often heard their master talk of me as of his particular friend.

My chief companion, when Sir Roger is diverting himself in the woods or the fields, is a very venerable man who is ever with Sir Roger, and has lived at his house in the nature of a chaplain above thirty years. This gentleman is a person of good sense and some learning, of a very regular life and obliging conversation : he heartily loves Sir Roger, and knows that he is very much in the old knight's esteem, so that he lives in the family rather as a relation than a dependant.

I have observed in several of my papers, that my friend Sir Roger, amidst all his good qualities, is something of a humorist ; and that his virtues, as well as imperfections, are, as it were, tinged by a certain extravagance, which makes them particularly his, and distinguishes them from those of other men. This cast of mind, as it is generally very innocent in itself, so it renders his conversation highly agreeable, and more delightful than the same degree of sense and virtue would appear in their common or ordinary colours. As I was walking with him last night, he asked me how I liked the good man whom I have just now mentioned ; and, without staying for my answer, told me that he was afraid of being insulted with Latin and Greek at his own table ; for which reason he desired a particular friend of his at the university to find him out a clergyman rather of plain sense than much learning, of a good aspect, a clear voice, a sociable temper : and, if possible, a man that understood a little of back-gammon. " My friend," says Sir Roger, " found me out this gentleman, who, besides the endowments required of him, is, they tell me, a good scholar, though he does not show it : I have given him the parsonage of the parish ; and because I know his value, have settled upon him a good annuity for life. If he outlives me, he shall find that he was higher in my esteem than perhaps he thinks he is. He has now been with me thirty years ; and though he does not know I have taken notice of it, has never in all that time asked anything of me for himself, though he is every day soliciting me for something in behalf of one or other of my tenants, his parishioners. There has not been a law-suit in the parish since he has lived among them ; if any dispute arises they apply themselves to him for the decision ; if they do not acquiesce in his judgment, which I think never happened above once or twice at most, they appeal to me. At his first settling with me, I made him a present of all the good sermons which have been printed in English, and only begged of him that every Sunday he would pronounce one of them in the pulpit. Accordingly, he has digested them into such a series, that they follow one another naturally, and make a continued system of practical divinity.

As Sir Roger was going on in his story, the gentleman we were talking of came up to us ; and upon the knight's asking him who preached to-morrow (for it was Saturday night) told us, the Bishop of St. Asaph in the morning, and Dr. South in the afternoon. He then showed us his list of preachers for the whole year, where I saw with a great deal of pleasure Archbishop Tillotson, Bishop Saunderson, Dr. Barrow, Dr. Calamy, with several living authors who have published discourses of practical divinity. I no sooner saw this venerable man in the pulpit, but I very much approved of my friend's insisting upon the qualifications of a good aspect and a clear voice ; for I was so charmed with the gracefulness of his figure and delivery, as well as with the discourses he pronounced, that I think I never passed any time more to my satisfaction. A sermon repeated after this manner, is like the composition of a poet in the mouth of a graceful actor.

I could heartily wish that more of our country clergy would follow this example ; and instead of wasting their spirits in laborious compositions of their own, would endeavour after a handsome elocution, and all those other talents that are proper to enforce what has been penned by greater masters. This would not only be more easy to themselves, but more edifying to the people.

SIR ROGER AT CHURCH

I AM always very well pleased with a country Sunday, and think, if keeping holy the seventh day were only a human institution, it would be the best method that could have been thought of for the polishing and civilising of mankind. It is certain the country people would soon degenerate into a kind of savages and barbarians, were there not such frequent returns of a stated time in which the whole village meet together with their best faces, and in their cleanliest habits, to converse with one another upon indifferent subjects, hear their duties explained to them, and join together in adoration of the Supreme Being. Sunday clears away the rust of the whole week, not only as it refreshes in their minds the notions of religion, but as it puts both the sexes upon appearing in their most agreeable forms, and exerting all such qualities as are apt to give them a figure in the eye of the village. A country fellow distinguishes himself as much in the churchyard, as a citizen does upon the Change, the whole parish politics being generally discussed in that place either after sermon or before the bell rings.

My friend Sir Roger, being a good churchman, has beautified the inside of his church with several texts of his own choosing ; he has likewise given a handsome pulpit-cloth, and railed in the communion table at his own expense. He has often told me, that at his coming to his estate he found his parishioners very irregular ; and that in order to make them kneel and join in the responses, he gave every one of them a hassock and a common prayer-book : and at the same time employed an itinerant singing master, who goes about the country for that purpose, to instruct them rightly in the tunes of the psalms ; upon which

they now very much value themselves, and indeed
outdo most of the country churches that I have ever
heard.

As Sir Roger is landlord to the whole congregation,
he keeps them in very good order, and will suffer
nobody to sleep in it besides himself; for if by
chance he has been surprised into a short nap at
sermon, upon recovering out of it he stands up and
looks about him, and if he sees anybody else nodding,
either wakes them himself, or sends his servants to
them. Several other of the old knight's particularities
break out upon these occasions: sometimes he
will be lengthening out a verse in the singing-psalms,
half a minute after the rest of the congregation have
done with it; sometimes, when he is pleased with the
matter of his devotion, he pronounces *Amen* three or
four times to the same prayer; and sometimes stands
up when everybody else is upon their knees, to count
the congregation, or see if any of his tenants are
missing.

I was yesterday very much surprised to hear my
old friend, in the midst of the service, calling out to
one John Matthews to mind what he was about, and
not disturb the congregation. This John Matthews
it seems is remarkable for being an idle fellow, and
at that time was kicking his heels for his diversion.
This authority of the knight, though exerted in that
odd manner which accompanies him in all circumstances of life, has a very good effect upon the parish,
who are not polite enough to see anything ridiculous
in his behaviour; besides that the general good sense
and worthiness of his character makes his friends
observe these little singularities as foils that rather
set off than blemish his good qualities.

As soon as the sermon is finished, nobody presumes
to stir till Sir Roger is gone out of the church. The
knight walks down from his seat in the chancel

between a double row of his tenants, that stand bowing to him on each side ; and every now and then inquires how such a one's wife, or mother, or son, or father do, whom he does not see at church ; which is understood as a secret reprimand to the person that is absent.

The chaplain has often told me, that upon a catechising day, when Sir Roger has been pleased with a boy that answers well, he has ordered a bible to be given him next day for his encouragement ; and sometimes accompanies it with a flitch of bacon to his mother. Sir Roger has likewise added five pounds a year to the clerk's place ; and that he may encourage the young fellows to make themselves perfect in the church service, has promised, upon the death of the present incumbent, who is very old, to bestow it according to merit.

The fair understanding between Sir Roger and his chaplain, and their mutual concurrence in doing good, is the more remarkable, because the very next village is famous for the differences and contentions that rise between the parson and the 'squire, who live in a perpetual state of war. The parson is always preaching at the 'squire, and the 'squire to be revenged on the parson never comes to church. The 'squire has made all his tenants atheists, and tithe-stealers ; while the parson instructs them every Sunday in the dignity of his order, and insinuates to them in almost every sermon that he is a better man than his patron. In short, matters are come to such an extremity, that the 'squire has not said his prayers either in public or private this half year ; and that the parson threatens him, if he does not mend his manners, to pray for him in the face of the whole congregation.

Feuds of this nature, though too frequent in the country, are very fatal to the ordinary people ; who are so used to be dazzled with riches, that they pay as much deference to the understanding of a man of an estate, as of a man of learning : and are very hardly brought to regard any truth, how important soever it may be, that is preached to them, when they know there are several men of five hundred a year who do not believe it.

SIR ROGER AT THE ASSIZES

A MAN'S first care should be to avoid the reproaches of his own heart ; his next, to escape the censures of the world ; if the last interferes with the former, it ought to be entirely neglected ; but otherwise there cannot be a greater satisfaction to an honest mind, than to see those approbations which it gives itself seconded by the applauses of the public : a man is more sure of his conduct, when the verdict which he passes upon his own behaviour is thus warranted and confirmed by the opinion of all that know him.

My worthy friend Sir Roger is one of those who is not only at peace within himself, but beloved and esteemed by all about him. He receives a suitable tribute for his universal benevolence to mankind, in the returns of affection and good-will, which are paid him by every one that lives within his neighbourhood. I lately met with two or three odd instances of that general respect which is shown to the good old knight. He would needs carry Will Wimble and myself with him to the county assizes : as we were upon the road Will Wimble joined a couple of plain men who rode before us, and conversed with them for some time ; during which my friend Sir Roger acquainted me with their characters.

" The first of them," says he, " that has a spaniel by

his side, is a yeoman of about a hundred pounds a year, an honest man : he is just within the game act, and qualified to kill a hare or a pheasant : he knocks down a dinner with his gun twice or thrice a week : and by that means lives much cheaper than those who have not so good an estate as himself. He would be a good neighbour if he did not destroy so many partridges : in short he is a very sensible man ; shoots flying ; and has been several times foreman of the petty jury.

"The other that rides along with him is Tom Touchy, a fellow famous for taking the law of every body. There is not one in the town where he lives that he has not sued at a quarter-sessions. The rogue had once the impudence to go to law with the widow. His head is full of costs, damages, and ejectments ; he plagued a couple of honest gentlemen so long for a trespass in breaking one of his hedges, till he was forced to sell the ground it enclosed to defray the charges of the prosecution : his father left him four-score pounds a year ; but he has cast and been cast so often, that he is not now worth thirty. I suppose he is going upon the old business of the willow tree."

As Sir Roger was giving me this account of Tom Touchy, Will Wimble and his two companions stopped short until we came up to them. After having paid their respects to Sir Roger, Will told him that Mr. Touchy and he must appeal to him upon a dispute that arose between them. Will it seems had been giving his fellow-traveller an account of his angling one day in such a hole ; when Tom Touchy, instead of hearing out his story, told him, that Mr. such a one, if he pleased, might *take the law of him* for fishing in that part of the river. My friend Sir Roger heard them both upon a round trot ; and after having paused some time, told them, with the air of a man who would not give his judgment rashly, that

57

much might be said on both sides. They were neither
of them dissatisfied with the knight's determination,
because neither of them found himself in the wrong
by it; upon which we made the best of our way to
the assizes.

The court was sat before Sir Roger came; but notwithstanding all the justices had taken their places
upon the bench, they made room for the old knight
at the head of them; who, for his reputation in the
country, took occasion to whisper in the judge's ear,
*that he was glad his lordship had met with so much good
weather in his circuit.* I was listening to the pro-
ceedings of the court with much attention, and
infinitely pleased with that great appearance and
solemnity which so properly accompanies such a
public administration of our laws; when, after about
an hour's sitting, I observed to my great surprise, in
the midst of a trial, that my friend Sir Roger was
getting up to speak. I was in some pain for him till
I found he had acquitted himself of two or three
sentences, with a look of much business and great
intrepidity.

Upon his first rising the court was hushed, and a
general whisper ran among the country people that
Sir Roger *was up.* The speech he made was so little
to the purpose, that I shall not trouble my readers
with an account of it; and I believe was not so much
designed by the knight himself to inform the court,
as to give him a figure in my eye, and keep up his
credit in the country.

I was highly delighted, when the court rose, to see
the gentlemen of the country gathering about my
old friend, and striving who should compliment him
most; at the same time that the ordinary people
gazed upon him at a distance, not a little admiring
his courage, that was not afraid to speak to the
judge.

In our return home we met with a very odd accident ; which I cannot forbear relating, because it shows how desirous all who know Sir Roger are of giving him marks of their esteem. When we were arrived upon the verge of his estate, we stopped at a little inn to rest ourselves and our horses. The man of the house had, it seems, been formerly a servant in the knight's family ; and to do honour to his old master, had some time since, unknown to Sir Roger, put him up in a sign-post before the door ; so that " the Knight's Head " had hung out upon the road about a week before he himself knew anything of the matter. As soon as Sir Roger was acquainted with it, finding that his servant's indiscretion proceeded wholly from affection and good-will, he only told him that he had made him too high a compliment ; and when the fellow seemed to think that could hardly be, added with a more decisive look, that it was too great an honour for any man under a duke ; but told him at the same time, that it might be altered with a very few touches, and that he himself would be at the charge of it. Accordingly, they got a painter by the knight's directions to add a pair of whiskers to the face, and by a little aggravation of the features to change it into the *Saracen's Head*. I should not have known this story, had not the innkeeper, upon Sir Roger's alighting, told him in my hearing, that his honour's head was brought back last night with the alterations that he had ordered to be made in it. Upon this my friend with his usual cheerfulness related the particulars above mentioned, and ordered the head to be brought into the room. I could not forbear discovering greater expressions of mirth than ordinary upon the appearance of this monstrous face, under which, notwithstanding it was made to frown and stare in a most extraordinary manner, I could still discover a distant resemblance

59

of my old friend. Sir Roger, upon seeing me laugh, desired me to tell him truly if I thought it possible for people to know him in that disguise. I at first kept my usual silence : but upon the knight conjuring me to tell him whether it was not still more like himself than a Saracen, I composed my countenance in the best manner I could, and replied, *That much might be said on both sides.*

These several adventures, with the knight's behaviour in them, gave me as pleasant a day as ever I met with in any of my travels.

SIR ROGER IN LONDON

I WAS this morning surprised with a great knocking at the door, when my landlady's daughter came up to me, and told me, that there was a man below desired to speak with me. Upon my asking her who it was, she told me it was a very grave elderly person, but that she did not know his name. I immediately went down to him, and found him to be the coachman of my worthy friend Sir Roger de Coverley. He told me that his master came to town last night, and would be glad to take a turn with me in Gray's Inn walks. As I was wondering in myself what had brought Sir Roger to town, not having lately received any letter from him, he told me that his master was come up to get a sight of Prince Eugene, and that he desired I would immediately meet him.

I was not a little pleased with the curiosity of the old knight, though I did not much wonder at it, having heard him say more than once in private discourse, that he looked upon Prince Eugenio (for so the knight always calls him) to be a greater man than Scanderbeg.

I was no sooner come into Gray's Inn walks, but I heard my friend upon the terrace hemming twice or thrice to himself with great vigour, for he loves to clear his pipes in good air (to make use of his own phrase), and is not a little pleased with any one who takes notice of the strength which he still exerts in his morning hems.

I was touched with a secret joy at the sight of the good old man, who before he saw me was engaged in conversation with a beggar man that had asked an alms of him. I could hear my friend chide him for not finding out some work, but at the same time saw him put his hand into his pocket and give him sixpence.

Our salutations were very hearty on both sides, consisting of many kind shakes of the hand, and several affectionate looks which we cast upon one another. After which the knight told me, my good friend his chaplain was very well, and much at my service, and that the Sunday before he had made a most incomparable sermon out of Dr. Barrow. " I have left," says he, " all my affairs in his hands, and being willing to lay an obligation upon him, have deposited with him thirty marks, to be distributed among his poor parishioners."

He then proceeded to acquaint me with the welfare of Will Wimble. Upon which he put his hand into his fob, and presented me in his name with a tobacco-stopper, telling me, that Will had been busy all the beginning of the winter in turning great quantities of them ; and that he made a present of one to every gentleman in the country who has good principles, and smokes. He added, that poor Will was at present under great tribulation, for that Tom Touchy had taken the law of him for cutting some hazel sticks out of one of his hedges.

Among other pieces of news which the knight

brought from his country-seat, he informed me that
Moll White was dead ; and that about a month after
her death the wind was so very high, that it blew
down the end of one of his barns. "But for my own
part," says Sir Roger, "I do not think that the old
woman had any hand in it."

He afterwards fell into an account of the diversions
which had passed in his house during the holidays ;
for Sir Roger, after the laudable custom of his
ancestors, always keeps open house at Christmas. I
learned from him, that he had killed eight fat hogs
for this season ; that he had dealt about his chines
very liberally amongst his neighbours ; and that in
particular he had sent a string of hog's-puddings
with a pack of cards to every poor family in the
parish. "I have often thought," says Sir Roger, "it
happens very well that Christmas should fall out in
the middle of winter. It is the most dead and uncomfortable time of the year, when the poor people
would suffer very much from their poverty and cold,
if they had not good cheer, warm fires, and Christmas
gambols to support them. I love to rejoice their poor
hearts at this season, and to see the whole village
merry in my great hall. I allow a double quantity of
malt to my small beer, and set it a-running for
twelve days to every one that calls for it. I have
always a piece of cold beef and a mince-pie upon the
table, and am wonderfully pleased to see my tenants
pass away a whole evening in playing their innocent
tricks, and smutting one another. Our friend Will
Wimble is as merry as any of them, and shows a
thousand roguish tricks upon these occasions."

I was very much delighted with the reflection of my
old friend, which carried so much goodness in it. He
then launched out into the praise of the late act of
parliament for securing the Church of England, and
told me, with great satisfaction, that he believed it

already began to take effect, for that a rigid dissenter who chanced to dine at his house on Christmas Day had been observed to eat very plentifully of his plum-porridge.

After having dispatched all our country matters, Sir Roger made several inquiries concerning the club, and particularly of his old antagonist Sir Andrew Freeport. He asked me with a kind of smile, whether Sir Andrew had not taken the advantage of his absence to vent among them some of his republican doctrines ; but soon after, gathering up his countenance into a more than ordinary seriousness, " Tell me truly," said he, " don't you think Sir Andrew had a hand in the pope's procession "—but without giving me time to answer him, " Well, well," says he, " I know you are a wary man, and do not care for talking of public matters."

The knight then asked me if I had seen Prince Eugenio, and made me promise to get him a stand in some convenient place where he might have a full sight of that extraordinary man, whose presence does so much honour to the British nation. He dwelt very long on the praises of this great general, and I found that, since I was with him in the country, he had drawn many observations together out of his reading in Baker's Chronicle, and other authors, who always lie in his hall window, which very much redound to the honour of this prince.

Having passed away the greatest part of the morning in hearing the knight's reflections, which were partly private and partly political, he asked me if I would smoke a pipe with him over a dish of coffee at Squire's. As I love the old man, I take delight in complying with every thing that is agreeable to him, and accordingly waited on him to the coffee-house, where his venerable aspect drew upon us the eyes of the whole room. He had no sooner seated himself at the upper end of the high table, but he called for a clean pipe, a paper of tobacco, a dish of coffee, a wax-candle, and the Supplement, with such an air of cheerfulness and good humour, that all the boys in the coffee-room (who seemed to take pleasure in serving him) were at once employed on his several errands, insomuch that nobody else could come at a dish of tea, till the knight had got all his conveniences about him.

THE DREAM—AN ALLEGORY

IT is a celebrated thought of Socrates, that if all the misfortunes of mankind were cast into a public stock, in order to be equally distributed among the whole species, those who now think themselves the most unhappy would prefer the share they are already possessed of, before that which would fall to them by such a division. Horace has carried this thought a great deal further, and implies that the hardships or misfortunes we lie under are more easy to us than those of any other person would be, in case we could change conditions with him.

As I was ruminating on these two remarks, and seated in my elbow-chair, I insensibly fell asleep ; when, on a sudden, methought there was a proclamation made by Jupiter, that every mortal should bring in his griefs and calamities, and throw them together in a heap. There was a large plain appointed for this purpose. I took my stand in the centre of it, and saw with a great deal of pleasure the whole human species marching one after another and throwing down their several loads, which immediately grew up into a prodigious mountain that seemed to rise above the clouds.

There was a certain lady of a thin airy shape, who was very active in this solemnity. She carried a magnifying glass in one of her hands and was clothed in a loose flowing robe, embroidered with several figures of fiends and spectres, that discovered themselves in a thousand chimerical shapes, as her garment hovered in the wind. There was something wild and distracted in her look. Her name was *Fancy*. She led up every mortal to the appointed place, after having very officiously assisted him in making up his pack, and laying it upon his shoulders. My heart melted within me to see my fellow-creatures groaning under their respective burdens, and to consider that prodigious bulk of human calamities which lay before me.

There were, however, several persons who gave me great diversion upon this occasion. I observed one bringing in a fardel very carefully concealed under an old embroidered cloak, which upon his throwing it into the heap, I discovered to be poverty. Another, after a great deal of puffing, threw down his luggage, which, upon examining, I found to be his wife.

There were multitudes of lovers saddled with very whimsical burdens composed of darts and flames ; but, what was very odd, though they sighed as if their hearts would break under these bundles of calamities, they could not persuade themselves to cast them into the heap when they came up to it ; but after a few faint efforts, shook their heads and marched away as heavy laden as they came.

I saw multitudes of old women throw down their wrinkles, and several young ones who stripped themselves of a tawny skin. There were very great heaps of red noses, large lips, and rusty teeth. The truth of it is, I was surprised to see the greatest part of the mountain made up of bodily deformities. Observing one advancing towards the heap with a larger cargo than ordinary upon his back, I found upon his near approach that it was only a natural hump, which he disposed of with great joy of heart among this collection of human miseries. There were likewise distempers of all sorts, though I could not but observe that there were many more imaginary than real. One little packet I could not but take notice of, which was a complication of all the diseases incident to human nature, and was in the hand of a great many fine people : this was called the spleen.

But what most of all surprised me was a remark I made, that there was not a single vice or folly thrown into the whole heap : at which I was very much astonished, having concluded within myself that every one would take this opportunity of getting rid of his passions, prejudices, and frailties.

I took notice in particular of a very profligate fellow, who I did not question came laden with his crimes, but upon searching into his bundle I found that, instead of throwing his guilt from him, he had only laid down his memory. He was followed by another worthless rogue who flung away his modesty instead of his ignorance.

When the whole race of mankind had thus cast their burdens, the phantom which had been so busy on this occasion, seeing me an idle spectator of what passed, approached towards me. I grew uneasy at her presence, when of a sudden she held her magnifying glass full before my eyes. I no sooner saw my face in it, but was startled at the shortness of it, which now appeared to me in its utmost aggravation. The immoderate breadth of the features made me very much out of humour with my own countenance, upon which I threw it from me like a mask.

It happened very luckily, that one who stood by me had just before thrown down his visage, which, it seems, was too long for him. It was indeed extended to a most shameful length ; I believe the very chin was, modestly speaking, as long as my whole face. We had both of us an opportunity of mending ourselves, and all the contributions being now brought in, every man was at liberty to exchange his misfortune for those of another person.

I saw, with unspeakable pleasure, the whole species thus delivered from its sorrows : though at the same time, as we stood round the heap, and surveyed the several materials of which it was composed, there was scarce a mortal in this vast multitude who did not discover what he thought pleasures and blessings of life ; and wondered how the owners of them came to look upon them as burdens and grievances.

As we were regarding very attentively this confusion of miseries, this chaos of calamity, Jupiter issued out a second proclamation, that every one was now at liberty to exchange his affliction, and to return to his habitation with any such bundle as should be delivered to him.

Upon this, Fancy began again to bestir herself, and parcelling out the whole heap with incredible activity, recommended to every one his particular packet. The hurry and confusion at this time was not to be expressed. Some observations, which I made upon the occasion, I shall communicate to the public.

A venerable gray-headed man, who had laid down the colic, and who I found wanted an heir to his estate, snatched up an undutiful son that had been thrown into the heap by his angry father. The graceless youth, in less than a quarter of an hour, pulled the old gentleman by the beard, and had like to have knocked his brains out ; so that meeting the true father, who came towards him in a fit of the gripes, he begged him to take his son again, and give him back his colic ; but they were incapable, either of them, to recede from the choice they had made.

A poor galley-slave, who had thrown down his chains, took up the gout in their stead, but made such wry faces, that one might easily perceive he was no great gainer by the bargain. It was pleasant enough to see the several exchanges that were made, for sickness against poverty, hunger against want of appetite, and care against pain.

The female world were very busy among themselves in bartering for features ; one was trucking a lock of gray hairs for a carbuncle, another was making over a short waist for a pair of round shoulders, and a third cheapening a bad face for a lost reputation: but on all these occasions, there was not one of them who did not think the new blemish, as soon as she had got it into her possession, much more disagreeable than the old one.

I made the same observation on every other misfortune or calamity, which every one in the assembly brought upon himself, in lieu of what he had parted with ; whether it be that all the evils which befall us are in some measure suited and proportioned to our strength, or that every evil becomes more supportable by our being accustomed to it, I shall not determine.

I must not omit my own particular adventure. My friend with the long visage, had no sooner taken upon him my short face, but he made such a grotesque figure in it, that as I looked upon him I could not forbear laughing at myself, insomuch that I put my own face out of countenance. The poor gentleman was so sensible of the ridicule, that I found he was ashamed of what he had done : on the other side, I found that I myself had no great reason to triumph, for as I went to touch my forehead I missed the place, and clapped my finger upon my upper lip. Besides, as my nose was exceeding prominent, I gave it two or three unlucky knocks as I was playing my hand about my face, and aiming at some other part of it.

I saw two other gentlemen by me who were in the same ridiculous circumstances. These had made a foolish swop between a couple of thick bandy legs, and two long trapsticks that had no calves to them. One of these looked like a man walking upon stilts, and was so lifted up into the air above his ordinary height, that his head turned round with it ; while the other made such awkward circles, as he attempted to walk, that he scarce knew how to move forward upon his new supporters. Observing him to be a pleasant kind of fellow, I stuck my cane in the ground, and told him I would lay him a bottle of wine that he did not march up to it on a line, that I drew for him, in a quarter of an hour.

The heap was at last distributed among the two sexes, who made a most piteous sight, as they wandered up and down under the pressure of their several burdens. The whole plain was filled with murmurs and complaints, groans and lamentations.

Jupiter at length, taking compassion on the poor mortals, ordered them a second time to lay down their loads, with a design to give every one his own again. They discharged themselves with a great deal of pleasure, after which the phantom, who had led them into such gross delusions, was commanded to disappear. There was sent in her stead a goddess of a quite different figure ; her motions were steady and composed, and her aspect serious but cheerful. She every now and then cast her eyes towards heaven, and fixed them upon Jupiter : her name was Patience.

She had no sooner placed herself by the Mount of Sorrows, but, what I thought very remarkable, the whole heap sunk to such a degree, that it did not appear a third part so big as it was before. She afterwards returned every man his own proper calamity, and teaching him how to bear it in the most commodious manner, he marched off with it contentedly, being very well pleased that he had not been left to his own choice as to the kind of evils which fell to his lot.

Besides the several pieces of morality to be drawn out of this vision, I learned from it, never to repine at my own misfortunes, or to envy the happiness of another, since it is impossible for any man to form a right judgment of his neighbour's sufferings ; for which reason also I have determined never to think too lightly of another's complaints, but to regard the sorrows of my fellow-creatures with sentiments of humanity and compassion.

REMARKS ON THE ENGLISH BY THE INDIAN KINGS

WHEN the four Indian kings were in this country about a twelvemonth ago, I often mixed with the rabble, and followed them a whole day together, being wonderfully struck with the sight of everything that is new or uncommon. I have, since their departure, employed a friend to make many inquiries of their landlord, the upholsterer, relating to their manners and conversation, as also concerning the remarks which they made in this country : for, next to the forming a right notion of such strangers, I should be desirous of learning what ideas they have conceived of us.

The upholsterer, finding my friend very inquisitive about these his lodgers, brought him some time since a little bundle of papers, which he assured him were written by King Sa Ga Yean Qua Rash Tow, and, as he supposes, left behind by some mistake. These papers are now translated, and contain abundance of very odd observations, which I find this little fraternity of kings made during their stay in the Isle of Great Britain. I shall present my reader with a short specimen of them in this paper, and may perhaps communicate more to him hereafter. In the article of London are the following words, which, without doubt, are meant of the Church of St. Paul.

" On the most rising part of the town there stands a huge house, big enough to contain the whole nation of which I am king. Our good brother E Tow O Koam, king of the rivers, is of opinion it was made by the hands of that great god to whom it is consecrated. The kings of Granajah, and of the six nations, believe that it was created with the earth, and produced on the same day with the sun and moon. But, for my own part, by the best information that I could get of this matter, I am apt to think, that this prodigious pile was fashioned into the shape it now bears by several tools and instruments, of which they have a wonderful variety in this country. It was probably at first a huge misshapen rock that grew upon the top of a hill, which the natives of the country (after having cut it into a kind of regular figure) bored and hollowed with incredible pains and industry, till they had wrought in it all those beautiful vaults and caverns into which it is divided at this day. As soon as this rock was thus curiously scooped to their liking, a prodigious number of hands must have been employed in chipping the outside of it, which is now as smooth as the surface of a pebble ; and is in several places hewn out into pillars, that stand like the trunks of so many trees bound about the top with garlands of leaves. It is probable that when this

71

great work was begun, which must have been many hundred years ago, there was some religion among this people, for they give it the name of a temple, and have a tradition that it was designed for men to pay their devotion in. And, indeed, there are several reasons which make us think, that the natives of this country had formerly among them some sort of worship : for they set apart every seventh day as sacred : but upon my going into one of these holy houses on that day, I could not observe any circumstance of devotion in their behaviour : there was, indeed, a man in black who was mounted above the rest, and seemed to utter something with a great deal of vehemence ; but as for those underneath him, instead of paying their worship to the deity of the place, they were most of them bowing and curtseying to one another, and a considerable number of them fast asleep.

" The queen of the country appointed two men to attend us, that had enough of our language to make themselves understood in some few particulars. But we soon perceived these two were great enemies to one another, and did not always agree in the same story. We could make a shift to gather out of one of them, that this island was very much infested with a monstrous kind of animals, in the shape of men, called Whigs ; and he often told us, that he hoped we should meet with none of them in our way, for that, if we did, they would be apt to knock us down for being kings.

" Our other interpreter used to talk very much of a kind of animal called a Tory, that was as great a monster as the Whig, and would treat us ill for being foreigners. These two creatures, it seems, are born with a secret antipathy to one another, and engage when they meet as naturally as the elephant and the rhinoceros. But as we saw none of either of these species, we are apt to think that our guides deceived us with misrepresentations and fictions, and amused us with an account of such monsters as are not really in their country.

" These particulars we made a shift to pick out from the discourse of our interpreters ; which we put together as well as we could, being able to understand but here and there a word of what they said, and afterwards making up the meaning of it among ourselves. The men of the country are very cunning and ingenious in handicraft works ; but withal so very idle, that we often saw young, lusty, raw-boned fellows carried up and down the streets in little covered rooms by a couple of porters, who are hired for that service. Their dress is likewise very barbarous, for they almost strangle themselves about the neck, and bind their bodies with many ligatures, that we are apt to think are the occasion of several distempers among them, which our country is entirely free from. Instead of those beautiful feathers with which we adorn our heads, they often buy up a monstrous bush of hair, which covers their heads, and falls down in a large fleece below the middle of their backs ; with which they walk up and down the streets, and are as proud of it as if it was of their own growth.

" We were invited to one of their public diversions, where we hoped to have seen the great men of their country running down a stag, or pitching a bar, that we might have discovered who were the persons of the greatest abilities among them ; but instead of that, they conveyed us into a huge room lighted up with abundance of candles, where this lazy people sat still above three hours to see several feats of ingenuity performed by others, who it seems were paid for it.

" As for the women of the country, not being able to talk with them, we could only make our remarks upon them at a distance. They let the hair of their heads grow to a great length ; but as the men make a great show with heads of hair that are none of their own, the women, who they say have very fine heads of hair, tie it up in a knot, and cover it from being seen. The women look like angels, and would be more beautiful than the sun, were it not for little black spots that are apt to break out in their faces, and sometimes rise in very odd figures. I have observed that those little blemishes wear off very soon ; but when they disappear in one part of the face, they are very apt to break out in another, insomuch that I have seen a spot upon the forehead in the afternoon, which was upon the chin in the morning."

The author then proceeds to show the absurdity of breeches and petticoats, with many other curious observations, which I shall reserve for another occasion. I cannot, however, conclude this paper without taking notice, that amidst these wild remarks, there now and then appears something very reasonable. I cannot likewise forbear observing, that we are all guilty in some measure of the same narrow way of thinking, which we meet with in this abstract of the Indian Journal, when we fancy the customs, dresses, and manners of other countries are ridiculous and extravagant, if they do not resemble those of our own.

MISCHIEFS OF PARTY SPIRIT

My worthy friend Sir Roger, when we are talking of the malice of parties, very frequently tells us an accident that happened to him when he was a school-

boy, which was at a time when the feuds ran high
between the Round-heads and Cavaliers. This
worthy knight being then but a stripling, had occasion
to inquire which was the way to St. Anne's Lane,
upon which the person whom he spoke to, instead
of answering his question, called him a young popish
cur, and asked him who had made Anne a saint !
The boy being in some confusion, inquired of the
next he met, which was the way to Anne's Lane ;
but was called a prick-eared cur for his pains ;
and instead of being shown the way, was told, that
she had been a saint before he was born, and would
be one after he was hanged. Upon this, says Sir
Roger, I did not think fit to repeat the former
question, but going into every lane of the neighbourhood, asked what they called the name of that lane.
By which ingenious artifice he found out the place
he inquired after, without giving any offence to any
party. Sir Roger generally closes this narrative with
reflections on the mischief that parties do in the
country ; how they spoil good neighbourhood, and
make honest gentlemen hate one another ; besides
that they manifestly tend to the prejudice of the land-
tax, and the destruction of the game.

There cannot a greater judgment befall a country
than such a dreadful spirit of division as rends a
government into two distinct people, and makes them
greater strangers and more averse to one another,
than if they were actually two different nations.
The effects of such a division are pernicious to the
last degree, not only with regard to those advantages
which they give the common enemy, but to those
private evils which they produce in the heart of
almost every particular person. This influence is
very fatal both to men's morals and their under-
standings ; it sinks the virtue of a nation, and not
only so, but destroys even common sense.

A furious party-spirit, when it rages in its full violence, exerts itself in civil war and bloodshed ; and when it is under its greatest restraints, naturally breaks out in falsehood, detraction, calumny, and a partial administration of justice. In a word, it fills a nation with spleen and rancour, and extinguishes all the seeds of good-nature, compassion, and humanity.

Plutarch says very finely, that a man should not allow himself to hate even his enemies, because, says he, if you indulge this passion in some occasions, it will rise of itself in others ; if you hate your enemies, you will contract such a vicious habit of mind, as by degrees will break out upon those who are your friends, or those who are indifferent to you. I might here observe how admirably this precept of morality (which derives the malignity of hatred from the passion itself, and not from its object) answers to that great rule which was dictated to the world about a hundred years before this philosopher wrote ; but instead of that, I shall only take notice, with a real grief of heart, that the minds of many good men among us appear soured with party-principles, and alienated from one another in such a manner, as seems to me altogether inconsistent with the dictates either of reason or religion. Zeal for a public cause is apt to breed passions in the hearts of virtuous persons, to which the regard of their own private interest would never have betrayed them.

If this party-spirit has so ill an effect on our morals, it has likewise a very great one upon our judgments. We often hear a poor insipid paper or pamphlet cried up, and sometimes a noble piece depreciated, by those who are of a different principle from the author. One who is actuated by this spirit, is almost under an incapacity of discerning either real blemishes or beauties. A man of merit in a different principle, is like an object seen in two different mediums, that appears crooked or broken, however straight and entire it may be in itself. For this reason there is scarce a person of any figure in England, who does not go by two contrary characters, as opposite to one another as light and darkness. Knowledge and learning suffer in a particular manner from this strange prejudice, which at present prevails amongst all ranks and degrees in the British nation. As men formerly became eminent in learned societies by their parts and acquisitions, they now distinguish themselves by the warmth and violence with which they espouse their respective parties. Books are valued upon the like considerations : an abusive, scurrilous style passes for satire, and a dull scheme of party-notions is called fine writing.

There is one piece of sophistry practised by both sides, and that is the taking any scandalous story that has been ever whispered or invented of a private man, for a known, undoubted truth, and raising suitable speculations upon it. Calumnies that have been never proved, or have been often refuted, are the ordinary postulatums of these infamous scribblers, upon which they proceed as upon first principles granted by all men, though in their hearts they know they are false, or at best very doubtful. When they have laid these foundations of scurrility, it is no wonder that their superstructure is every way answerable to them. If this shameless practice of the present age endures much longer, praise and reproach will cease to be motives of action in good men.

There are certain periods of time in all governments when this inhuman spirit prevails. Italy was long torn in pieces by the Guelfes and Gibelines, and France by those who were for and against the League : but it is very unhappy for a man to be born in such a stormy and tempestuous season. It is the restless ambition of artful men that thus breaks a people into factions, and draws several well-meaning persons to their interest by a specious concern for their country. How many honest minds are filled with uncharitable and barbarous notions, out of their zeal for the public good ! What cruelties and outrages would they not commit against men of an adverse party, whom they would honour and esteem, if, instead of considering them as they are represented, they knew them as they are ? Thus are persons of the greatest probity seduced into shameful errors and prejudices, and made bad men even by that noblest of principles, the love of their country. I cannot here forbear mentioning the famous Spanish proverb, " If there were neither fools nor knaves in the world, all people would be of one mind."

For my own part I could heartily wish that all honest men would enter into an association, for the support of one another against the endeavours of those whom they ought to look upon as their common enemies, whatsoever side they may belong to. Were there such an honest body of neutral forces, we should never see the worst of men in great figures of life, because they are useful to a party ; nor the best unregarded, because they are above practising those methods which would be grateful to their faction. We should then single every criminal out of the herd, and hunt him down, however formidable and overgrown he might appear : on the contrary, we should shelter distressed innocence, and defend virtue, however beset with contempt or ridicule, envy or defamation. In short, we should not any longer regard our fellow-subjects as Whigs and Tories, but should make the man of merit our friend, and the villain our enemy.

OLIVER GOLDSMITH

WAR

Were an Asiatic politician to read the treaties of peace and friendship that have been annually making for more than a hundred years among the inhabitants of Europe, he would probably be surprised how it should ever happen that Christian princes could quarrel among each other. Their compacts for peace are drawn up with the utmost precision, and ratified with the greatest solemnity : to these each party promises a sincere and inviolable obedience, and all wears the appearance of open friendship and unreserved reconciliation.

Yet, notwithstanding those treaties, the people of Europe are almost continually at war. There is nothing more easy than to break a treaty ratified in all the usual forms, and yet neither party be the aggressor. One side, for instance, breaks a trifling article by mistake ; the opposite party, upon this, makes a small but premeditated reprisal ; this brings on a return of greater from the other ; both sides complain of injuries and infractions ; war is declared ; they beat—are beaten ; some two or three hundred thousand men are killed ; they grow tired ; leave off just where they began ; and so sit coolly down to make new treaties.

The English and French seem to place themselves foremost among the champion states of Europe. Though parted by a narrow sea, yet are they entirely of opposite characters ; and, from their vicinity, are taught to fear and admire each other. They are at present engaged in a very destructive war, have already spilled much blood, are excessively irritated, and all upon account of one side's desiring to wear greater quantities of *furs* than the other.

The pretext of the war is about some lands a thousand leagues off,—a country cold, desolate, and hideous—a country belonging to a people who were in possession for time immemorial. The savages of Canada claim a property in the country in dispute ; they have all the pretensions which long possession can confer. Here they had reigned for ages without rivals in dominion, and knew no enemies but the prowling bear or insidious tiger ; their native forests produced all the necessaries of life, and they found ample luxury in the enjoyment. In this manner they might have continued to live to eternity, had not the English been informed that those countries produced furs in great abundance. From that moment the country became an object of desire : it was found that furs were things very much wanted in England ; the ladies edged some of their clothes with furs, and muffs were worn both by gentlemen and ladies. In short, furs were found indispensably necessary for the happiness of the state ; and the king was consequently petitioned to grant, not only the country of Canada, but all the savages belonging to it, to the subjects of England, in order to have the people supplied with proper quantities of this necessary commodity.

So very reasonable a request was immediately complied with, and large colonies were sent abroad to procure furs, and take possession. The French, who were equally in want of furs (for they were as fond of muffs and tippets as the English), made the very same request to their monarch, and met with the same gracious reception from their king, who generously granted what was not his to give. Wherever the French landed, they called the country their own ;

and the English took possession wherever they came, upon the same equitable pretensions. The harmless savages made no opposition; and, could the intruders have agreed together, they might peaceably have shared this desolate country between them; but they quarrelled about the boundaries of their settlements, about grounds and rivers to which neither side could show any other right than that of power, and which neither could occupy but by usurpation. Such is the contest, that no honest man can heartily wish success to either party.

The war has continued for some time with various success. At first the French seemed victorious; but the English have of late dispossessed them of the whole country in dispute. Think not, however, that success on one side is the harbinger of peace; on the contrary, both parties must be heartily tired, to effect even a temporary reconciliation. It should seem the business of the victorious party to offer terms of peace: but there are many in England who, encouraged by success, are for still protracting the war.

The best English politicians, however, are sensible, that to keep their present conquests would be rather a burden than an advantage to them; rather a diminution of their strength than an increase of power. It is in the politic as in the human constitution: if the limbs grow too large for the body, their size, instead of improving, will diminish the vigour of the whole. The colonies should always bear an exact proportion to the mother country: when they grow populous, they grow powerful, and, by becoming powerful, they become independent also: thus subordination is destroyed, and a country swallowed up in the extent of its own dominions. The Turkish empire would be more formidable, were it less extensive—were it not for those countries which it can neither command nor give entirely away, which it is obliged to protect, but from which it has no power to exact obedience.

Yet, obvious as these truths are, there are many Englishmen who are for transplanting new colonies into this late acquisition, for peopling the deserts of America with the refuse of their countrymen, and (as they express it) with the waste of an exuberant nation. But who are those unhappy creatures who are to be thus drained away ? Not the sickly, for they are unwelcome guests abroad as well as at home ; nor the idle, for they would starve as well behind the Apalachian mountains as in the streets of London. This refuse is composed of the laborious and enter-prising—of such men as can be serviceable to their country at home—of men who ought to be regarded as the sinews of the people, and cherished with every degree of political indulgence. And what are the commodities which this colony, when established, is to produce in return ? Why, raw silk, hemp, and tobacco. England, therefore, must make an ex-change of her best and bravest subjects for raw silk, hemp, and tobacco ; her hardy veterans and honest tradesmen must be trucked for a box of snuff or a silk petticoat. Strange absurdity ! Surely the politics of the Daures are not more strange, who sell their religion, their wives, and their liberty, for a glass bead or a paltry penknife.

DOCTORS

WHATEVER may be the merits of the English in other sciences, they seem peculiarly excellent in the art of healing. There is scarcely a disorder incident to humanity, against which they are not possessed

with a most infallible antidote. The professors of
other arts confess the inevitable intricacy of things ;
talk with doubt, and decide with hesitation : but
doubting is entirely unknown in medicine ; the
advertising professors here delight in cases of difficulty.
Be the disorder never so desperate or radical, you will
find numbers in every street, who, by levelling a pill
at the part affected, promise a certain cure, without
loss of time, knowledge of a bedfellow, or hindrance
of business.

When I consider the assiduity of this profession,
their benevolence amazes me. They not only in
general give their medicines for half value, but use
the most persuasive remonstrances to induce the sick
to come and be cured. Sure, there must be something strangely obstinate in an English patient who
refuses so much health upon such easy terms. Does
he take a pride in being bloated with a dropsy ?
does he find pleasure in the alternations of an intermittent fever ? or feel as much satisfaction in nursing
up his gout, as he found pleasure in acquiring it ?
He must, otherwise he would not reject such repeated
assurances of instant relief. What can be more con-
vincing than the manner in which the sick are invited
to be well ? The doctor first begs the most earnest
attention of the public to what he is going to propose :
he solemnly affirms the pill was never found to want
success ; he produces a list of those who have been
rescued from the grave by taking it : yet, notwithstanding all this, there are many here who now and
then think proper to be sick. Only sick, did I say ?
there are some who even think proper to die ! Yes,
by the head of Confucius ! they die ; though they
might have purchased the health-restoring specific for
half-a-crown at every corner.

I am amazed, my dear Fum Hoam, that these
doctors, who know what an obstinate set of people

they have to deal with, have never thought of attempting to revive the dead. When the living are found to reject their prescriptions, they ought in conscience to apply to the dead, from whom they can expect no such mortifying repulses : they would find in the dead the most complying patients imaginable ; and what gratitude might they not expect from the patient's son, now no longer an heir, and his wife, now no longer a widow !

Think not, my friend, that there is any thing chimerical in such an attempt ; they already perform cures equally strange. What can be more truly astonishing, than to see old age restored to youth, and vigour to the most feeble constitutions ? Yet this is performed here every day : a simple electuary effects these wonders, even without the bungling ceremonies of having the patient boiled up in a kettle, or ground down in a mill.

Few physicians here go through the ordinary courses of education, but receive all their knowledge of medicine by immediate inspiration from Heaven. Some are thus inspired even in the womb ; and, what is very remarkable, understand their profession as well at three years old, as at threescore. Others have spent a great part of their lives unconscious of any latent excellence, till a bankruptcy, or residence in gaol, have called their miraculous powers into exertion. And others still there are indebted to their superlative ignorance alone for success ; the more ignorant the practitioner, the less capable is he thought of deceiving. The people here judge as they do in the East, where it is thought absolutely requisite that a man should be an idiot, before he pretend to be either a conjurer or a doctor.

When a physician by inspiration is sent for, he never perplexes the patient by previous examination ; he asks very few questions, and those only for form sake. He knows every disorder by intuition; he administers the pill or drop for every distemper; nor is more inquisitive than the farrier while he drenches a horse. If the patient lives, then has he one more to add to the surviving list; if he dies, then it may be justly said of the patient's disorder, that, as it was not cured, the disorder was incurable.

THE STORY OF THE MAN IN BLACK

As there appeared something reluctantly good in the character of my companion, I must own it surprised me what could be his motives for thus concealing virtues which others take such pains to display. I was unable to repress my desire of knowing the history of a man who thus seemed to act under continual restraint, and whose benevolence was rather the effect of appetite than reason.

It was not, however, till after repeated solicitations he thought proper to gratify my curiosity. " If you are fond," says he, " of hearing hairbreadth 'scapes, my history must certainly please; for I have been for twenty years upon the very verge of starving, without ever being starved.

" My father, the younger son of a good family, was possessed of a small living in the church. His education was above his fortune, and his generosity greater than his education. Poor as he was, he had his flatterers, still poorer than himself; for every dinner he gave them they returned an equivalent in praise, and this was all he wanted. The same ambition that actuates a monarch at the head of an army influenced my father at the head of his table : he told the story of the ivy-tree, and that was laughed at; he repeated the jest of the two scholars and one pair of breeches, and the company laughed at that ; but the story of Taffy in the sedan-chair was sure to set the table in a roar : thus his pleasure increased in proportion to the pleasure he gave ; he loved all the world, and he fancied all the world loved him.

" As his fortune was but small, he lived up to the very extent of it ; he had no intentions of leaving his children money, for that was dross ; he was resolved they should have learning ; for learning, he used to observe, was better than silver or gold. For this purpose, he undertook to instruct us himself ; and took as much pains to form our morals as to improve our understanding. We were told that universal benevolence was what first cemented society : we were taught to consider all the wants of mankind as our own ; to regard the human face divine with affec-tion and esteem ; he wound us up to be mere machines of pity, and rendered us incapable of withstanding the slightest impulse made either by real or fictitious distress : in a word, we were perfectly instructed in the art of giving away thousands, before we were taught the more necessary qualifications of getting a farthing.

" I cannot avoid imagining, that thus refined by his lessons out of all my suspicion, and divested of even all the little cunning which nature had given me, I resembled, upon my first entrance into the busy and insidious world, one of those gladiators who were exposed without armour in the amphitheatre at Rome. My father, however, who had only seen the world on one side, seemed to triumph in my superior discern-ment ; though my whole stock of wisdom consisted in being able to talk like himself upon subjects that once were useful, because they were then topics of the busy world, but that now were utterly useless, because connected with the busy world no longer.

" The first opportunity he had of finding his expectations disappointed was in the very middling
figure I made at the university; he had flattered
himself that he should soon see me rising into the
foremost rank in literary reputation, but was mortified
to find me utterly unnoticed and unknown. His disappointment might have been partly ascribed to his
having overrated my talents, and partly to my dislike
of mathematical reasonings, at a time when my
imagination and memory, yet unsatisfied, were more
eager after new objects than desirous of reasoning
upon those I knew. This did not, however, please
my tutor, who observed, indeed, that I was a little
dull; but at the same time allowed, that I seemed to
be very good-natured, and had no harm in me.

" After I had resided at college seven years, my
father died, and left me—his blessing. Thus shoved
from shore without ill-nature to protect, or cunning
to guide, or proper stores to subsist me in so dangerous
a voyage, I was obliged to embark in the wide world
at twenty-two. But, in order to settle in life, my
friends advised (for they always advise when they
begin to despise us), they advised me, I say, to go
into orders.

" To be obliged to wear a long wig, when I liked a
short one, or a black coat, when I generally dressed
in brown, I thought was such a restraint upon my
liberty, that I absolutely rejected the proposal. A
priest in England is not the same mortified creature
with a bonze in China: with us, not he that fasts
best, but eats best, is reckoned the best liver; yet I
rejected a life of luxury, indolence, and ease, from no
other consideration but that boyish one of dress. So
that my friends were now perfectly satisfied I was
undone; and yet they thought it a pity for one who
had not the least harm in him and was so very good-
natured.

" Poverty naturally begets dependence, and I was admitted as flatterer to a great man. At first, I was surprised that the situation of a flatterer at a great man's table could be thought disagreeable : there was no great trouble in listening attentively when his lordship spoke, and laughing when he looked round for applause. This even good manners might have obliged me to perform. I found, however, too soon, that his lordship was a greater dunce than myself ; and from that very moment my power of flattery was at an end. I now rather aimed at setting him right, than at receiving his absurdities with submission : to flatter those we do not know is an easy task ; but to flatter our intimate acquaintances, all whose foibles are strongly in our eye, is drudgery insupportable. Every time I now opened my lips in praise, my falsehood went to my conscience ; his lordship soon perceived me to be unfit for service ; I was therefore discharged ; my patron at the same time being graciously pleased to observe, that he believed I was tolerably good-natured, and had not the least harm in me.

" Disappointed in ambition, I had recourse to love. A young lady, who lived with her aunt, and was possessed of a pretty fortune in her own disposal, had given me, as I fancied, some reason to expect success. The symptoms by which I was guided were striking. She had always laughed with me at her awkward acquaintance, and at her aunt among the number ; she always observed, that a man of sense would make a better husband than a fool, and I as constantly applied the observation in my own favour. She continually talked, in my company, of friendship and the beauties of the mind, and spoke of Mr. Shrimp my rival's high-heeled shoes with detestation. These were circumstances which I thought strongly in my favour ; so, after resolving and resolving, I had courage enough to tell her my mind. Miss heard my proposal with serenity, seeming at the same time to study the figures of her fan. Out at last it came. There was but one small objection to complete our happiness, which was no more than——that she was married three months before to Mr. Shrimp, with high-heeled shoes ! By way of consolation, however, she observed, that, though I was disappointed in her, my addresses to her aunt would probably kindle her into sensibility ; as the old lady always allowed me to be very good-natured, and not to have the least share of harm in me.

" Yet still I had friends, numerous friends, and to them I was resolved to apply. O friendship ! thou fond soother of the human breast, to thee we fly in every calamity ; to thee the wretched seek for succour ; on thee the care-tired son of misery fondly relies : from thy kind assistance the unfortunate always hopes relief, and may be ever sure of—disappointment. My first application was to a city scrivener, who had frequently offered to lend me money, when he knew I did not want it. I informed him, that now was the time to put his friendship to the test ; that I wanted to borrow a couple of hundred for a certain occasion, and was resolved to take it up from him. ' And pray, sir,' cried my friend, ' do you want all this money ? '—' Indeed, I never wanted it more,' returned I.—' I am sorry for that,' cries the scrivener, ' with all my heart ; for they who want money when they come to borrow, will always want money when they should come to pay.'

" From him I flew, with indignation, to one of the best friends I had in the world, and made the same request. ' Indeed, Mr. Drybone,' cries my friend, ' I always thought it would come to this. You know, sir, I would not advise you but for your own good ; but your conduct has hitherto been ridiculous in the highest degree, and some of your acquaintance always thought you a very silly fellow. Let me see— you want two hundred pounds. Do you only want two hundred, sir, exactly?'—'To confess a truth, returned I, ' I shall want three hundred; but then, I have another friend, from whom I can borrow the rest.'—' Why, then,' replied my friend, ' if you would take my advice, (and you know I should not presume to advise you but for your own good,) I would recommend it to you to borrow the whole sum from that other friend; and then one note will serve for all, you know.'

" Poverty now began to come fast upon me; yet instead of growing more provident or cautious as I grew poor, I became every day more indolent and simple. A friend was arrested for fifty pounds; I was unable to extricate him, except by becoming his bail. When at liberty, he fled from his creditors, and left me to take his place. In prison I expected greater satisfactions than I enjoyed at large. I hoped to converse with men in this new world, simple and believing like myself; but I found them as cunning and as cautious as those in the world I had left behind. They spunged up my money while it lasted, borrowed my coals and never paid for them, and cheated me when I played at cribbage. All this was done because they believed me to be very good-natured, and knew that I had no harm in me.

" Upon my first entrance into this mansion, which is to some the abode of despair, I felt no sensations different from those I experienced abroad. I was now on one side the door, and those who were unconfined were on the other : this was all the difference between us. At first, indeed, I felt some uneasiness, in considering how I should be able to provide this week for the wants of the week ensuing; but after some time, if I found myself sure of eating one day,

I never troubled my head how I was to be supplied another. I seized every precarious meal with the utmost good-humour ; indulged no rants of spleen at my situation ; never called down Heaven and all the stars to behold me dining upon a halfpenny-worth of radishes ; my very companions were taught to believe that I liked salad better than mutton. I contented myself with thinking, that all my life I should either eat white bread or brown ; considered that all that happened was best ; laughed when I was not in pain, took the world as it went, and read Tacitus often for want of more books and company.

" How long I might have continued in this torpid state of simplicity I cannot tell, had I not been roused by seeing an old acquaintance, whom I knew to be a prudent blockhead, preferred to a place in the government. I now found that I had pursued a wrong track, and that the true way of being able to relieve others was first to aim at independence myself : my immediate care, therefore, was to leave my present habitation and make an entire reformation in my conduct and behaviour. For a free, open, un-designing deportment, I put on that of closeness, prudence, and economy. One of the most heroic actions I ever performed, and for which I shall praise myself as long as I live, was the refusing half-a-crown to an old acquaintance, at the time when he wanted it, and I had it to spare : for this alone I deserve to be decreed an ovation.

" I now therefore pursued a course of uninterrupted frugality, seldom wanted a dinner, and was con-sequently invited to twenty. I soon began to get the character of a saving hunks that had money, and insensibly grew into esteem. Neighbours have asked my advice in the disposal of their daughters ; and I have always taken care not to give any. I have con-tracted a friendship with an alderman, only by observing, that if we take a farthing from a thousand pounds, it will be a thousand pounds no longer. I have been invited to a pawnbroker's table, by pretending to hate gravy; and am now actually upon treaty of marriage with a rich widow, for only having observed that the bread was rising. If ever I am asked a question, whether I know it or not, instead of answering, I only smile and look wise. If a charity is proposed, I go about with the hat, but put nothing in myself. If a wretch solicits my pity, I observe that the world is filled with impostors, and take a certain method of not being deceived by never relieving. In short, I now find the truest way of finding esteem, even from the indigent, is to give away nothing, and thus have much in our power to give."

PARLIAMENTARY ELECTIONS

The English are at present employed in celebrating a feast, which becomes general every seventh year; the parliament of the nation being then dissolved, and another appointed to be chosen. This solemnity falls infinitely short of our Feast of the Lanterns in magnificence and splendour; it is also surpassed by others of the East in unanimity and pure devotion; but no festival in the world can compare with it for eating. Their eating, indeed, amazes me; had I five hundred heads, and were each head furnished with brains, yet would they all be insufficient to compute the number of cows, pigs, geese, and turkeys, which, upon this occasion, die for the good of their country.

To say the truth, eating seems to make a grand ingredient in all English parties of zeal, business, or amusement. When a church is to be built, or a hospital endowed, the directors assemble, and instead

94

of consulting upon it, they eat upon it, by which means the business goes forward with success. When the poor are to be relieved, the officers appointed to dole out public charity assemble and eat upon it. Nor has it ever been known that they filled the bellies of the poor, till they had previously satisfied their own. But in the election of magistrates the people seem to exceed all bounds : the merits of a candidate are often measured by the number of his treats ; his constituents assemble, eat upon him, and lend their applause, not to his integrity or sense, but to the quantities of his beef and brandy.

And yet I could forgive this people their plentiful meals on this occasion, as it is extremely natural for every man to eat a great deal when he gets it for nothing ; but what amazes me is, that all this good living no way contributes to improve their good humour. On the contrary, they seem to lose their temper as they lose their appetites ; every morsel they swallow, and every glass they pour down, serves to increase their animosity. Many an honest man, before as harmless as a tame rabbit, when loaded with a single election dinner, has become more dangerous than a charged culverin. Upon one of these occasions I have actually seen a bloody-minded man-milliner sally forth at the head of a mob, determined to face a desperate pastrycook, who was general of the opposite party.

But you must not suppose they are without a pretext for thus beating each other. On the contrary, no man here is so uncivilized as to beat his neighbour without producing very sufficient reasons. One candidate, for instance, treats with gin, a spirit of their own manufacture ; another always drinks brandy, imported from abroad. Brandy is a wholesome liquor ; gin, a liquor wholly their own. This, then, furnishes an obvious cause of quarrel,—Whether

95

it be most reasonable to get drunk with gin, or get drunk with brandy ? The mob meet upon the debate, fight themselves sober, and then draw off to get drunk again, and charge for another encounter. So that the English may now properly be said to be engaged in war ; since, while they are subduing their enemies abroad, they are breaking each other's heads at home.

I lately made an excursion to a neighbouring village, in order to be a spectator of the ceremonies practised upon this occasion. I left town in company with three fiddlers, nine dozen of hams, and a corporation poet, which were designed as reinforcements to the gin-drinking party. We entered the town with a very good face ; the fiddlers, no way intimidated by the enemy, kept handling their arms up the principal street. By this prudent manœuvre, they took peaceable possession of their head-quarters, amidst the shouts of multitudes, who seemed perfectly rejoiced at hearing their music, but above all at seeing their bacon.

I must own, I could not avoid being pleased to see all ranks of people, on this occasion, levelled into an equality, and the poor, in some measure, enjoying the primitive privileges of nature. If there was any distinction shown, the lowest of the people seemed to receive it from the rich. I could perceive a cobbler with a levee at his door, and a haberdasher giving audience from behind his counter.

But my reflections were soon interrupted by a mob, who demanded whether I was for the distillery or the brewery ? As these were terms with which I was totally unacquainted, I chose at first to be silent ; however, I know not what might have been the consequence of my reserve, had not the attention of the mob been called off to a skirmish between a brandy-drinker's cow and a gin-drinker's mastiff, which turned out, greatly to the satisfaction of the mob, in favour of the mastiff.

This spectacle, which afforded high entertainment, was at last ended by the appearance of one of the candidates, who came to harangue the mob : he made a very pathetic speech upon the late excessive importation of foreign drams, and the downfall of the distillery ; I could see some of the audience shed tears. He was accompanied in his procession by Mrs. Deputy and Mrs. Mayoress. Mrs. Deputy was not in the least in liquor ; and as for Mrs. Mayoress, one of the spectators assured me in my ear, that—she was a very fine woman before she had the small-pox.

Mixing with the crowd, I was now conducted to the hall where the magistrates are chosen : but what tongue can describe this scene of confusion ! the whole crowd seemed equally inspired with anger, jealousy, politics, patriotism, and punch. I re-marked one figure that was carried up by two men upon this occasion. I at first began to pity his in-firmities as natural, but soon found the fellow so drunk that he could not stand ; another made his appearance to give his vote, but though he could stand, he actually lost the use of his tongue, and remained silent ; a third, who, though excessively drunk, could both stand and speak, being asked the candidate's name for whom he voted, could be pre-vailed upon to make no other answer but " Tobacco and brandy." In short, an election hall seems to be a theatre, where every passion is seen without disguise ; a school where fools may readily become worse, and where philosophers may gather wisdom.

A REVERIE

SCARCELY a day passes in which we do not hear compliments paid to Dryden, Pope, and other writers of the last age, while not a month comes forward that is not loaded with invectives against the writers of this. Strange, that our critics should be fond of giving their favours to those who are insensible of the obligation, and their dislike to those who, of all mankind, are most apt to retaliate the injury.

Even though our present writers had not equal merit with their predecessors, it would be politic to use them with ceremony. Every compliment paid them would be more agreeable, in proportion as they least deserved it. Tell a lady with a handsome face that she is pretty, she only thinks it her due ; it is what she has heard a thousand times before from others, and disregards the compliment : but assure a lady the cut of whose visage is something more plain that she looks killing to-day, she instantly bridles up, and feels the force of the well-timed flattery the whole day after. Compliments which we think are deserved, we accept only as debts, with indifference ; but those which conscience informs us we do not merit, we receive with the same gratitude that we do favours given away.

Our gentlemen, however, who preside at the distribution of literary fame, seem resolved to part with praise neither from motives of justice or generosity : one would think, when they take pen in hand, that it was only to blot reputations, and to put their seals to the packet which consigns every new-born effort to oblivion.

Yet, notwithstanding the republic of letters hangs at present so feebly together—though those friendships which once promoted literary fame seem now to be discontinued—though every writer who now draws the quill seems to aim at profit, as well as applause,— many among them are probably laying in stores for immortality, and are provided with a sufficient stock of reputation to last the whole journey.

As I was indulging these reflections, in order to eke out the present page, I could not avoid pursuing the metaphor of going a journey in my imagination, and formed the following Reverie, too wild for allegory, and too regular for a dream.

I fancied myself placed in the yard of a large inn, in which there were an infinite number of waggons and stage-coaches, attended by fellows who either invited the company to take their places, or were busied in packing their baggage. Each vehicle had its inscription, showing the place of its destination. On one I could read, The Pleasure Stage Coach ; on another, The Waggon of Industry ; on a third, The Vanity Whim ; and on a fourth, The Landau of Riches. I had some inclination to step into each of these, one after another ; but, I know not by what means, I passed them by, and at last fixed my eye upon a small carriage, Berlin fashion, which seemed the most convenient vehicle at a distance in the world ; and upon my nearer approach found it to be The Fame Machine.

I instantly made up to the coachman, whom I found to be an affable and seemingly good-natured fellow. He informed me, that he had but a few days ago returned from the Temple of Fame, to which he had been carrying Addison, Swift, Pope, Steele, Congreve, and Colley Cibber ; that they made but indifferent company by the way ; and that he once or twice was going to empty his berlin of the whole cargo : " However," says he, " I got them all safe home, with no other damage than a black eye, which Colley gave Mr. Pope, and am now returned for another coachful."—" If that be all, friend," said I, " and if you are in want of company, I'll make one with all my heart. Open the door : I hope the machine rides easy."—" Oh, for that, sir, extremely easy." But still keeping the door shut, and measuring

me with his eye, " Pray, sir, have you no luggage ?
You seem to be a good-natured sort of gentleman ;
but I don't find you have got any luggage, and I
never permit any to travel with me but such as have
something valuable to pay for coach-hire." Examining my pockets, I own I was not a little disconcerted
at this unexpected rebuff ; but considering that I
carried a number of the BEE under my arm, I was
resolved to open it in his eyes, and dazzle him with the
splendour of the page. He read the title and contents,
however, without any emotion, and assured me he
had never heard of it before. " In short, friend," said
he, now losing all his former respect, " you must not
come in : I expect better passengers ; but as you
seem a harmless creature, perhaps, if there be room
left, I may let you ride a while for charity."

I now took my stand by the coachman at the door ;
and since I could not command a seat, was resolved
to be as useful as possible, and earn by my assiduity
what I could not by my merit.

The next that presented for a place was a most
whimsical figure indeed. He was hung round with
papers of his own composing, not unlike those who
sing ballads in the streets, and come dancing up to
the door with all the confidence of instant admittance.
The volubility of his motion and address prevented
my being able to read more of his cargo than the word
Inspector, which was written in great letters at the
top of some of the papers. He opened the coach-door
himself without any ceremony, and was just slipping
in, when the coachman, with as little ceremony,
pulled him back. Our figure seemed perfectly angry
at this repulse, and demanded gentleman's satisfaction. " Lord, sir ! " replied the coachman, " instead
of proper luggage, by your bulk you seem loaded for
a West India vogage. You are big enough, with all
your papers, to crack twenty stage-coaches. Excuse

me, indeed, sir, for you must not enter." Our figure now began to expostulate: he assured the coachman, that though his baggage seemed so bulky, it was perfectly light, and that he would be contented with the smallest corner of room. But Jehu was inflexible, and the carrier of the Inspectors was sent to dance back again, with all his papers fluttering in the wind. We expected to have no more trouble from this quarter, when, in a few minutes, the same figure changed his appearance, like harlequin upon the stage, and with the same confidence again made his approaches, dressed in lace, and carrying nothing but a nosegay. Upon coming nearer, he thrust the nosegay to the coachman's nose, grasped the brass, and seemed now resolved to enter by violence. I found the struggle soon begin to grow hot, and the coachman, who was a little old, unable to continue the contest; so, in order to ingratiate myself, I stepped in to his assistance, and our united efforts sent our literary Proteus, though worsted, unconquered still, clear off, dancing a rigadoon, and smelling to his own nosegay.

The person who after him appeared as candidate for a place in the stage came up with an air not quite so confident, but somewhat, however, theatrical; and, instead of entering, made the coachman a very low bow, which the other returned, and desired to see his baggage; upon which he instantly produced some farces, a tragedy, and other miscellany productions. The coachman, casting his eye upon the cargo, assured him, at present he could not possibly have a place, but hoped in time he might aspire to one, as he seemed to have read in the book of nature, without a careful perusal of which none ever found entrance at the Temple of Fame. "What!" replied the disappointed poet, "shall my tragedy, in which I have vindicated the cause of liberty and virtue——"—

" Follow nature," returned the other, " and never expect to find lasting fame by topics which only please from their popularity. Had you been first in the cause of freedom, or praised in virtue more than an empty name, it is possible you might have gained admittance ; but at present I beg, sir, you will stand aside for another gentleman whom I see approaching."

This was a very grave personage, whom at some distance I took for one of the most reserved, and even disagreeable, figures I had seen ; but as he approached his appearance improved, and when I could distinguish him thoroughly, I perceived that, in spite of the severity of his brow, he had one of the most good-natured countenances that could be imagined. Upon coming to open the stage door, he lifted a parcel of folios into the seat before him, but our inquisitorial coachman at once shoved them out again. " What ! not take in my Dictionary ? " exclaimed the other in rage. " Be patient, sir," replied the coachman : " I have drove a coach, man and boy, these two thousand years ; but I do not remember to have carried above one dictionary during the whole time. That little book which I perceive peeping from one of your pockets, may I presume to ask what it contains ? "—" A mere trifle," replied the author ; " it is called the Rambler."—" The Rambler ! " says the coachman : " I beg, sir, you'll take your place ; I have heard our ladies in the court of Apollo frequently mention it with rapture ; and Clio, who happens to be a little grave, has been heard to prefer it to the Spectator ; though others have observed, that the reflections, by being refined, sometimes become minute."

This grave gentleman was scarcely seated, when another, whose appearance was something more modern, seemed willing to enter, yet afraid to ask. He carried in his hand a bundle of essays, which the coachman was curious enough to inquire the contents. " These," replied the gentleman, " are rhapsodies against the religion of my country."— " And how can you expect to come into my coach, after thus choosing the wrong side of the question ? " —" Ay, but I am right," replied the other ; " and if you give me leave, I shall, in a few minutes, state the argument."—" Right or wrong," said the coachman, " he who disturbs religion is a blockhead, and he shall never travel in a coach of mine."—" If, then," said the gentleman, mustering up all his courage, " if I am not to have admittance as an essayist, I hope I shall not be repulsed as an historian ; the last volume of my history met with applause."—" Yes," replied the coachman, " but I have heard only the first approved at the Temple of Fame ; and as I see you have it about you, enter, without further ceremony." My attention was now diverted to a crowd who were pushing forward a person that seemed more inclined to the Stage-coach of Riches ; but by their means he was driven forward to the same machine, which he, however, seemed heartily to despise. Impelled, however, by their solicitations, he steps up, flourishing a voluminous history, and demanding admittance. " Sir, I have formerly heard your name mentioned," says the coachman, " but never as an historian. Is there no other work upon which you may claim a place ? "—" None," replied the other, " except a romance ; but this is a work of too trifling a nature to claim future attention."—" You mistake," says the inquisitor ; " a well-written romance is no such easy task as is generally imagined. I remember formerly to have carried Cervantes and Segrais ; and if you think fit, you may enter."

Upon our three literary travellers coming into the same coach, I listened attentively to hear what might be the conversation that passed upon this extraordinary occasion ; when, instead of agreeable or entertaining dialogue, I found them grumbling at each other, and each seemed discontented with his companions. Strange ! thought I to myself, that they who are thus born to enlighten the world, should still preserve the narrow prejudices of childhood, and, by disagreeing, make even the highest merit ridiculous. Were the learned and the wise to unite against the dunces of society, instead of sometimes siding into opposite parties with them, they might throw a lustre upon each other's reputation, and teach every rank of sub-ordinate merit, if not to admire, at least not to avow dislike.

In the midst of these reflections I perceived the coachman, unmindful of me, had now mounted the box. Several were approaching to be taken in whose pretensions I was sensible were very just ; I therefore desired him to stop, and take in more passengers : but he replied, as he had now mounted the box, it would be improper to come down ; but that he should take them all, one after the other, when he should return. So he drove away ; and for myself, as I could not get in, I mounted behind, in order to hear the conversation on the way.

CHARLES LAMB

THE LONDONER

I was born under the shadow of St. Dunstan's steeple, just where the conflux of the eastern and western inhabitants of this twofold city meet and jostle in friendly opposition at Temple Bar. The same day which gave me to the world saw London happy in the celebration of her great annual feast. This I cannot help looking upon as a lively omen of the future good-will which I was destined to bear toward the city, resembling in kind that solicitude which every Chief Magistrate is supposed to feel for whatever concerns her interests and well-being. Indeed I consider myself in some sort a speculative Lord Mayor of London ; for though circumstances unhappily preclude me from the hope of ever arriving at the dignity of a gold chain and Spital Sermon, yet thus much will I say of myself in truth, that Whittington with his Cat (just emblem of vigilance and a furred gown) never went beyond me in affection, which I bear to the citizens.

I was born, as you have heard, in a crowd. This has begot in me an entire affection for that way of life, amounting to an almost insurmountable aversion from solitude and rural scenes. This aversion was never interrupted or suspended, except for a few years in the younger part of my life, during a period in which I had set my affections upon a charming young woman. Every man, while the passion is upon him, is for a time at least addicted to groves and meadows and purling streams. During this short period of my existence, I contracted just familiarity enough with rural *objects* to understand tolerably well ever after the *poets*, when they declaim in such passionate terms in favour of a country life.

For my own part, now the fit is past, I have no hesitation in declaring, that a mob of happy faces crowding up at the pit door of Drury Lane Theatre, just at the hour of six, gives me ten thousand sincerer pleasures, than I could ever receive from all the flocks of silly sheep that ever whitened the plains of Arcadia or Epsom Downs.

This passion for crowds is nowhere feasted so full as in London. The man must have a rare *recipe* for melancholy, who can be dull in Fleet Street. I am naturally inclined to hypochondria, but in London it vanishes, like all other ills. Often, when I have felt a weariness or distaste at home, have I rushed out into her crowded Strand, and fed my humour, till tears have wetted my cheek for inutterable sympathies with the multitudinous moving picture, which she never fails to present at all hours, like the scenes of a shifting pantomime.

The very deformities of London, which give distaste to others, from habit do not displease me. The endless succession of shops where *Fancy mis-called Folly* is supplied with perpetual gauds and toys, excite in me no puritanical aversion. I gladly behold every appetite supplied with its proper food. The obliging customer, and the obliged tradesman—things which live by bowing, and things which exist but for homage —do not affect me with disgust; from habit I perceive nothing but urbanity, where other men, more refined, discover meanness : I love the very smoke of London, because it has been the medium most familiar to my vision. I see grand principles of honour at work in the dirty ring which encompasses two combatants with fists, and principles of no less eternal justice in the detection of a pick-pocket. The salutary astonishment with which an execution is surveyed, convinces me more forcibly than a hundred volumes of abstract polity, that the universal instinct of man in all ages has leaned to order and good government.

Thus an art of extracting morality from the commonest incidents of a town life, is attained by the same well-natured alchemy, with which the Foresters of Arden, in a beautiful country,

" Found tongues in trees, books in the running brooks,
    Sermons in stones, and good in everything."

Where has spleen her food but in London ! Humour, Interest, Curiosity, suck at her measureless breasts without a possibility of being satiated. Nursed amid her noise, her crowds, her beloved smoke, what have I been doing all my life, if I have not lent out my heart with usury to such scenes !

ALL FOOLS' DAY

THE compliments of the season to my worthy masters, and a merry first of April to us all !

Many happy returns of this day to you—and you—and *you*, Sir—nay, never frown, man, nor put a long face upon the matter. Do not we know one another ? what need of ceremony among friends ? we have all a touch of *that same*—you understand me—a speck of the motley. Beshrew the man who on such a day as this, the *general festival*, should affect to stand aloof. I am none of those sneakers. I am free of the corporation, and care not who knows it. He that meets me in the forest to-day, shall meet with no wise-acre, I can tell him. *Stultus sum.* Translate me that, and take the meaning of it to yourself for your pains. What ! man, we have four quarters of the globe on our side, at the least computation.

Fill us a cup of that sparkling gooseberry—we will drink no wise, melancholy, politic port on this day— and let us troll the catch of Amiens—*duc ad me—duc ad me*—how goes it ?

> " Here shall he see
> Gross fools as he."

Now would I give a trifle to know, historically and authentically, who was the greatest fool that ever lived. I would certainly give him in a bumper. Marry, of the present breed, I think I could without much difficulty name you the party.

Remove your cap a little further, if you please : it hides my bauble. And now each man bestride his hobby, and dust away his bells to what tune he pleases. I will give you, for my part,

> "——The crazy old church clock,
> And the bewildered chimes."

Good master Empedocles,* you are welcome. It is long since you went a salamander-gathering down Ætna. Worse than samphire-picking by some odds. 'Tis a mercy your worship did not singe your mustachios.

Ha ! Cleombrotus ! † and what salads in faith did you light upon at the bottom of the Mediterranean ? You were founder, I take it, of the disinterested sect of the Calenturists.

Gebir, my old free-mason, and prince of plasterers

[* ——He who, to be deem'd
  A god, leap'd fondly into Etna flames—]
[† ——He who, to enjoy
  Plato's Elysium, leap'd into the sea—]

at Babel,* bring in your trowel, most Ancient Grand ! You have claim to a seat here at my right hand, as patron of the stammerers. You left your work, if I remember Herodotus correctly, at eight hundred million toises, or thereabout, above the level of the sea. Bless us, what a long bell you must have pulled, to call your top workmen to their nuncheon on the low grounds of Shinar. Or did you send up your garlic and onions by a rocket ? I am a rogue if I am not ashamed to show you our Monument on Fishstreet Hill, after your altitudes. Yet we think it somewhat.

What, the magnanimous Alexander in tears ?—cry, baby, put its finger in its eye, it shall have another globe, round as an orange, pretty moppet !

Mister Adams——'odso, I honour your coat—pray do us the favour to read to us that sermon, which you lent to Mistress Slipslop—the twenty and second in your portmanteau there—on Female Incontinence— the same—it will come in most irrelevantly and impertinently seasonable to the time of the day.

Good Master Raymund Lully, you look wise. Pray correct that error.——

Duns, spare your definitions. I must fine you a bumper, or a paradox. We will have nothing said or done syllogistically this day. Remove those logical forms, waiter, that no gentleman break the tender shins of his apprehension stumbling across them.

Master Stephen, you are late.—Ha ! Cokes, is it you ?—Aguecheek, my dear knight, let me pay my devoir to you.—Master Shallow, your worship's poor servant to command.—Master Silence, I will use few words with you.—Slender, it shall go hard if I edge not you in somewhere.—You six will engross all the poor wit of the company to-day.—I know it, I know it.

Ha ! honest R——, my fine old Librarian of

[* The builders next of Babel on the plain
Of Senaar—]

Ludgate, time out of mind, art thou here again ? Bless
thy doublet, it is not over-new, threadbare as thy
stories :—what dost thou flitting about the world at
this rate ?—Thy customers are extinct, defunct, bed-
rid, have ceased to read long ago.—Thou goest still
amongst them, seeing if, peradventure, thou canst
hawk a volume or two.—Good Granville S——, thy
last patron is flown.

> " King Pandion, he is dead,
>   All thy friends are lapt in lead.—"

Nevertheless, noble R——, come in, and take your
seat here, between Armado and Quisada ; for in true
courtesy, in gravity, in fantastic smiling to thyself, in
courteous smiling upon others, in the goodly ornature
of well-apparelled speech, and the commendation of
wise sentences, thou art nothing inferior to those
accomplished Dons of Spain. The spirit of chivalry
forsake me for ever, when I forget thy singing the
song of Macheath, which declares that he might be
happy with either, situated between those two ancient
spinsters—when I forget the inimitable formal love
which thou didst make, turning now to the one, and
now to the other, with that Malvolian smile—as if
Cervantes, not Gay, had written it for his hero ; and
as if thousands of periods must revolve, before the
mirror of courtesy could have given his invidious preference between a pair of so goodly-propertied and
meritorious-equal damsels.   *   *   *   *

To descend from these altitudes, and not to protract
our Fools' Banquet beyond its appropriate day,—for
I fear the second of April is not many hours distant—
in sober verity I will confess a truth to thee, reader.
I love a *Fool*—as naturally as if I were of kith and kin
to him. When a child, with child-like apprehensions,
that dived not below the surface of the matter, I read
those *Parables*—not guessing at the involved wisdom—

I had more yearnings towards that simple architect, that built his house upon the sand, than I entertained for his more cautious neighbour : I grudged at the hard censure pronounced upon the quiet soul that kept his talent ; and—prizing their simplicity beyond the more provident, and, to my apprehension, somewhat *unfeminine* wariness of their competitors—I felt a kindliness, that almost amounted to a *tendre*, for those five thoughtless virgins.—I have never made an acquaintance since, that lasted : or a friendship, that answered ; with any that had not some tincture of the absurd in their characters. I venerate an honest obliquity of understanding. The more laughable blunders a man shall commit in your company, the more tests he giveth you, that he will not betray or overreach you. I love the safety which a palpable hallucination warrants ; the security, which a word out of season ratifies. And take my word for this, reader, and say a fool told it to you, if you please, that he who hath not a dram of folly in his mixture, hath pounds of much worse matter in his composition. It is observed that, " the foolisher the fowl or fish,— woodcocks,—dotterels—cods'-heads, etc., the finer the flesh thereof," and what are commonly the world's received fools but such whereof the world is not worthy ? and what have been some of the kindliest patterns of our species, but so many darlings of absurdity, minions of the goddess, and her white boys ? —Reader, if you wrest my words beyond their fair construction, it is you, and not I, that are the *April Fool*.

MODERN GALLANTRY

IN comparing modern with ancient manners, we are pleased to compliment ourselves upon the point of gallantry ; a certain obsequiousness, or deferential respect, which we are supposed to pay to females, as females.

I shall believe that this principle actuates our conduct, when I can forget, that in the nineteenth century of the era from which we date our civility, we are but just beginning to leave off the very frequent practice of whipping females in public, in common with the coarsest male offenders.

I shall believe it to be influential, when I can shut my eyes to the fact that in England women are still occasionally—hanged.

I shall believe in it, when actresses are no longer subject to be hissed off a stage by gentlemen.

I shall believe in it when Dorimant hands a fish-wife across the kennel ; or assists the apple-woman to pick up her wandering fruit, which some unlucky dray has just dissipated.

I shall believe in it, when the Dorimants in humbler life, who would be thought in their way notable adepts in this refinement, shall act upon it in places where they are not known, or think themselves not observed—when I shall see the traveller for some rich tradesman part with his admired box-coat, to spread it over the defenceless shoulders of the poor woman, who is passing to her parish on the roof of the same stage-coach with him, drenched in the rain—when I shall no longer see a woman standing up in the pit of a London theatre, till she is sick and faint with the exertion, with men about her, seated at their ease, and jeering at her distress ; till one, that seems to have more manners or conscience than the rest, significantly declares " she should be welcome to his seat, if she were a little younger and handsomer." Place this dapper warehouseman, or that rider, in a circle of their own female acquaintance, and you shall confess you have not seen a politer-bred man in Lothbury.

Lastly, I shall begin to believe that there is some such principle influencing our conduct, when more than one-half of the drudgery and coarse servitude of the world shall cease to be performed by women.

Until that day comes I shall never believe this boasted point to be anything more than a conventional fiction ; a pageant got up between the sexes, in a certain rank, and at a certain time of life, in which both find their account equally.

I shall be even disposed to rank it among the salutary fictions of life, when in polite circles I shall see the same attentions paid to age as to youth, to homely features as to handsome, to coarse complexions as to clear—to the woman, as she is a woman, not as she is a beauty, a fortune, or a title.

I shall believe it to be something more than a name, when a well-dressed gentleman in a well-dressed company can advert to the topic of *female old age* without exciting, and intending to excite, a sneer :— when the phrases " antiquated virginity," and such a one has " overstood her market," pronounced in good company, shall raise immediate offence in man, or woman, that shall hear them spoken.

Joseph Paice, of Bread-street-hill, merchant, and one of the Directors of the South Sea company—the same to whom Edwards, the Shakespeare commentator, has addressed a fine sonnet—was the only pattern of consistent gallantry I have met with. He took me under his shelter at an early age, and bestowed some pains upon me. I owe to his precepts and example whatever there is of the man of business (and that is not much) in my composition. It was not his fault that I did not profit more. Though bred a Presbyterian, and brought up a merchant, he was the finest gentleman of his time. He had not *one* system of attention to females in the drawing-room, and *another* in the shop, or at the stall. I do not mean that he made no distinction. But he never lost sight of sex, or overlooked it in the casualties of a disadvantageous situation. I have seen him stand bareheaded—smile if you please—to a poor servant-girl, while she has been inquiring of him the way to some street—in such a posture of unforced civility, as neither to embarrass her in the acceptance, nor himself in the offer, of it. He was no dangler, in the common acceptation of the word, after women ; but he reverenced and upheld, in every form in which it came before him, *womanhood*. I have seen him—nay, smile not—tenderly escorting a market-woman, whom he had encountered in a shower, exalting his umbrella over her poor basket of fruit, that it might receive no damage, with as much carefulness as if she had been a countess. To the reverend form of Female Eld he would yield the wall (though it were to an ancient beggar-woman) with more ceremony than we can afford to show our grandams. He was the Preux Chevalier of Age ; the Sir Calidore, or Sir Tristan, to those who have no Calidores or Tristans to defend them. The roses, that had long faded thence, still bloomed for him in those withered and yellow cheeks.

He was never married, but in his youth he paid his addresses to the beautiful Susan Winstanley—old Winstanley's daughter of Clapton—who dying in the early days of their courtship, confirmed in him the resolution of perpetual bachelorship. It was during their short courtship, he told me, that he had been one day treating his mistress with a profusion of civil speeches—the common gallantries—to which kind of thing she had hitherto manifested no repugnance—but in this instance with no effect. He could not obtain from her a decent acknowledgment in return. She rather seemed to resent his compliments. He could not set it down to caprice, for the lady had always shown herself above that littleness. When he ventured on the following day, finding her a little better humoured, to expostulate with her on her coldness of yesterday, she confessed, with her usual frankness, that she had no sort of dislike to his attentions; that she could even endure some high-flown compliments; that a young woman placed in her situation had a right to expect all sorts of civil things said to her; that she hoped she could digest a dose of adulation, short of insincerity, with as little injury to her humility as most young women; but that—a little before he had commenced his compliments—she had overheard him by accident, in rather rough language, rating a young woman, who had not brought home his cravats quite to the appointed time, and she thought to herself, "As I am Miss Susan Winstanley, and a young lady —a reputed beauty, and known to be a fortune—I can have my choice of the finest speeches from the mouth of this very fine gentleman who is courting me,—but if I had been poor Mary Such-a-one (*naming the milliner*)—and had failed of bringing home the cravats to the appointed hour—though perhaps I had sat up half the night to forward them—what sort of compliments should I have received then?—And my woman's pride came to my assistance; and I thought, that if it were only to do *me* honour, a female, like myself, might have received handsomer usage; and I was determined not to accept any fine speeches to the compromise of that sex, the belonging to which was after all my strongest claim and title to them."

I think the lady discovered both generosity, and a just way of thinking, in this rebuke which she gave her lover; and I have sometimes imagined, that the uncommon strain of courtesy, which through life regulated the actions and behaviour of my friend towards all of womankind indiscriminately, owed its happy origin to this seasonable lesson from the lips of his lamented mistress.

I wish the whole female world would entertain the same notion of these things that Miss Winstanley showed. Then we should see something of the spirit of consistent gallantry ; and no longer witness the anomaly of the same man—a pattern of true politeness to a wife—of cold contempt, or rudeness, to a sister—the idolater of his female mistress—the disparager and despiser of his no less female aunt, or unfortunate—still female—maiden cousin. Just so much respect as a woman derogates from her own sex, in whatever condition placed—her hand-maid, or dependent—she deserves to have diminished from herself on that score ; and probably will feel the diminution, when youth, and beauty, and advantages, not inseparable from sex, shall lose of their attraction. What a woman should demand of a man in courtship, or after it, is first—respect for her as she is a woman ; —and next to that—to be respected by him above all other women. But let her stand upon her female character as upon a foundation ; and let the attentions, incident to individual preference, be so many pretty additaments and ornaments—as many, and as fanciful, as you please—to that main structure. Let her first lesson be with sweet Susan Winstanley—to *reverence her sex.*

MY FIRST PLAY

AT the north end of Cross-court there yet stands a portal, of some architectural pretensions, though reduced to humble use, serving at present for an entrance to a printing-office. This old door-way, if you are young, reader, you may not know was the identical pit entrance to old Drury—Garrick's Drury—all of it that is left. I never pass it without shaking some forty years from off my shoulders, recurring to the evening when I passed through it to see *my first play*. The afternoon had been wet, and the condition of our going (the elder folks and myself) was, that the rain should cease. With what a beating heart did I watch from the window the puddles, from the stillness of which I was taught to prognosticate the desired cessation ! I seem to remember the last spurt, and the glee with which I ran to announce it.

We went with orders, which my godfather F. had sent us. He kept the oil shop (now Davies's) at the corner of Featherstone-buildings, in Holborn. F. was a tall grave person, lofty in speech, and had pretensions above his rank. He associated in those days with John Palmer, the comedian, whose gait and bearing he seemed to copy ; if John (which is quite as likely) did not rather borrow somewhat of his manner from my godfather. He was also known to and visited by Sheridan. It was to his house in Holborn that young Brinsley brought his first wife on her elopement with him from a boarding-school at Bath—the beautiful Maria Linley. My parents were present (over a quadrille table) when he arrived in the evening with his harmonious charge. From either of these connections it may be inferred that my god-father could command an order for the then Drury-lane theatre at pleasure—and, indeed, a pretty liberal issue of those cheap billets, in Brinsley's easy autograph, I have heard him say was the sole re-muneration which he had received for many years' nightly illumination of the orchestra and various avenues of that theatre—and he was content it should be so. The honour of Sheridan's familiarity—or supposed familiarity—was better to my godfather than money.

F. was the most gentlemanly of oilmen ; grandiloquent, yet courteous. His delivery of the commonest matters of fact was Ciceronian. He had two Latin words almost constantly in his mouth (how odd sounds Latin from an oilman's lips !), which my better knowledge since has enabled me to correct. In strict pronunciation they should have been sounded *vice versâ*—but in those young years they impressed me with more awe than they would now do, read aright from Seneca or Varro—in his own peculiar pronunciation, monosyllabically elaborated, or Anglicised, into something like *verse verse*. By an imposing manner, and the help of these distorted syllables, he climbed (but that was little) to the highest parochial honours which St. Andrew's has to bestow.

He is dead—and thus much I thought due to his memory, both for my first orders (little wondrous talismans !—slight keys, and insignificant to outward sight, but opening to me more than Arabian paradises!) and, moreover, that by his testamentary beneficence I came into possession of the only landed property which I could ever call my own—situate near the road-way village of pleasant Puckeridge, in Hertfordshire. When I journeyed down to take possession, and planted foot on my own ground, the stately habits of the donor descended upon me, and I strode (shall I confess the vanity ?) with larger paces over my allotment of three-quarters of an acre, with its commodious mansion in the midst, with the feeling of an English freeholder that all betwixt sky and centre was my own. The estate has passed into more prudent hands, and nothing but an agrarian can restore it.

In those days were pit orders. Beshrew the uncomfortable manager who abolished them !—with one of these we went. I remember the waiting at the door —not that which is left—but between that and an inner door in shelter—O when shall I be such an expectant again !—with the cry of nonpareils, an indispensable play-house accompaniment in those days. As near as I can recollect, the fashionable pronunciation of the theatrical fruiteresses then was, " Chase some oranges, chase some numparels, chase a bill of the play ;"—chase *pro* chuse. But when we got in, and I beheld the green curtain that veiled a heaven to my imagination, which was soon to be disclosed—the breathless anticipations I endured ! I had seen something like it in the plate prefixed to *Troilus and Cressida*, in Rowe's *Shakespeare*—the tent scene with Diomede—and a sight of that plate can always bring back in a measure the feeling of that evening.—The boxes at that time, full of well-dressed women of quality, projected over the pit ; and the pilasters reaching down were adorned with a glistening substance (I know not what) under glass (as it seemed), resembling—a homely fancy—but I judged it to be a sugar-candy—yet, to my raised imagination, divested of its homelier qualities, it appeared a glorified candy !—The orchestra lights at length rose, those " fair Auroras ! " Once the bell sounded. It was to ring out yet once again—and, incapable of the anticipation, I reposed my shut eyes in a sort of resignation upon the maternal lap. It rang the second time. The curtain drew up—I was not past six years old, and the play was *Artaxerxes* !

I had dabbled a little in the Universal History—the ancient part of it—and here was the court of Persia.—It was being admitted to a sight of the past. I took no proper interest in the action going on, for I understood not its import—but I heard the word Darius, and I was in the midst of Daniel. All feeling was absorbed in vision. Gorgeous vests, gardens, palaces, princesses, passed before me. I knew not players. I was in Persepolis for the time, and the burning idol of their devotion almost converted me into a worshipper. I was awe-struck, and believed

those significations to be something more than elemental fires. It was all enchantment and a dream.
No such pleasure has since visited me but in dreams.—
Harlequin's invasion followed ; where, I remember,
the transformation of the magistrates into reverend
beldams seemed to me a piece of grave historic justice,
and the tailor carrying his own head to be as sober a
verity as the legend of St. Denys.

The next play to which I was taken was *The Lady
of the Manor*, of which, with the exception of some
scenery, very faint traces are left in my memory. It
was followed by a pantomime, called *Lun's Ghost*—
a satiric touch, I apprehend, upon Rich, not long
since dead—but to my apprehension (too sincere for
satire), Lun was as remote a piece of antiquity as
Lud—the father of a line of Harlequins—transmitting
his dagger of lath (the wooden sceptre) through countless ages. I saw the primeval Motley come from his
silent tomb in a ghastly vest of white patchwork, like
the apparition of a dead rainbow. So Harlequins
(thought I) look when they are dead.

My third play followed in quick succession. It was
the *Way of the World*. I think I must have sat at it
as grave as a judge ; for I remember the hysteric
affectations of good Lady Wishfort affected me
like some solemn tragic passion. *Robinson Crusoe*
followed ; in which Crusoe, man Friday, and the
parrot, were as good and authentic as in the story.—
The clownery and pantaloonery of these panto-
mimes have clean passed out of my head. I believe,
I no more laughed at them, than at the same age I
should have been disposed to laugh at the grotesque
Gothic heads (seeming to me then replete with devout
meaning) that gape, and grin, in stone around the
inside of the old Round Church (my church) of the
Templars.

I saw these plays in the season 1781-1782, when I

was from six to seven years old. After the intervention of six or seven other years (for at school all play-going was inhibited) I again entered the doors of a theatre. That old *Artaxerxes* evening had never done ringing in my fancy. I expected the same feelings to come again with the same occasion. But we differ from ourselves less at sixty and sixteen, than the latter does from six. In that interval what had I not lost ! At the first period I knew nothing, understood nothing, discriminated nothing. I felt all, loved all, wondered all—

> " Was nourished, I could not tell how— "

I had left the temple a devotee, and was returned a rationalist. The same things were there materially ; but the emblem, the reference, was gone !—The green curtain was no longer a veil, drawn between two worlds, the unfolding of which was to bring back past ages, to present a " royal ghost,"—but a certain quantity of green baize, which was to separate the audience for a given time from certain of their fellow-men who were to come forward and pretend those parts. The lights—the orchestra lights—came up a clumsy machinery. The first ring, and the second ring, was now but a trick of the prompter's bell—which had been, like the note of the cuckoo, a phantom of a voice, no hand seen or guessed at which ministered to its warning. The actors were men and women painted. I thought the fault was in them ; but it was in myself, and the alteration which those many centuries—of six short twelvemonths—had wrought in me.—Perhaps it was fortunate for me that the play of the evening was but an indifferent comedy, as it gave me time to crop some unreasonable expectations, which might have interfered with the genuine emotions with which I was soon after enabled to enter upon the first appearance to me of Mrs. Siddons in *Isabella.* Comparison and retrospection soon yielded to the present attraction of the scene ; and the theatre became to me, upon a new stock, the most delightful of recreations.

THE SUPERANNUATED MAN

Sera tamen respexit
Libertas.   VIRGIL.
A Clerk I was in London gay.—O'KEEFE.

IF peradventure, Reader, it has been thy lot to waste the golden years of thy life—thy shining youth —in the irksome confinement of an office ; to have thy prison days prolonged through middle age down to decrepitude and silver hairs, without hope of release or respite ; to have lived to forget that there are such things as holidays, or to remember them but as the prerogatives of childhood ; then, and then only, will you be able to appreciate my deliverance.

It is now six-and-thirty years since I took my seat at the desk in Mincing Lane. Melancholy was the transition at fourteen from the abundant playtime, and the frequently-intervening vacations of school days, to the eight, nine, and sometimes ten hours' a-day attendance at the counting-house. But time partially reconciles us to anything. I gradually became content—doggedly contented, as wild animals in cages.

It is true I had my Sundays to myself ; but Sundays, admirable as the institution of them is for purposes of worship, are for that very reason the very worst adapted for days of unbending and recreation. In particular, there is a gloom for me attendant upon a city Sunday, a weight in the air. I miss the cheerful

cries of London, the music, and the ballad-singers—
the buzz and stirring murmur of the streets. Those
eternal bells depress me. The closed shops repel me.
Prints, pictures, all the glittering and endless succession
of knacks and gewgaws, and ostentatiously displayed
wares of tradesmen, which make a weekday saunter
through the less busy parts of the metropolis so
delightful—are shut out. No book-stalls deliciously
to idle over—no busy faces to recreate the idle man
who contemplates them ever passing by—the very
face of business a charm by contrast to his temporary
relaxation from it. Nothing to be seen but unhappy
countenances—or half-happy at best—of emancipated
'prentices and little tradesfolks, with here and there
a servant-maid that has got leave to go out, who,
slaving all the week, with the habit has lost almost
the capacity of enjoying a free hour ; and livelily
expressing the hollowness of a day's pleasuring. The
very strollers in the fields on that day look anything
but comfortable.

But besides Sundays, I had a day at Easter, and a
day at Christmas, with a full week in the summer to
go and air myself in my native fields of Hertfordshire.
This last was a great indulgence ; and the prospect of
its recurrence, I believe, alone kept me up through the
year, and made my durance tolerable. But when
the week came round, did the glittering phantom
of the distance keep touch with me, or rather was it not
a series of seven uneasy days, spent in restless pursuit
of pleasure, and a wearisome anxiety to find out how
to make the most of them ? Where was the quiet,
where the promised rest ? Before I had a taste of it,
it was vanished. I was at the desk again, counting
upon the fifty-one tedious weeks that must intervene
before such another snatch would come. Still the
prospect of its coming threw something of an illumination upon the darker side of my captivity. Without

it, as I have said, I could scarcely have sustained my thraldom.

Independently of the rigours of attendance, I have ever been haunted with a sense (perhaps a mere caprice) of incapacity for business. This, during my latter years, had increased to such a degree, that it was visible in all the lines of my countenance. My health and my good spirits flagged. I had perpetually a dread of some crisis, to which I should be found unequal. Besides my daylight servitude, I served over again all night in my sleep, and would awake with terrors of imaginary false entries, errors in my accounts, and the like. I was fifty years of age, and no prospect of emancipation presented itself. I had grown to my desk, as it were ; and the wood had entered into my soul.

My fellows in the office would sometimes rally me upon the trouble legible in my countenance ; but I did not know that it had raised the suspicions of any of my employers, when, on the fifth of last month, a day ever to be remembered by me, L——, the junior partner in the firm, calling me on one side, directly taxed me with my bad looks, and frankly inquired the cause of them. So taxed, I honestly made confession of my infirmity, and added that I was afraid I should eventually be obliged to resign his service. He spoke some words of course to hearten me, and there the matter rested. A whole week I remained labouring under the impression that I had acted imprudently in my disclosure ; that I had foolishly given a handle against myself, and had been anticipating my own dismissal. A week passed in this manner —the most anxious one, I verily believe, in my whole life—when on the evening of the 12th of April, just as I was about quitting my desk to go home (it might be about eight o'clock), I received an awful summons to attend the presence of the whole assembled firm in the formidable back parlour. I thought now my time is surely come, I have done for myself, I am going to be told that they have no longer occasion for me. L——, I could see, smiled at the terror I was in, which was a little relief to me,—when to my utter astonishment B——, the eldest partner, began a formal harangue to me on the length of my services, my very meritorious conduct during the whole of the time (the deuce, thought I, how did he find out that ? I protest I never had the confidence to think as much). He went on to descant on the expediency of retiring at a certain time of life (how my heart panted !) and asking me a few questions as to the amount of my own property, of which I have a little, ended with a proposal, to which his three partners nodded a grave assent, that I should accept from the house, which I had served so well, a pension for life to the amount of two-thirds of my accustomed salary—a magnificent offer ! I do not know what I answered between surprise and gratitude, but it was understood that I accepted their proposal, and I was told that I was free from that hour to leave their service. I stammered out a bow, and at just ten minutes after eight I went home—for ever. This noble benefit—gratitude forbids me to conceal their names—I owe to the kindness of the most munificent firm in the world—the house of Boldero, Merryweather, Bosanquet, and Lacy.

" Esto perpetua ! "

For the first day or two I felt stunned—overwhelmed. I could only apprehend my felicity ; I was too confused to taste it sincerely. I wandered about, thinking I was happy, and knowing that I was not. I was in the condition of a prisoner in the old Bastile, suddenly let loose after a forty years' confinement. I could scarce trust myself with myself. It was like passing out of Time into Eternity—for it

is a sort of Eternity for a man to have his Time all to
himself. It seemed to me that I had more time on
my hands than I could ever manage. From a poor
man, poor in Time, I was suddenly lifted up into a
vast revenue ; I could see no end of my possessions ;
I wanted some steward, or judicious bailiff, to manage
my estates in Time for me. And here let me caution
persons grown old in active business, not lightly, nor
without weighing their own resources, to forego their
customary employment all at once, for there may be
danger in it. I feel it by myself, but I know that my
resources are sufficient ; and now that those first
giddy raptures have subsided, I have a quiet home-
feeling of the blessedness of my condition. I am in
no hurry. Having all holidays, I am as though I had
none. If Time hung heavy upon me, I could walk it
away ; but I do *not* walk all day long, as I used to do
in those old transient holidays, thirty miles a day, to
make the most of them. If Time were troublesome,
I could read it away ; but I do *not* read in that violent
measure, with which, having no Time my own but
candlelight Time, I used to weary out my head and
eyesight in bygone winters. I walk, read, or scribble
(as now) just when the fit seizes me. I no longer hunt
after pleasure ; I let it come to me. I am like the man

"———— that's born, and has his years come to him,
In some green desert."

" Years ! " you will say ; " what is this superannuated
simpleton calculating upon ? He has already told us
he is past fifty."

I have indeed lived nominally fifty years, but deduct
out of them the hours which I have lived to other
people, and not to myself, and you will find me still
a young fellow. For *that* is the only true Time, which
a man can properly call his own—that which he has
all to himself ; the rest, though in some sense he may

be said to live it, is other people's Time, not his.
The remnant of my poor days, long or short, is at
least multiplied for me threefold. My ten next years,
if I stretch so far, will be as long as any preceding
thirty. 'Tis a fair rule-of-three sum.

Among the strange fantasies which beset me at the
commencement of my freedom, and of which all
traces are not yet gone, one was, that a vast tract of
time had intervened since I quitted the Counting
House. I could not conceive of it as an affair of
yesterday. The partners, and the clerks with whom
I had for so many years, and for so many hours in
each day of the year, been closely associated—being
suddenly removed from them—they seemed as dead
to me. There is a fine passage, which may serve to
illustrate this fancy, in a *Tragedy* by Sir Robert
Howard, speaking of a friend's death :—

"————— 'Twas but just now he went away ;
I have not since had time to shed a tear ;
And yet the distance does the same appear
As if he had been a thousand years from me.
Time takes no measure in Eternity."

To dissipate this awkward feeling, I have been fain
to go among them once or twice since ; to visit my
old desk-fellows—my co-brethren of the quill—that
I had left below in the state militant. Not all the
kindness with which they received me could quite
restore to me that pleasant familiarity, which I had
heretofore enjoyed among them. We cracked some
of our old jokes, but methought they went off but
faintly. My old desk ; the peg where I hung my
hat, were appropriated to another. I knew it must
be, but I could not take it kindly. D——l take me,
if I did not feel some remorse—beast, if I had not—
at quitting my old compeers, the faithful partners
of my toils for six-and-thirty years, that soothed for

me with their jokes and conundrums the ruggedness of my professional road. Had it been so rugged then, after all ? or was I a coward simply ? Well, it is too late to repent ; and I also know that these suggestions are a common fallacy of the mind on such occasions. But my heart smote me. I had violently broken the bands betwixt us. It was at least not courteous. I shall be some time before I get quite reconciled to the separation. Farewell, old cronies, yet not for long, for again and again I will come among ye, if I shall have your leave. Farewell, Ch——, dry, sarcastic, and friendly ! Do——, mild, slow to move, and gentlemanly ! Pl——k, officious to do, and to volunteer, good services !—and thou, thou dreary pile, fit mansion for a Gresham or a Whittington of old, stately house of Merchants ; with thy labyrinthine passages, and light-excluding, pent-up offices, where candles for one-half the year supplied the place of the sun's light ; unhealthy contributor to my weal, stern fosterer of my living, farewell ! In thee remain, and not in the obscure collection of some wandering bookseller, my " works ! " There let them rest, as I do from my labours, piled on thy massy shelves, more MSS. in folio than ever Aquinas left, and full as useful ! My mantle I bequeath among ye.

A fortnight has passed since the date of my first communication. At that period I was approaching to tranquillity, but had not reached it. I boasted of a calm indeed, but it was comparative only. Something of the first flutter was left ; an unsettling sense of novelty ; the dazzle to weak eyes of unaccustomed light. I missed my old chains, forsooth, as if they had been some necessary part of my apparel. I was a poor Carthusian, from strict cellular discipline suddenly by some revolution returned upon the world. I am now as if I had never been other than my own master. It is natural for me to go where I please, to do what I please. I find myself at 11 o'clock in the day in Bond Street, and it seems to me that I have been sauntering there at that very hour for years past. I digress into Soho, to explore a bookstall. Methinks I have been thirty years a collector. There is nothing strange nor new in it. I find myself before a fine picture in the morning. Was it ever otherwise ? What is become of Fish Street Hill ? Where is Fenchurch Street ? Stones of old Mincing Lane, which I have worn with my daily pilgrimage for six-and-thirty years, to the footsteps of what toil-worn clerk are your everlasting flints now vocal ? I indent the gayer flags of Pall Mall. It is 'Change time, and I am strangely among the Elgin marbles. It was no hyperbole when I ventured to compare the change in my condition to passing into another world. Time stands still in a manner to me. I have lost all distinction of season. I do not know the day of the week or of the month. Each day used to be individually felt by me in its reference to the foreign post days ; in its distance from, or propinquity to, the next Sunday. I had my Wednesday feelings, my Saturday nights' sensations. The genius of each day was upon me distinctly during the whole of it, affecting my appetite, spirits, etc. The phantom of the next day, with the dreary five to follow, sate as a load upon my poor Sabbath recreations. What charm has washed the Ethiop white ? What is gone of Black Monday ? All days are the same. Sunday itself—that unfortunate failure of a holiday, as it too often proved, what with my sense of its fugitiveness, and over-care to get the greatest quantity of pleasure out of it—is melted down into a week-day. I can spare to go to church now, without grudging the huge cantle which it used to seem to cut out of the holiday. I have time for everything. I can visit a sick friend. I can interrupt the man of much occupation when he is busiest. I can insult over him with an invitation to take a day's pleasure with me to Windsor this fine May-morning. It is Lucretian pleasure to behold the poor drudges, whom I have left behind in the world, carking and caring ; like horses in a mill, drudging on in the same eternal round—and what is it all for ? A man can never have too much Time to himself, nor too little to do. Had I a little son, I would christen him NOTHING-TO-DO ; he should do nothing. Man, I verily believe, is out of his element as long as he is operative. I am altogether for the life contemplative. Will no kindly earthquake come and swallow up those accursed cotton-mills ? Take me that lumber of a desk there, and bowl it down

"As low as to the fiends."

I am no longer ******, clerk to the Firm of, etc. I am Retired Leisure. I am to be met with in trim gardens. I am already come to be known by my vacant face and careless gesture, perambulating at no fixed pace, nor with any settled purpose. I walk about ; not to and from. They tell me, a certain *cum dignitate* air, that has been buried so long with my other good parts, has begun to shoot forth in my person. I grow into gentility perceptibly. When I take up a newspaper, it is to read the state of the opera. *Opus operatum est.* I have done all that I came into this world to do. I have worked task-work, and have the rest of the day to myself.

REJOICINGS UPON THE NEW YEAR'S COMING OF AGE

THE *Old Year* being dead, and the *New Year* coming of age, which he does, by Calendar Law, as soon as the breath is out of the old gentleman's body, nothing would serve the young spark but he must give a dinner upon the occasion, to which all the *Days* in the year were invited. The *Festivals*, whom he deputed as his stewards, were mightily taken with the notion. They had been engaged time out of mind, they said, in providing mirth and good cheer for mortals below ; and it was time they should have a taste of their own bounty. It was stiffly debated among them whether the *Fasts* should be admitted. Some said the appearance of such lean, starved guests, with their mortified faces, would pervert the ends of the meeting. But the objection was overruled by *Christmas Day*, who had a design upon *Ash Wednesday* (as you shall hear), and a mighty desire to see how the old Domine would behave himself in his cups. Only the *Vigils* were requested to come with their lanterns, to light the gentlefolks home at night.

All the *Days* came to their day. Covers were provided for three hundred and sixty-five guests at the principal table ; with an occasional knife and fork at the side-board for the *Twenty-Ninth of February*.

I should have told you that cards of invitation had been issued. The carriers were the *Hours ;* twelve little, merry, whirligig foot-pages, as you should desire to see, that went all round, and found out the persons invited well enough, with the exception of *Easter Day*, *Shrove Tuesday*, and a few such *Moveables*, who had lately shifted their quarters.

Well, they all met at last—foul *Days*, fine *Days*, all sorts of *Days*, and a rare din they made of it. There was nothing but, Hail ! fellow *Day*, well met— brother *Day*—sister *Day*—only *Lady Day* kept a little on the aloof, and seemed somewhat scornful. Yet some said *Twelfth Day* cut her out and out, for she came in a tiffany suit, white and gold, like a queen on a frost-cake, all royal, glittering, and *Epiphanous*.

The rest came, some in green, some in white—but old *Lent and his family* were not yet out of mourning. Rainy *Days* came in, dripping ; and sunshiny *Days* helped them to change their stockings. *Wedding Day* was there in his marriage finery, a little the worse for wear. *Pay Day* came late, as he always does ; and *Doomsday* sent word—he might be expected.

April Fool (as my young lord's jester) took upon himself to marshal the guests, and wild work he made with it. It would have posed old Erra Pater to have found out any given *Day* in the year to erect a scheme upon—good *Days*, bad *Days*, were so shuffled together, to the confounding of all sober horoscopy.

He had stuck the *Twenty-First of June* next to the *Twenty-Second of December*, and the former looked like a Maypole siding a marrow-bone. *Ash Wednesday* got wedged in (as was concerted) betwixt *Christmas* and *Lord Mayor's Days*. Lord ! how he laid about him ! Nothing but barons of beef and turkeys would go down with him—to the great greasing and detriment of his new sackcloth bib and tucker. And still *Christmas Day* was at his elbow, plying him with the wassail-bowl, till he roared, and hiccupp'd, and protested there was no faith in dried ling, but commended it to the devil for a sour, windy, acrimonious, censorious, hy-po-crit-crit-critical mess, and no dish for a gentleman. Then he dipt his fist into the middle of the great custard that stood before his *left-hand neighbour*, and daubed his hungry beard all over with it, till you would have taken him for the *Last Day in December*, it so hung in icicles.

At another part of the table, *Shrove Tuesday* was helping the *Second of September* to some cock broth,— which courtesy the latter returned with the delicate thigh of a hen pheasant—so that there was no love lost for that matter. The *Last of Lent* was spunging upon *Shrove-tide's* pancakes ; which *April Fool* perceiving, told him that he did well, for pancakes were proper to a *good fry-day*.

In another part, a hubbub arose about the *Thirtieth of January*, who, it seems, being a sour, puritanic character, that thought nobody's meat good or sanctified enough for him, had smuggled into the room a calf's head, which he had had cooked at home for that purpose, thinking to feast thereon incontinently ; but as it lay in the dish, *March Many-weathers*, who is a very fine lady, and subject to the meagrims, screamed out there was a " human head in the platter," and raved about Herodias' daughter to that degree, that the obnoxious viand was obliged to be removed ; nor did she recover her stomach till she had gulped down a *Restorative*, confected of *Oak Apple*, which the merry *Twenty-Ninth of May* always carries about with him for that purpose.

The King's health * being called for after this, a notable dispute arose between the *Twelfth of August* (a zealous old Whig gentlewoman) and the *Twenty-Third of April* (a new-fangled lady of the Tory stamp), as to which of them should have the honour to propose it. *August* grew hot upon the matter, affirming time out of mind the prescriptive right to have lain with her, till her rival had basely supplanted her ; whom she represented as little better than a *kept* mistress, who went about in *fine clothes*, while she (the legitimate BIRTHDAY) had scarcely a rag, etc.

April Fool being made mediator, confirmed the right, in the strongest form of words, to the appellant, but decided for peace' sake, that the exercise of it should remain with the present possessor. At the same time, he slyly rounded the first lady in the ear, that an action might lie against the Crown for *bi-geny*.

It beginning to grow a little duskish, *Candlemas* lustily bawled out for lights, which was opposed by

* King George IV.

all the *Days*, who protested against burning daylight. Then fair water was handed round in silver ewers, and the *same lady* was observed to take an unusual time in *Washing* herself.

May Day, with that sweetness which is peculiar to her, in a neat speech proposing the health of the founder, crowned her goblet (and by her example the rest of the company) with garlands. This being done, the lordly *New Year*, from the upper end of the table, in a cordial but somewhat lofty tone, returned thanks. He felt proud on an occasion of meeting so many of his worthy father's late tenants, promised to improve their farms, and at the same time to abate (if anything was found unreasonable) in their rents.

At the mention of this, the four *Quarter Days* involuntarily looked at each other, and smiled ; *April Fool* whistled to an old tune of " New Brooms " ; and a surly old rebel at the farther end of the table (who was discovered to be no other than the *Fifth of November*) muttered out, distinctly enough to be heard by the whole company, words to this effect—that " when the old one is gone, he is a fool that looks for a better." Which rudeness of his, the guests resenting, unanimously voted his expulsion ; and the malcontent was thrust out neck and heels into the cellar, as the properest place for such a *boutefeu* and firebrand as he had shown himself to be.

Order being restored—the young lord (who, to say truth, had been a little ruffled, and put beside his oratory) in as few and yet as obliging words as possible, assured them of entire welcome ; and, with a graceful turn, singling out poor *Twenty-Ninth of February*, that had sate all this while mumchance at the sideboard, begged to couple his health with that of the good company before him—which he drank accordingly ; observing that he had not seen his honest face any time these four years—with a number of endearing expressions besides. At the same time removing the solitary *Day* from the forlorn seat which had been assigned him, he stationed him at his own board, somewhere between the *Greek Calends* and *Latter Lammas*.

Ash Wednesday, being now called upon for a song, with his eyes fast stuck in his head, and as well as the Canary he had swallowed would give him leave, struck up a Carol, which *Christmas Day* had taught him for the nonce ; and was followed by the latter, who gave " Miserere " in fine style, hitting off the mumping notes and lengthened drawl of *Old Mortification* with infinite humour. *April Fool* swore they had exchanged conditions ; but *Good Friday* was observed to look extremely grave ; and *Sunday* held her fan before her face that she might not be seen to smile.

Shrove-tide, *Lord Mayor's Day*, and *April Fool*, next joined in a glee—

" Which is the properest day to drink ? "

in which all the *Days* chiming in, made a merry burden.

They next fell to quibbles and conundrums. The question being proposed, who had the greatest number of followers—the *Quarter Days* said, there could be no question as to that ; for they had all the creditors in the world dogging their heels. But *April Fool* gave it in favour of the *Forty Days before Easter ;* because the debtors in all cases outnumbered the creditors, and they kept *Lent* all the year.

All this while *Valentine's Day* kept courting pretty *May*, who sate next him, slipping amorous *billets-doux* under the table, till the *Dog Days* (who are naturally of a warm constitution) began to be jealous, and to bark and rage exceedingly. *April Fool*, who likes a bit of sport above measure, and had some pretensions to the lady besides, as being but a cousin once removed,—clapped and halloo'd them on ; and

137

as fast as their indignation cooled, those mad wags, the *Ember Days*, were at it with their bellows, to blow it into a flame ; and all was in a ferment, till old Madam *Septuagesima* (who boasts herself the *Mother of the Days*) wisely diverted the conversation with a tedious tale of the lovers which she could reckon when she was young, and of one Master *Rogation Day* in particular, who was for ever putting the *question* to her ; but she kept him at a distance, as the chronicle would tell—by which I apprehend she meant the Almanack. Then she rambled on to the *Days that were gone*, the *good old Days*, and so to the *Days before the Flood*—which plainly showed her old head to be little better than crazed and doited.

Day being ended, the *Days* called for their cloaks and greatcoats, and took their leave. *Lord Mayor's Day* went off in a Mist, as usual ; *Shortest Day* in a deep black Fog, that wrapt the little gentleman all round like a hedge-hog. Two *Vigils*—so watchmen are called in heaven—saw *Christmas Day* safe home— they had been used to the business before. Another *Vigil*—a stout, sturdy patrole, called the *Eve of St. Christopher*—seeing *Ash Wednesday* in a condition little better than he should be—e'en whipt him over his shoulders, pick-a-back fashion, and *Old Mortification* went floating home singing—

" On the bat's back do I fly,"

and a number of old snatches besides, between drunk and sober ; but very few Aves or Penitentiaries (you may believe me) were among them. *Longest Day* set off westward in beautiful crimson and gold—the rest, some in one fashion, some in another ; but *Valentine* and pretty *May* took their departure together in one of the prettiest silvery twilights a Lover's Day could wish to set in.

OLD CHINA

I HAVE an almost feminine partiality for old china. When I go to see any great house, I inquire for the china-closet, and next for the picture-gallery. I cannot defend the order of preference, but by saying that we have all some taste or other, of too ancient a date to admit of our remembering distinctly that it was an acquired one. I can call to mind the first play, and the first exhibition, that I was taken to ; but I am not conscious of a time when china jars and saucers were introduced into my imagination.

I had no repugnance then—why should I now have ?—to those little, lawless, azure-tinctured grotesques, that, under the notion of men and women, float about, uncircumscribed by any element, in that world before perspective—a china tea-cup.

I like to see my old friends—whom distance cannot diminish—figuring up in the air (so they appear to our optics), yet on *terra firma* still—for so we must in courtesy interpret that speck of deeper blue, which the decorous artist, to prevent absurdity, had made to spring up beneath their sandals.

I love the men with women's faces, and the women, if possible, with still more womanish expressions.

Here is a young and courtly Mandarin, handing tea to a lady from a salver—two miles off. See how distance seems to set off respect ! And here the same lady, or another—for likeness is identity on tea-cups —is stepping into a little fairy boat, moored on the hither side of this calm garden river, with a dainty mincing foot, which in a right angle of incidence (as angles go in our world) must infallibly land her in the midst of a flowery mead—a furlong off on the other side of the same strange stream !

Farther on—if far or near can be predicated of

139

their world—see horses, trees, pagodas, dancing the hays.

Here—a cow and rabbit couchant, and coextensive —so objects show, seen through the lucid atmosphere of fine Cathay.

I was pointing out to my cousin last evening, over our Hyson (which we are old-fashioned enough to drink unmixed still of an afternoon), some of these *speciosa miracula* upon a set of extraordinary old blue china (a recent purchase) which we were now for the first time using ; and could not help remarking, how favourable circumstances had been to us of late years, that we could afford to please the eye sometimes with trifles of this sort—when a passing sentiment seemed to overshade the brows of my companion. I am quick at detecting these summer clouds in Bridget.

" I wish the good old times would come again," she said, " when we were not quite so rich. I do not mean that I want to be poor ; but there was a middle state "—so she was pleased to ramble on,—" in which I am sure we were a great deal happier. A purchase is but a purchase, now that you have money enough and to spare. Formerly it used to be a triumph. When we coveted a cheap luxury (and, O ! how much ado I had to get you to consent in those times !) —we were used to have a debate two or three days before, and to weigh the *for* and *against*, and think what we might spare it out of, and what saving we could hit upon, that should be an equivalent. A thing was worth buying then, when we felt the money that we paid for it.

" Do you remember the brown suit, which you made to hang upon you, till all your friends cried shame upon you, it grew so threadbare—and all because of that folio Beaumont and Fletcher, which you dragged home late at night from Barker's in Covent Garden ? Do you remember how we eyed it for weeks before we could make up our minds to the purchase, and had not come to a determination till it was near ten o'clock of the Saturday night, when you set off from Islington, fearing you should be too late—and when the old bookseller with some grumbling opened his shop, and by the twinkling taper (for he was setting bedwards) lighted out the relic from his dusty treasures—and when you lugged it home, wishing it were twice as cumbersome—and when you presented it to me—and when we were exploring the perfectness of it (*collating*, you called it)—and while I was repairing some of the loose leaves with paste, which your impatience would not suffer to be left till day-break—was there no pleasure in being a poor man? or can those neat black clothes which you wear now, and are so careful to keep brushed, since we have become rich and finical—give you half the honest vanity with which you flaunted it about in that overworn suit—your old corbeau—for four or five weeks longer than you should have done, to pacify your conscience for the mighty sum of fifteen —or sixteen shillings was it?—a great affair we thought it then—which you had lavished on the old folio. Now you can afford to buy any book that pleases you, but I do not see that you ever bring me home any nice old purchases now.

" When you came home with twenty apologies for laying out a less number of shillings upon that print after Lionardo, which we christened the ' Lady Blanch '; when you looked at the purchase, and thought of the money—and thought of the money, and looked again at the picture—was there no pleasure in being a poor man? Now, you have nothing to do but to walk into Colnaghi's, and buy a wilderness of Lionardos. Yet do you?

" Then, do you remember our pleasant walks to Enfield, and Potter's Bar, and Waltham, when we

had a holyday—holydays and all other fun are gone
now we are rich—and the little hand-basket in which
I used to deposit our day's fare of savoury cold lamb
and salad—and how you would pry about at noon-
tide for some decent house, where we might go in
and produce our store—only paying for the ale that
you must call for—and speculate upon the looks of
the landlady, and whether she was likely to allow us a
tablecloth—and wish for such another honest hostess as
Izaak Walton has described many a one on the pleasant
banks of the Lea, when we went a-fishing—and sometimes they would prove obliging enough, and sometimes they would look grudgingly upon us—but we
had cheerful looks still for one another, and would
eat our plain food savourily, scarcely grudging
Piscator his Trout Hall ? Now—when we go out a
day's pleasuring, which is seldom, moreover, we *ride*
part of the way, and go into a fine inn, and order the
best of dinners, never debating the expense—which,
after all, never has half the relish of those chance
country snaps, when we were at the mercy of uncertain usage, and a precarious welcome.

" You are too proud to see a play anywhere now
but in the pit. Do you remember where it was we
used to sit, when we saw the Battle of Hexham, and
the Surrender of Calais, and Bannister and Mrs.
Bland in the Children in the Wood—when we
squeezed out our shillings apiece to sit three or four
times in a season in the one-shilling gallery—where
you felt all the time that you ought not to have
brought me—and more strongly I felt obligation to
you for having brought me—and the pleasure was the
better for a little shame—and when the curtain drew
up, what cared we for our place in the house, or
what mattered it where we were sitting, when our
thoughts were with Rosalind in Arden, or with Viola
at the Court of Illyria ? You used to say that the

Gallery was the best place of all for enjoying a play socially—that the relish of such exhibitions must be in proportion to the infrequency of going—that the company we met there, not being in general readers of plays, were obliged to attend the more, and did attend, to what was going on, on the stage—because a word lost would have been a chasm, which it was impossible for them to fill up. With such reflections we consoled our pride then—and I appeal to you whether, as a woman, I met generally with less attention and accommodation than I have done since in more expensive situations in the house? The getting in, indeed, and the crowding up those inconvenient staircases, was bad enough—but there was still a law of civility to woman recognised to quite as great an extent as we ever found in the other passages—and how a little difficulty overcome heightened the snug seat and the play, afterwards! Now we can only pay our money and walk in. You cannot see, you say, in the galleries now. I am sure we saw, and heard too, well enough then—but sight, and all, I think, is gone with our poverty.

" There was pleasure in eating strawberries, before they became quite common—in the first dish of peas, while they were yet dear—to have them for a nice supper, a treat. What treat can we have now? If we were to treat ourselves now—that is, to have dainties a little above our means, it would be selfish and wicked. It is the very little more that we allow ourselves beyond what the actual poor can get at, that makes what I call a treat—when two people, living together as we have done, now and then indulge themselves in a cheap luxury, which both like ; while each apologises, and is willing to take both halves of the blame to his single share. I see no harm in people making much of themselves, in that sense of the word. It may give them a hint how to make much of others. But now—what I mean by the word—we never *do* make much of ourselves. None but the poor can do it. I do not mean the veriest poor of all, but persons as we were, just above poverty.

" I know what you were going to say, that it is mighty pleasant at the end of the year to make all meet,—and much ado we used to have every Thirty-first Night of December to account for our exceedings —many a long face did you make over your puzzled accounts, and in contriving to make it out how we had spent so much—or that we had not spent so much—or that it was impossible we should spend so much next year—and still we found our slender capital decreasing—but then,—betwixt ways, and projects, and compromises of one sort or another, and talk of curtailing this charge, and doing without that for the future—and the hope that youth brings, and laughing spirits (in which you were never poor till now), we pocketed up our loss, and in conclusion, with ' lusty brimmers ' (as you used to quote it out of *hearty cheerful Mr. Cotton*, as you called him), we used to welcome in the ' coming guest.' Now we have no reckoning at all at the end of the old year—no flattering promises about the new year doing better for us."

Bridget is so sparing of her speech on most occasions, that when she gets into a rhetorical vein, I am careful how I interrupt it. I could not help, however, smiling at the phantom of wealth which her dear imagination had conjured up out of a clear income of poor —— hundred pounds a year. " It is true we were happier when we were poorer, but we were also younger, my cousin. I am afraid we must put up with the excess, for if we were to shake the superflux into the sea, we should not much mend ourselves. That we have had much to struggle with, as we grew up together, we have reason to be most thankful. It strengthened and knit

our compact closer. We could never have been what
we have been to each other, if we had always had
the sufficiency which you now complain of. The
resisting power—those natural dilations of the youth-
ful spirit, which circumstances cannot straiten—with
us are long since passed away. Competence to age
is supplementary youth, a sorry supplement indeed,
but I fear the best that is to be had. We must ride
where we formerly walked : live better and lie softer
—and shall be wise to do so—than we had means to
do in those good old days you speak of. Yet could
those days return—could you and I once more walk
our thirty miles a day—could Bannister and Mrs.
Bland again be young, and you and I be young to see
them—could the good old one-shilling gallery days
return—they are dreams, my cousin, now—but could
you and I at this moment, instead of this quiet argument, by our well-carpeted fireside, sitting on this
luxurious sofa—be once more struggling up those inconvenient staircases, pushed about and squeezed, and
elbowed by the poorest rabble of poor gallery
scramblers—could I once more hear those anxious
shrieks of yours—and the delicious *Thank God, we are
safe*, which always followed when the topmost stair,
conquered, let in the first light of the whole cheerful
theatre down beneath us—I know not the fathom
line that ever touched a descent so deep as I would
be willing to bury more wealth in than Crœsus had,
or the great Jew R—— is supposed to have, to purchase it. And now do just look at that merry little
Chinese waiter holding an umbrella, big enough for
a bed-tester, over the head of that pretty insipid half
Madonna-ish chit of a lady in that very blue summer-
house."

WILLIAM HAZLITT

ON A SUN-DIAL

To carve out dials quaintly, point by point.
SHAKESPEARE

HORAS non numero nisi serenas—is the motto of a
sun-dial near Venice. There is a softness and a har-
mony in the words and in the thought unparalleled.
Of all conceits it is surely the most classical. " I
count only the hours that are serene." What a bland
and care-dispelling feeling ! How the shadows seem
to fade on the dial-plate as the sky lours, and time
presents only a blank unless as its progress is marked
by what is joyous, and all that is not happy sinks into
oblivion ! What a fine lesson is conveyed to the mind
—to take no note of time but by its benefits, to watch
only for the smiles and neglect the frowns of fate, to
compose our lives of bright and gentle moments,
turning always to the sunny side of things, and letting
the rest slip from our imaginations, unheeded or
forgotten ! How different from the common art of
self-tormenting ! For myself, as I rode along the
Brenta, while the sun shone hot upon its sluggish,
slimy waves, my sensations were far from comfortable ; but the reading this inscription on the side of
a glaring wall in an instant restored me to myself ;
and still, whenever I think of or repeat it, it has the
power of wafting me into the region of pure and bliss-
ful abstraction. . . . Some monk of the dark ages
must have invented and bequeathed it to us, who,
loitering in trim gardens and watching the silent
march of time, as his fruits ripened in the sun or his

F   149

flowers scented the balmy air, felt a mild languor pervade his senses, and having little to do or to care for, determined (in imitation of his sun-dial) to efface that little from his thoughts or draw a veil over it, making of his life one long dream of quiet ! *Horas non numero nisi serenas*—he might repeat, when the heavens were overcast and the gathering storm scattered the falling leaves, and turn to his books and wrap himself in his golden studies ! Out of some such mood of mind, indolent, elegant, thoughtful, this exquisite device (speaking volumes) must have originated.

Of the several modes of counting time, that by the sun-dial is perhaps the most apposite and striking, if not the most convenient or comprehensive. It does not obtrude its observations, though it " morals on the time," and, by its stationary character, forms a contrast to the most fleeting of all essences. It stands *sub dio*—under the marble air, and there is some connection between the image of infinity and eternity. I should also like to have a sun-flower growing near it with bees fluttering round. It should be of iron to denote duration, and have a dull, leaden look. I hate a sun-dial made of wood, which is rather calculated to show the variations of the seasons, than the progress of time, slow, silent, imperceptible, chequered with light and shade. If our hours were all serene, we might probably take almost as little note of them, as the dial does of those that are clouded. It is the shadow thrown across, that gives us warning of their flight. Otherwise, our impressions would take the same undistinguishable hue ; we should scarce be conscious of our existence. Those who have had none of the cares of this life to harass and disturb them, have been obliged to have recourse to the hopes and fears of the next to vary the prospect before them. Most of the methods for measuring the lapse of time have, I believe, been the contrivance of monks and religious recluses, who, finding time hang heavy on their hands, were at some pains to see how they got rid of it. The hour-glass is, I suspect, an older invention; and it is certainly the most defective of all. Its creeping sands are not indeed an unapt emblem of the minute, countless portions of our existence; and the manner in which they gradually slide through the hollow glass and diminish in number till not a single one is left, also illustrates the way in which our years slip from us by stealth : but as a mechanical invention, it is rather a hindrance than a help, for it requires to have the time, of which it pretends to count the precious moments, taken up in attention to itself, and in seeing that when one end of the glass is empty, we turn it round, in order that it may go on again, or else all our labour is lost, and we must wait for some other mode of ascertaining the time before we can recover our reckoning and proceed as before. The philosopher in his cell, the cottager at her spinning-wheel, must, however, find an invaluable acquisition in this " companion of the lonely hour," as it has been called,* which not only serves to tell how the time goes, but to fill up its vacancies. What a treasure must not the little box seem to hold, as if it were a sacred deposit of the very grains and fleeing sands of life ! What a business, in lieu of other more important avocations, to see it out to the last sand, and then to renew the process again on the instant, that there may not be the least flaw or error in the account ! What a strong sense must be brought home to the mind of the value and irrecoverable nature of the time that is fled ; what a thrilling, incessant consciousness of the slippery tenure

* Once more, companion of the lonely hour,
    I'll turn thee up again.
    Bloomfield's Poems, " The Widow to her Hour-glass."

by which we hold what remains of it ! Our very existence must seem crumbling to atoms, and running down (without a miraculous reprieve) to the last fragment. " Dust to dust and ashes to ashes " is a text that might be fairly inscribed on an hour-glass : it is ordinarily associated with the scythe of Time and a Death's-head, as a *memento mori ;* and has, no doubt, furnished many a tacit hint to the apprehensive and visionary enthusiast in favour of a resurrection to another life !

The French give a different turn to things, less *sombre* and less edifying. A common and also a very pleasing ornament to a clock, in Paris, is a figure of Time seated in a boat which Cupid is rowing along, with the motto, *L'Amour fait passer le Temps*—which the wits again have travestied into *Le Temps fait passer l'Amour.* All this is ingenious and well ; but it wants sentiment. I like a people who have something that they love and something that they hate, and with whom everything is not alike a matter of indifference or *pour passer le temps.* The French attach no importance to anything, except for the moment ; they are only thinking how they shall get rid of one sensation for another ; all their ideas are *in transitu.* Everything is detached, nothing is accumulated. It would be a million of years before a Frenchman would think of the *Horas non numero nisi serenas.* Its impassioned repose and *ideal* voluptuousness are as far from their breasts as the poetry of that line in Shakespeare—" How sweet the moonlight sleeps upon this bank ! " * They never arrive at the classical— or the romantic. They blow the bubbles of vanity, fashion, and pleasure ; but they do not expand their perceptions into refinement, or strengthen them into solidity. Where there is nothing fine in the ground-work of the imagination, nothing fine in the super-

* *Merchant of Venice,* V. I.

structure can be produced. They are light, airy, fanciful (to give them their due)—but when they attempt to be serious (beyond mere good sense) they are either dull or extravagant. When the volatile salt has flown off, nothing but a *caput mortuum* remains. They have infinite crotchets and caprices with their clocks and watches, which seem made for anything but to tell the hour—gold repeaters, watches with metal covers, clocks with hands to count the seconds. There is no escaping from quackery and impertinence, even in our attempts to calculate the waste of time. The years gallop fast enough for me, without re-marking every moment as it flies ; and further, I must say I dislike a watch (whether of French or English manufacture) that comes to me like a footpad with its face muffled, and does not present its clear, open aspect like a friend, and point with its finger to the time of day. All this opening and shutting of dull, heavy cases (under pretence that the glass lid is liable to be broken, or lets in the dust or air and obstructs the movements of the watch), is not to husband time, but to give trouble. It is mere pomposity and self-importance, like consulting a mysterious oracle that one carries about with one in one's pocket, instead of asking a common question of an acquaintance or companion. There are two clocks which strike the hour in the room where I am. This I do not like. In the first place, I do not want to be reminded twice how the time goes (it is like the second tap of a saucy servant at your door when perhaps you have no wish to get up) : in the next place, it is starting a difference of opinion on the subject, and I am averse to every appearance of wrangling and disputation. Time moves on the same, whatever disparity there may be in our mode of keeping count of it, like true fame in spite of the cavils and contradictions of the critics. I am no friend to repeating watches. The only pleasant association I have with them is the account given by Rousseau of some French lady, who sat up reading the *New Eloise* when it first came out, and ordering her maid to sound the repeater, found it was too late to go to bed, and continued reading on till morning. Yet how different is the interest excited by this story from the account which Rousseau somewhere else gives of his sitting up with his father reading romances, when a boy, till they were startled by the swallows twittering in their nests at daybreak, and the father cried out, half angry and ashamed— " *Allons, mon fils ; je suis plus enfant que toi !* " In general, I have heard repeating watches sounded in stage-coaches at night, when some fellow-traveller suddenly awaking and wondering what was the hour, another has very deliberately taken out his watch, and pressing the spring, it has counted out the time ; each petty stroke acting like a sharp puncture on the ear, and informing me of the dreary hours I had already passed, and of the more dreary ones I had to wait till morning.

The great advantage, it is true, which clocks have over watches and other dumb reckoners of time is, that for the most part they strike the hour—that they are as it were the mouth-pieces of time ; that they not only point it to the eye, but impress it on the ear ; that they " lend it both an understanding and a tongue." Time thus speaks to us in an audible and warning voice. Objects of sight are easily distinguished by the sense, and suggest useful reflections to the mind ; sounds, from their intermittent nature, and perhaps other causes, appeal more to the imagination, and strike upon the heart. But to do this, they must be unexpected and involuntary—there must be no trick in the case—they should not be squeezed out with a finger and a thumb ; there should be nothing optional, personal in their occurrence ; they should be like stern, inflexible monitors, that nothing can prevent from discharging their duty. Surely, if there is anything with which we should not mix up our vanity and self-consequence, it is with Time, the most independent of all things. All the sublimity, all the superstition that hang upon this palpable mode of announcing its flight, are chiefly attached to this circumstance. Time would lose its abstracted character, if we kept it like a curiosity or a jack-in-a-box : its prophetic warnings would have no effect, if it obviously spoke only at our prompting like a paltry ventriloquism. The clock that tells the coming, dreaded hour—the castle bell, that " with its brazen throat and iron tongue, sounds *one* unto the drowsy ear of night "—the curfew, " swinging slow with sullen roar " o'er wizard stream or fountain, are like a voice from other worlds, big with unknown events. The last sound, which is still kept up as an old custom in many parts of England, is a great favourite with me. I used to hear it when a boy. It tells a tale of other times. The days that are past, the generations that are gone, the tangled forest glades and hamlets brown of my native country, the woodman's art, the Norman warrior armed for the battle or in his festive hall, the conqueror's iron rule and peasant's lamp extinguished, all start up at the clamorous peal, and fill my mind with fear and wonder. I confess, nothing at present interests me but what has been—the recollection of the impressions of my early life, or events long past, of which only the dim traces remain in a mouldering ruin or half-obsolete custom. That *things should be that are now no more*, creates in my mind the most unfeigned astonishment. I cannot solve the mystery of the past, nor exhaust my pleasure in it. The years, the generations to come, are nothing to me. We care no more about the world in the year 2300 than we do about one of the planets. We might as well make a voyage to the moon as think of stealing a march upon Time with impunity. *De non apparentibus et non existentibus eadem est ratio.* Those who are to come after us and push us from the stage seem like upstarts and pretenders, that may be said to exist *in vacuo*, we know not upon what, except as they are blown up with vanity and self-conceit by their patrons among the moderns. But the ancients are true and *bona fide* people, to whom we are bound by aggregate knowledge and filial ties, and in whom, seen by the mellow light of history, we feel our own existence doubled and our pride consoled, as we ruminate on the vestiges of the past. The public in general, however, do not carry this speculative indifference about the future to what is to happen to themselves, or to the part they are to act in the busy scene. For my own part, I do ; and the only wish I can form, or that ever prompts the passing sigh, would be to live some of my years over again—they would be those in which I enjoyed and suffered most !

The ticking of a clock in the night has nothing very interesting nor very alarming in it, though superstition has magnified it into an omen. In a state of vigilance or debility, it preys upon the spirits like the persecution of a teasing, pertinacious insect ; and haunting the imagination after it has ceased in reality, is converted into the death-watch. Time is rendered vast by contemplating its minute portions thus repeatedly and painfully urged upon its attention, as the ocean in its immensity is composed of water-drops. A clock striking with a clear and silver sound is a great relief in such circumstances, breaks the spell, and resembles a sylph-like and friendly spirit in the room. Foreigners with all their tricks and contrivances upon clocks and time-pieces, are strangers to the sound of village bells, though perhaps a people that can dance may dispense

with them. They impart a pensive, wayward pleasure
to the mind, and are a kind of chronology of happy
events, often serious in the retrospect—births, marriages, and so forth. Coleridge calls them " the poor
man's only music." A village spire in England
peeping from its cluster of trees, is always associated
in imagination with this cheerful accompaniment, and
may be expected to pour its joyous tidings on the gale.
In Catholic countries, you are stunned with the everlasting tolling of bells to prayers or for the dead. In
the Apennines, and other wild and mountainous
districts of Italy, the little chapel-bell with its simple
tinkling sound has a romantic and charming effect.
The monks in former times appear to have taken a
pride in the construction of bells as well as churches ;
and some of those of the great cathedrals abroad (as
at Cologne and Rouen) may be fairly said to be hoarse
with counting the flight of ages. The chimes in
Holland are a nuisance. They dance in the hours and
the quarters. They leave no respite to the imagination. Before one set has done ringing in your ears,
another begins. You do not know whether the hours
move or stand still, go backwards or forwards, so
fantastical and perplexing are their accompaniments.
Time is a more staid personage, and not so full of
gambols. It puts you in mind of a tune with variations,
or of an embroidered dress. Surely, nothing is more
simple than Time. His march is straightforward ;
but we should have leisure allowed us to look back
upon the distance we have come, and not be counting
his steps every moment. Time in Holland is a foolish
old fellow with all the antics of a youth, who " goes to
church in a coranto, and lights his pipe in a cinquepace." The chimes with us, on the contrary, as they
come in every three or four hours, are like stages in
the journey of the day. They give a fillip to the lazy,
creeping hours, and relieve the lassitude of country-

places. At noon, their desultory, trivial song is diffused through the hamlet with the odour of rashers of bacon ; at the close of day they send the toil-worn sleepers to their beds. Their discontinuance would be a great loss to the thinking or unthinking public. Mr. Wordsworth has painted their effect on the mind when he makes his friend Matthew, in a fit of inspired dotage,

> " Sing those witty rhymes
> About the crazy old church-clock
> And the bewilder'd chimes."

The tolling of the bell for deaths and executions is a fearful summons, though, as it announces, not the advance of time but the approach of fate, it happily makes no part of our subject. Otherwise, the " sound of the bell " for Macheath's execution in the *Beggar's Opera*, or for that of the Conspirators in *Venice Preserved*, with the roll of the drum at a soldier's funeral, and a digression to that of my Uncle Toby, as it is so finely described by Sterne, would furnish ample topics to descant upon. If I were a moralist, I might disapprove the ringing in the new and ringing out the old year.

" Why dance ye, mortals, o'er the grave of Time ? "

St. Paul's bell tolls only for the death of our English kings, or a distinguished personage or two, with long intervals between.*

Those who have no artificial means of ascertaining the progress of time, are in general the most acute in discerning its immediate signs, and are most retentive of individual dates. The mechanical aids to knowledge are not sharpeners of the wits. The understanding of

---

* Rousseau has admirably described the effect of bells on the imagination in a passage in the *Confessions*, beginning, " *Le son des cloches m'a toujours singulièrement affecté,*" etc.

a savage is a kind of natural almanac, and more true in its prognostication of the future. In his mind's eye he sees what has happened or what is likely to happen to him, " as in a map the voyager his course." Those who read the times and seasons in the aspect of the heavens and the configuration of the stars, who count by moons and know when the sun rises and sets, are by no means ignorant of their own affairs or of the common concatenation of events. People in such situations have not their faculties distracted by any multiplicity of inquiries beyond what befalls themselves, and the outward appearances that mark the change. There is, therefore, a simplicity and clearness in the knowledge they possess, which often puzzles the more learned. I am sometimes surprised at a shepherd-boy by the road-side, who sees nothing but the earth and sky, asking me the time of day—he ought to know so much better than anyone how far the sun is above the horizon. I suppose he wants to ask a question of a passenger, or to see if he has a watch. Robinson Crusoe lost his reckoning in the monotony of his life and that bewildering dream of solitude, and was fain to have recourse to the notches in a piece of wood. What a diary was his ! And how time must have spread its circuit round him, vast and pathless as the ocean !

For myself, I have never had a watch nor any other mode of keeping time in my possession, nor ever wish to learn how time goes. It is a sign I have had little to do, few avocations, few engagements. When I am in a town, I can hear the clock ; and when I am in the country, I can listen to the silence. What I like best is to lie whole mornings on a sunny bank on Salisbury Plain, without any object before me, neither knowing nor caring how time passes, and thus " with light-winged toys of feathered Idleness " to melt down hours to moments. Perhaps some such thoughts as I have here set down float before me like motes before my half-shut eyes, or some vivid image of the past by forcible contrast rushes by me—" Diana and her fawn, and all the glories of the antique world " ; then I start away to prevent the iron from entering my soul, and let fall some tears into that stream of time which separates me farther and farther from all I once loved ! At length I rouse myself from my reverie, and home to dinner, proud of killing time with thought, nay even without thinking. Somewhat of this idle humour I inherit from my father, though he had not the same freedom from *ennui*, for he was not a metaphysician ; and there were stops and vacant intervals in his being which he did not know how to fill up. He used in these cases, and as an obvious resource, carefully to wind up his watch at night, and " with lack-lustre eye " more than once in the course of the day look to see what o'clock it was. Yet he had nothing else in his character in common with the elder Mr. Shandy. Were I to attempt a sketch of him, for my own or the reader's satisfaction, it would be after the following manner——But now I recollect I have done something of the kind once before, and were I to resume the subject here, some bat or owl of a critic, with spectacled gravity, might swear I had stolen the whole of this Essay from myself—or (what is worse) from him ! So I had better let it go as it is.

ON NICKNAMES

Hæ nugæ in seria ducunt.

THIS is a more important subject than it seems at first sight. It is as serious in its results as it is contemptible in the means by which these results are brought about. Nicknames, for the most part, govern the world. The history of politics, of religion, of literature, of morals, and of private life, is too often little less than the history of nicknames. What are one-half the convulsions of the civilised world—the frequent overthrow of states and kingdoms—the shock and hostile encounters of mighty continents— the battles by sea and land—the intestine commotions —the feuds of the Vitelli and Orsini, of the Guelphs and Ghibellines—the civil wars in England and the League in France—the jealousies and heart-burnings of cabinets and councils—the uncharitable proscriptions of creeds and sects, Turk, Jew, Pagan, Papist and Puritan, Quaker, and Methodist—the persecutions and massacres—the burnings, tortures, imprisonments, and lingering deaths, inflicted for a different profession of faith—but so many illustrations of the power of this principle ? Foxe's *Book of Martyrs*, and Neale's *History of the Puritans*, are comments on the same text. The fires in Smithfield were fanned by nicknames, and a nickname set its seal on the unopened dungeons of the Holy Inquisition. Nicknames are the talismans and spells that collect and set in motion all the combustible part of men's passions and prejudices, which have hitherto played so much more successful a game, and done their work so much more effectually than reason, in all the grand concerns and petty details of human life, and do not yet seem tired of the task assigned them. Nicknames are the convenient, portable tools by which they simplify the process of mischief, and get through their job with the least time and trouble. These worthless, unmeaning, irritating, envenomed words of reproach are the established signs by which the different compartments of society are ticketed, labelled, and marked out for each other's hatred and contempt. They are to be had, ready cut and dry, of all sorts and sizes, wholesale and retail, for foreign exportation or for home consumption, and for all occasions in life. " The priest calls the lawyer a cheat, the lawyer beknaves the divine." The Frenchman hates the Englishman because he is an Englishman ; and the Englishman hates the Frenchman for as good a reason. The Whig hates the Tory, and the Tory the Whig. The Dissenter hates the Church of England man, and the Church of England man hates the Dissenter, as if they were of a different species, because they have a different designation. The Mussulman calls the worshipper of the Cross " Christian dog," spits in his face, and kicks him from the pavement, by virtue of a nickname ; and the Christian retorts the indignity upon the Infidel and the Jew by the same infallible rule of right. In France they damn Shakespeare in the lump, by calling him a *barbare;* and we talk of Racine's *verbiage* with inexpressible contempt and self-complacency. Among ourselves, an anti-Jacobin critic denounces a Jacobin poet and his friends, at a venture, " as infidels and fugitives, who have left their wives destitute, and their children fatherless "—whether they have wives and children or not. The unenlightened savage makes a meal of his enemy's flesh, after reproaching him with the name of his tribe, because he is differently tattooed ; and the literary cannibal cuts up the character of his opponent by the help of a nickname. The jest of all this is, that a party nickname is always a relative term, and has its countersign, which has just the same force and meaning, so that both must be perfectly ridiculous and insignificant. A Whig implies a Tory ; there must be " Malcontents " as well as " Malignants " ; Jacobins and anti-Jacobins ; English and French. These sorts of *noms-de-guerre* derive all their force from their contraries. Take away the meaning of the one, and you take the sting out of the other.

They could not exist but upon the strength of mutual and irreconcilable antipathies; there must be no love lost between them. What is there in the names themselves to give them a preference over each other? " Sound them, they do become the mouth as well; weigh them, they are as heavy; conjure with them, one will raise a spirit as soon as the other." If there were not fools and madmen who hated both, there could not be fools and madmen bigoted to either. I have heard an eminent character boast that he had done more to produce the late war by nicknaming Buonaparte " the Corsican," than all the state papers and documents on the subject put together. And yet Mr. Southey asks triumphantly, " Is it to be supposed that it is England, *our* England, to whom that war was owing ? " As if, in a dispute between two countries, the conclusive argument, which lies in the pronoun *our*, belonged only to one of them. I like Shakespeare's version of the matter better :—

" Hath Britain all the sun that shines ? Day, night,
Are they not but in Britain ? I' the world's volume
Our Britain seems as of it, but not in 't;
In a great pool a swan's nest, prithee, think
There's livers out of Britain."

In all national disputes, it is common to appeal to the numbers on your side as decisive on the point. If everybody in England thought the late war right, everybody in France thought it wrong. There were ten millions on one side of the question (or rather of the water), and thirty millions on the other side— that's all. I remember some one arguing, in justification of our Ministers interfering without occasion, " That governments would not go to war for nothing "; to which I answered : " Then they could not go to war at all; for, at that rate, neither of them could be in the wrong, and yet both of them

must be in the right, which was absurd." The only
meaning of these vulgar nicknames and party distinctions, where they are urged most violently and
confidently, is that others differ from you in some
particular or other (whether it be opinion, dress,
clime, or complexion), which you highly disapprove
of, forgetting that, by the same rule, they have the
very same right to be offended at you because you
differ from them. Those who have reason on their
side do not make the most obstinate and grievous
appeals to prejudice and abusive language. I know
but of one exception to this general rule, and that is
where the things that excite disgust are of such a
kind that they cannot well be gone into without
offence to decency and good manners ; but it is
equally certain in this case, that those who are most
shocked at the things are not those who are most
forward to apply the names. A person will not be
fond of repeating a charge, or adverting to a subject,
that inflicts a wound on his own feelings, even for the
sake of wounding the feelings of another. A man
should be very sure that he himself is not what he has
always in his mouth. The greatest prudes have been
often accounted the greatest hypocrites, and a satirist
is at best but a suspicious character. The loudest
and most unblushing invectives against vice and
debauchery will as often proceed from a desire to
inflame and pamper the passions of the writer, by
raking into a nauseous subject, as from a wish to
excite virtuous indignation against it in the public
mind, or to reform the individual. To familiarise the
mind to gross ideas is not the way to increase your
own or the general repugnance to them. But to
return to the subject of nicknames.

The use of this figure of speech is, that it excites a
strong idea without requiring any proof. It is a short-
hand, compendious mode of getting at a conclusion,

and never troubling yourself or anybody else with the
formalities of reasoning or the dictates of common
sense. It is superior to all evidence, for it does not
rest upon any, and operates with the greatest force
and certainty in proportion to the utter want of
probability. Belief is only a stray impression, and
the malignity or extravagance of the accusation passes
for a proof of the crime. " Brevity is the soul of wit " ;
and of all eloquence a nickname is the most concise,
of all arguments the most unanswerable. It gives
carte-blanche to the imagination, throws the reins on
the neck of the passions, and suspends the use of the
understanding altogether. It does not stand upon
ceremony, on the nice distinctions of right and wrong.
It does not wait the slow processes of reason, or stop
to unravel the wit of sophistry. It takes everything
for granted that serves for nourishment for the spleen.
It is instantaneous in its operations. There is nothing
to interpose between the effect and it. It is passion
without proof, and action without thought—" the
unbought grace of life, the cheap defence of nations."
It does not, as Mr. Burke expresses it, " leave the
will puzzled, undecided, and sceptical in the moment
of action." It is a word and a blow. The " No
Popery " cry raised a little while ago let loose all the
lurking spite and prejudice which had lain rankling
in the proper receptacles for them for above a century,
without any knowledge of the past history of the
country which had given rise to them, or any reference
to their connection with present circumstances ; for
the knowledge of the one would have prevented the
possibility of their application to the other. Facts
present a tangible and definite idea to the mind, a
train of causes and consequences, accounting for each
other, and leading to a positive conclusion—but no
farther. But a nickname is tied down to no such
limited service ; it is a disposable force, that is almost

always perverted to mischief. It clothes itself with all the terrors of uncertain abstraction, and there is no end of the abuse to which it is liable but the cunning of those who employ, or the credulity of those who are gulled by it. It is a reserve of the ignorance, bigotry, and intolerance of weak and vulgar minds, brought up where reason fails, and always ready, at a moment's warning, to be applied to any, the most absurd purposes. If you bring specific charges against a man, you thereby enable him to meet and repel them, if he thinks it worth his while; but a nickname baffles reply, by the very vagueness of the inferences from it, and gives increased activity to the confused, dim, and imperfect notions of dislike connected with it, from their having no settled ground to rest upon. The mind naturally irritates itself against an unknown object of fear or jealousy, and makes up for the blindness of its zeal by an excess of it. We are eager to indulge our hasty feelings to the utmost, lest, by stopping to examine, we should find that there is no excuse for them. The very consciousness of the injustice we may be doing another makes us only the more loud and bitter in our invectives against him. We keep down the admonitions of returning reason, by calling up a double portion of gratuitous and vulgar spite. The will may be said to act with most force *in vacuo;* the passions are the most ungovernable when they are blindfolded. That malignity is always the most implacable which is accompanied with a sense of weakness, because it is never satisfied of its own success or safety. A nickname carries the weight of the pride, the indolence, the cowardice, the ignorance, and the ill-nature of mankind on its side. It acts by mechanical sympathy on the nerves of society. Any one who is without character himself may make himself master of the reputation of another by the application of a nickname, as, if you do not mind soiling your fingers, you may always throw dirt on another. No matter how undeserved the imputation, it will stick ; for, though it is sport to the bystanders to see you bespattered, they will not stop to see you wipe out the stains. You are not heard in your own defence ; it has no effect, it does not tell, excites no sensation, or it is only felt as a disappointment of their triumph over you. Their passions and prejudices are inflamed by the charge, " As rage with rage doth sympathise " ; by vindicating yourself, you merely bring them back to common sense, which is a very sober, mawkish state. *Give a dog an ill name and hang him*, is a proverb. " A nickname is the heaviest stone that the devil can throw at a man." It is a bugbear to the imagination, and, though we do not believe in it, it still haunts our apprehensions. Let a nickname be industriously applied to our dearest friend, and let us know that it is ever so false and malicious, yet it will answer its end ; it connects the person's name and idea with an ugly association, you think of them with pain together, or it requires an effort of indignation or magnanimity on your part to disconnect them ; it becomes an uneasy subject, a sore point, and you will sooner desert your friend, or join in the conspiracy against him, than be constantly forced to repel charges without truth or meaning, and have your penetration or character called in question by a rascal. Nay, such is the unaccountable construction of language and of the human mind, that the affixing the most innocent or praiseworthy appellation to any individual, or set of individuals, *as a nickname*, has all the effect of the most opprobrious epithets. Thus the cant name, " the Talents," was successfully applied as a stigma to the Whigs at one time ; it held them up to ridicule, and made them obnoxious to public feeling, though it was notorious to everybody that the Whig leaders were " the

Talents," and that their adversaries nicknamed them so from real hatred and pretended derision. Call a man short by his Christian name, as Tom or Dick such-a-one, or by his profession (however respectable), as Canning pelted a noble lord with his left-off title of Doctor, and you undo him for ever, if he has a reputation to lose. Such is the tenaciousness of spite and ill-nature, or the jealousy of public opinion, even this will be peg enough to hang doubtful inuendos, weighty dilemmas upon. " With so small a web as this will I catch so great a fly as Cassio." The public do not like to see their favourites treated with impertinent familiarity ; it lowers the tone of admiration very speedily. It implies that some one stands in no great awe of their idol, and he perhaps may know as much about the matter as they do. It seems as if a man whose name, with some contemptuous abbreviation, is always dinned in the public ear, was distinguished for nothing else. By repeating a man's name in this manner you may soon make him sick of it, and of his life too. Children do not like to be *called out of their names :* it is questioning their personal identity. There are political writers who have fairly worried their readers into conviction by abuse and nicknames. People surrender their judgments to escape the persecution of their style, and the disgust and indignation which their incessant violence and vulgarity excite, at last make you hate those who are the objects of it. *Causa causæ causa causati.* They make people sick of a subject by making them sick of their arguments.

A parrot may be taught to call names ; and if the person who keeps the parrot has a spite to his neighbours, he may give them a great deal of annoyance without much wit, either in the employer or the puppet. The insignificance of the instrument has nothing to do with the efficacy of the means. Hotspur would have had " a *starling* taught to speak nothing but Mortimer," in the ears of his enemy. Nature, it is said, has given arms to all creatures the most proper to defend themselves, and annoy others : to the lowest she has given the use of nicknames.

There are some droll instances of the effect of proper names combined with circumstances. A young student had come up to London from Cambridge, and went in the evening and planted himself in the pit of the playhouse. He had not been seated long, when in one of the front boxes near him he discovered one of his college tutors, with whom he felt an immediate and strong desire to claim acquaintance, and accordingly called out, in a low and respectful voice, " Dr. Topping ! " The appeal was, however, ineffectual. He then repeated in a louder tone, but still in an under key, so as not to excite the attention of any one but his friend, " Dr. Topping ! " The Doctor took no notice. He then grew more impatient, and repeated " Dr. Topping, Dr. Topping ! " two or three times pretty loud, to see whether the Doctor did not or would not hear him. Still the Doctor remained immovable. The joke began at length to get round, and one or two persons, as he continued his invocation of the Doctor's name, joined in with him ; these were reinforced by others calling out, " Dr. Topping, Dr. Topping ! " on all sides, so that he could no longer avoid perceiving it, and at length the whole pit rose and roared, " Dr. Topping ! " with loud and repeated cries, and the Doctor was forced to retire precipitately, frightened at the sound of his own name.

The calling people by their Christian or surname is a proof of affection, as well as of hatred. They are generally the best of good fellows with whom their friends take this sort of liberty. *Diminutives* are titles of endearment. Dr. Johnson's calling Goldsmith

" Goldy " did equal honour to both. It showed the regard he had for him. This familiarity may perhaps imply a certain want of formal respect; but formal respect is not necessary to, if it is consistent with, cordial friendship. Titles of honour are the reverse of nicknames : they convey the idea of respect, as the others do of contempt, but they equally mean little or nothing. Junius's motto, *Stat nominis umbra*, is a very significant one; it might be extended farther. A striking instance of the force of names, standing by themselves, is in the respect felt towards Michael Angelo in this country. We know nothing of him but his name. It is an abstraction of fame and greatness. Our admiration of him supports itself, and our idea of his superiority seems self-evident, because it is attached to his name only.

JOHN CAVANAGH

Died at his house in Burbage Street, St. Giles's, John Cavanagh, the famous hand fives-player. When a person dies who does any one thing better than any one else in the world, which so many others are trying to do well, it leaves a gap in society. It is not likely that any one will now see the game of fives played in its perfection for many years to come—for Cavanagh is dead, and has not left his peer behind him. It may be said that there are things of more importance than striking a ball against a wall—there are things, indeed, that make more noise and do as little good, such as making war and peace, making speeches and answering them, making verses and blotting them, making money and throwing it away. But the game of fives is what no one despises who has ever played at it. It is the finest exercise for the body, and the best relaxation for the mind. The Roman poet said that " Care mounted behind the horseman and stuck to his skirts." But this remark would not have applied to the fives-player. He who takes to playing at fives is twice young. He feels neither the past nor future " in the instant." Debts, taxes, " domestic treason, foreign levy, nothing can touch him further." He has no other wish, no other thought, from the moment the game begins, but that of striking the ball, of placing it, of *making* it ! This Cavanagh was sure to do. Whenever he touched the ball there was an end of the chase. His eye was certain, his hand fatal, his presence of mind complete. He could do what he pleased, and he always knew exactly what to do. He saw the whole game, and played it ; took instant advantage of his adversary's weakness, and recovered balls, as if by a miracle and from sudden thought, that every one gave for lost. He had equal power and skill, quickness and judgment. He could either outwit his antagonist by finesse, or beat him by main strength. Sometimes, when he seemed preparing to send the ball with the full swing of his arm, he would by a slight turn of his wrist drop it within an inch of the line. In general, the ball came from his hand, as if from a racket, in a straight, horizontal line ; so that it was in vain to attempt to overtake or stop it. And it was said of a great orator that he never was at a loss for a word, and for the properest word, so Cavanagh always could tell the degree of force necessary to be given to a ball, and the precise direction in which it should be sent. He did his work with the greatest ease ; never took more pains than was necessary ; and while others were fagging themselves to death, was as cool and collected as if he had just entered the court. His style of play was as remarkable as his power of execution. He had no affectation, no trifling. He did not throw away the game to show off an attitude or try an experiment. He was a fine, sensible, manly player, who did what he could, but that was more than any one else could even affect to do. His blows were not undecided and ineffectual—lumbering like Mr. Wordsworth's epic poetry, nor wavering like Mr. Coleridge's lyric prose, nor short of the mark like Mr. Brougham's speeches, nor wide of it like Mr. Canning's wit, nor foul like the *Quarterly*, nor *let* balls like the *Edinburgh Review*. Cobbett and Junius together would have made a Cavanagh. He was the best *up-hill* player in the world ; even when his adversary was fourteen, he would play on the same or better, and as he never flung away the game through carelessness and conceit, he never gave it up through laziness or want of heart. The only peculiarity of his play was that he never *volleyed*, but let the balls hop ; but if they rose an inch from the ground he never missed having them. There was not only nobody equal, but nobody second to him. It is supposed that he could give any other player half the game, or beat them with his left hand. His service was tremendous. He once played Woodward and Meredith together (two of the best players in England) in the Fives-court, St. Martin's Street, and made seven and twenty aces following by services alone—a thing unheard of. He another time played Peru, who was considered a first-rate fives-player, a match of the best out of five games, and in the three first games, which of course decided the match, Peru got only one ace. Cavanagh was an Irishman by birth, and a housepainter by profession. He had once laid aside his working-dress, and walked up, in his smartest clothes, to the Rosemary Branch to have an afternoon's pleasure. A person accosted him, and asked him if he would have a game. So they agreed to play for half a crown a game and a bottle of cider. The first game began—it was seven, eight, ten, thirteen, four-

teen, all. Cavanagh won it. The next was the same.
They played on, and each game was hardly contested.
"There," said the unconscious fives-player, "there
was a stroke that Cavanagh could not take : I never
played better in my life, and yet I can't win a game.
I don't know how it is ! " However, they played on,
Cavanagh winning every game, and the bystanders
drinking the cider and laughing all the time. In the
twelfth game, when Cavanagh was only four, and the
stranger thirteen, a person came in and said, " What !
are you here, Cavanagh ? " The words were no
sooner pronounced than the astonished player let the
ball drop from his hand, and saying, " What ! have I
been breaking my heart all this time to beat
Cavanagh ? " refused to make another effort. " And
yet, I give you my word," said Cavanagh, telling the
story with some triumph, " I played all the while
with my clenched fist."—He used frequently to play
matches at Copenhagen House for wagers and dinners.
The wall against which they play is the same that
supports the kitchen-chimney, and when the wall
resounded louder than usual, the cooks exclaimed,
" Those are the Irishman's balls," and the joints
trembled on the spit !—Goldsmith consoled himself
that there were places where he too was admired :
and Cavanagh was the admiration of all the fives-
courts where he ever played. Mr. Powell, when he
played matches in the Court in St. Martin's Street,
used to fill his gallery at half a crown a head with
amateurs and admirers of talent in whatever department it is shown. He could not have shown himself
in any ground in England but he would have been
immediately surrounded with inquisitive gazers, trying
to find out in what part of his frame his unrivalled
skill lay, as politicians wonder to see the balance of
Europe suspended in Lord Castlereagh's face, and
admire the trophies of the British Navy lurking under

Mr. Croker's hanging brow. Now Cavanagh was as good-looking a man as the Noble Lord, and much better looking than the Right Hon. Secretary. He had a clear, open, countenance, and did not look sideways or down, like Mr. Murray the bookseller. He was a young fellow of sense, humour, and courage. He once had a quarrel with a waterman at Hungerford Stairs, and, they say, served him out in great style. In a word, there are hundreds at this day who cannot mention his name without admiration, as the best fives-player that perhaps ever lived (the greatest excellence of which they have any notion) ; and the noisy shout of the ring happily stood him in stead of the unheard voice of posterity !—The only person who seems to have excelled as much in another way as Cavanagh did in his was the late John Davies, the racket-player. It was remarked of him that he did not seem to follow the ball, but the ball seemed to follow him. Give him a foot of wall, and he was sure to make the ball. The four best racket-players of that day were Jack Spines, Jem Harding, Armitage, and Church. Davies could give any one of these two hands a time, that is, half the game, and each of these, at their best, could give the best player now in London the same odds. Such are the gradations in all exertions of human skill and art. He once played four capital players together, and beat them. He was also a first-rate tennis player and an excellent fives-player. In the Fleet or King's Bench he would have stood against Powell, who was reckoned the best open-ground player of this time. This last-mentioned player is at present the keeper of the Fives-court, and we might recommend to him for a motto over his door, " Who enters here, forgets himself, his country, and his friends." And the best of it is, that by the calculation of the odds, none of the three are worth remembering !—Cavanagh died from the bursting of a blood-vessel, which prevented him from playing for the last two or three years. This, he was often heard to say, he thought hard upon him. He was fast recovering, however, when he was suddenly carried off, to the regret of all who knew him. As Mr. Peel made it a qualification of the present Speaker, Mr. Manners Sutton, that he was an excellent moral character, so Jack Cavanagh was a zealous Catholic, and could not be persuaded to eat meat on a Friday, the day on which he died. We have paid this willing tribute to his memory.

> " Let no rude hand deface it,
> And his forlorn ' *Hic Jacet*.' "

R. L. STEVENSON

AN APOLOGY FOR IDLERS

BOSWELL: We grow weary when idle.
JOHNSON: That is, sir, because others being busy,
we want company; but if we were idle, there
would be no growing weary; we should all entertain
one another.

JUST now, when every one is bound, under pain of
a decree in absence convicting them of *lèse*-respect-
ability, to enter on some lucrative profession, and
labour therein with something not far short of enthusiasm, a cry from the opposite party who are
content when they have enough, and like to look on
and enjoy in the meanwhile, savours a little of
bravado and gasconade. And yet this should not be.
Idleness so called, which does not consist in doing
nothing, but in doing a great deal not recognised in
the dogmatic formularies of the ruling class, has as
good a right to state its position as industry itself. It
is admitted that the presence of people who refuse to
enter in the great handicap race for sixpenny pieces,
is at once an insult and a disenchantment for those
who do. A fine fellow (as we see so many) takes his
determination, votes for the sixpences, and in the
emphatic Americanism, " goes for " them. And
while such an one is ploughing distressfully up the
road, it is not hard to understand his resentment,
when he perceives cool persons in the meadows by
the wayside, lying with a handkerchief over their
ears and a glass at their elbow. Alexander is touched
in a very delicate place by the disregard of Diogenes.
Where was the glory of having taken Rome for these

tumultuous barbarians, who poured into the Senate house, and found the Fathers sitting silent and unmoved by their success? It is a sore thing to have laboured along and scaled the arduous hilltops, and when all is done, find humanity indifferent to your achievement. Hence physicists condemn the unphysical; financiers have only a superficial toleration for those who know little of stocks; literary persons despise the unlettered; and people of all pursuits combine to disparage those who have none.

But though this is one difficulty of the subject, it is not the greatest. You could not be put in prison for speaking against industry, but you can be sent to Coventry for speaking like a fool. The greatest difficulty with most subjects is to do them well; therefore, please to remember this is an apology. It is certain that much may be judiciously argued in favour of diligence; only there is something to be said against it, and that is what, on the present occasion, I have to say. To state one argument is not necessarily to be deaf to all others, and that a man has written a book of travels in Montenegro, is no reason why he should never have been to Richmond.

It is surely beyond a doubt that people should be a good deal idle in youth. For though here and there a Lord Macaulay may escape from school honours with all his wits about him, most boys pay so dear for their medals that they never afterwards have a shot in their locker, and begin the world bankrupt. And the same holds true during all the time a lad is educating himself, or suffering others to educate him. It must have been a very foolish old gentleman who addressed Johnson at Oxford in these words: " Young man, ply your book diligently now, and acquire a stock of knowledge; for when years come upon you, you will find that poring upon books will be but an irksome task." The old gentleman seems to have been unaware that many other things besides reading grow irksome, and not a few become impossible, by the time a man has to use spectacles and cannot walk without a stick. Books are good enough in their own way, but they are a mighty bloodless substitute for life. It seems a pity to sit, like the Lady of Shalott, peering into a mirror, with your back turned on all the bustle and glamour of reality. And if a man reads very hard, as the old anecdote reminds us, he will have little time for thought.

If you look back on your own education, I am sure it will not be the full, vivid, instructive hours of truantry that you regret ; you would rather cancel some lack-lustre periods between sleep and waking in the class. For my own part, I have attended a good many lectures in my time. I still remember that the spinning of a top is a case of Kinetic Stability. I still remember that Emphyteusis is not a disease, nor Stillicide a crime. But though I would not willingly part with such scraps of science, I do not set the same store by them as by certain other odds and ends that I came by in the open street while I was playing truant. This is not the moment to dilate on that mighty place of education, which was the favourite school of Dickens and of Balzac, and turns out yearly many inglorious masters in the Science of the Aspects of Life. Suffice it to say this : if a lad does not learn in the streets, it is because he has no faculty of learning Nor is the truant always in the streets, for if he prefers, he may go out by the gardened suburbs into the country. He may pitch on some tuft of lilacs over a burn, and smoke innumerable pipes to the tune of the water on the stones. A bird will sing in the thicket. And there he may fall into a vein of kindly thought, and see things in a new perspective. Why, if this be not education, what is ? We may

conceive Mr. Worldly Wiseman accosting such an one,
and the conversation that should thereupon ensue :—

" How now, young fellow, what dost thou here ? "

" Truly, sir, I take mine ease."

" Is not this the hour of the class ? and should'st
thou not be plying thy Book with diligence, to the
end thou mayest obtain knowledge ? "

" Nay, but thus also I follow after Learning, by
your leave."

" Learning, quotha ! After what fashion, I pray
thee ? Is it mathematics ? "

" No, to be sure."

" Is it metaphysics ? "

" Nor that."

" Is it some language ? "

" Nay, it is no language."

" Is it a trade ? "

" Nor a trade neither."

" Why, then, what is't ? "

" Indeed, sir, as a time may soon come for me to
go upon Pilgrimage, I am desirous to note what is
commonly done by persons in my case, and where
are the ugliest Sloughs and Thickets on the Road ;
as also, what manner of Staff is of the best service.
Moreover, I lie here, by this water, to learn by root-
of-heart a lesson which my master teaches me to call
Peace, or Contentment."

Hereupon Mr. Worldly Wiseman was much com-
moved with passion, and shaking his cane with a
very threatful countenance, broke forth upon this
wise : " Learning, quotha ! " said he ; " I would
have all such rogues scourged by the Hangman ! "

And so he would go his way, ruffling out his cravat
with a crackle of starch, like a turkey when it spreads
its feathers.

Now this, of Mr. Wiseman's, is the common opinion.
A fact is not called a fact, but a piece of gossip, if it

does not fall into one of your scholastic categories. An inquiry must be in some acknowledged direction, with a name to go by ; or else you are not inquiring at all, only lounging ; and the workhouse is too good for you. It is supposed that all knowledge is at the bottom of a well or the far end of a telescope. Sainte-Beuve, as he grew older, came to regard all experience as a single great book, in which to study for a few years ere we go hence ; and it seemed all one to him whether you should read in Chapter xx., which is the differential calculus, or in Chapter xxxix., which is hearing the band play in the gardens. As a matter of fact, an intelligent person, looking out of his eyes and hearkening in his ears, with a smile on his face all the time, will get more true education than many another in a life of heroic vigils. There is certainly some chill and arid knowledge to be found upon the summits of formal and laborious science ; but it is round about you, and for the trouble of looking, that you will acquire the warm and palpitating facts of life. While others are filling their memory with a lumber of words, one-half of which they will forget before the week be out, your truant may learn some really useful art : to play the fiddle, to know a good cigar, or to speak with ease and opportunity to all varieties of men. Many who have " plied their book diligently," and know all about some one branch or another of accepted lore, come out of the study with an ancient and owl-like demeanour, and prove dry, stockish, and dyspeptic in all the better and brighter parts of life. Many make a large fortune, who remain underbred and pathetically stupid to the last. And meantime there goes the idler, who began life along with them—by your leave, a different picture. He has had time to take care of his health and his spirits ; he has been a great deal in the open air, which is the most salutary of all things for both body and mind ; and if he has never read the great Book in very recondite places, he has dipped into it and skimmed it over to excellent purpose. Might not the student afford some Hebrew roots, and the business man some of his half-crowns, for a share of the idler's knowledge of life at large, and Art of Living ? Nay, and the idler has another and more important quality than these. I mean his wisdom. He who has much looked on at the childish satisfaction of other people in their hobbies, will regard his own with only a very ironical indulgence. He will not be heard among the dogmatists. He will have a great and cool allowance for all sorts of people and opinions. If he finds no out-of-the-way truths, he will identify himself with no very burning falsehood. His way takes him along a by-road, not much frequented, but very even and pleasant, which is called Commonplace Lane, and leads to the Belvedere of Common-sense. Thence he shall command an agreeable, if no very noble prospect ; and while others behold the East and West, the Devil and the Sunrise, he will be contentedly aware of a sort of morning hour upon all sublunary things, with an army of shadows running speedily and in many different directions into the great daylight of Eternity. The shadows and the generations, the shrill doctors and the plangent wars, go by into ultimate silence and emptiness ; but underneath all this, a man may see, out of the Belvedere windows, much green and peaceful landscape ; many firelit parlours ; good people laughing, drinking, and making love as they did before the Flood or the French Revolution ; and the old shepherd telling his tale under the hawthorn.

Extreme *busyness*, whether at school or college, kirk or market, is a symptom of deficient vitality ; and a faculty for idleness implies a catholic appetite and a strong sense of personal identity. There is a sort of dead-alive, hackneyed people about, who are scarcely conscious of living except in the exercise of some conventional occupation. Bring these fellows into the country, or set them aboard ship, and you will see how they pine for their desk or study. They have no curiosity ; they cannot give themselves over to random provocations , they do not take pleasure in the exercise of their faculties for its own sake ; and unless Necessity lays about them with a stick, they will even stand still. It is no good speaking to such folk : they *cannot* be idle, their nature is not generous enough ; and they pass those hours in a sort of coma, which are not dedicated to furious moiling in the gold-mill. When they do not require to go to the office, when they are not hungry and have no mind to drink, the whole breathing world is a blank to them. If they have to wait an hour or so for a train, they fall into a stupid trance with their eyes open. To see them, you would suppose there was nothing to look at and no one to speak with ; you would imagine they were paralysed or alienated ; and yet very possibly they are hard workers in their own way, and have good eyesight for a flaw in a deed or a turn of the market. They have been to school and college, but all the time they had their eye on the medal ; they have gone about in the world and mixed with clever people, but all the time they were thinking of their own affairs. As if a man's soul were not too small to begin with, they have dwarfed and narrowed theirs by a life of all work and no play ; until here they are forty, with a listless attention, a mind vacant of all material of amusement, and not one thought to rub against another, while they wait for the train. Before he was breeched, he might have clambered on the boxes ; when he was twenty, he would have stared at the girls ; but now the pipe is smoked out, the snuff-box empty, and my gentleman sits bolt upright upon a bench, with lamentable eyes. This does not appeal to me as being Success in Life.

But it is not only the person himself who suffers from his busy habits, but his wife and children, his friends and relations, and down to the very people he sits with in a railway carriage or an omnibus. Perpetual devotion to what a man calls his business, is only to be sustained by perpetual neglect of many other things. And it is not by any means certain that a man's business is the most important thing he has to do. To an impartial estimate it will seem clear that many of the wisest, most virtuous, and most beneficent parts that are to be played upon the Theatre of Life are filled by gratuitous performers, and pass, among the world at large, as phases of idleness. For in that Theatre, not only the walking gentlemen, singing chambermaids, and diligent fiddlers in the orchestra, but those who look on and clap their hands from the benches, do really play a part and fulfil important offices towards the general result. You are no doubt very dependent on the care of your lawyer and stockbroker, of the guards and signalmen who convey you rapidly from place to place, and the policemen who walk the streets for your protection; but is there not a thought of gratitude in your heart for certain other benefactors who set you smiling when they fall in your way, or season your dinner with good company? Colonel Newcome helped to lose his friend's money; Fred Bayham had an ugly trick of borrowing shirts; and yet they were better people to fall among than Mr. Barnes. And though Falstaff was neither sober nor very honest, I think I could name one or two long-faced Barabbases whom the world could better have done without. Hazlitt mentions that he was more sensible of obligation to Northcote, who had never done him anything he could call a service, than to his whole circle of ostentatious friends; for he thought a good companion emphatically the greatest benefactor. I know there are people in the world who cannot feel grateful unless the favour has been done them at the cost of pain and difficulty. But this is a churlish disposition. A man may send you six sheets of letter-paper covered with the most entertaining gossip, or you may pass half an hour pleasantly, perhaps profitably, over an article of his ; do you think the service would be greater, if he had made the manuscript in his heart's blood, like a compact with the devil ? Do you really fancy you should be more beholden to your correspondent, if he had been damning you all the while for your importunity ? Pleasures are more beneficial than duties because, like the quality of mercy, they are not strained, and they are twice blest. There must always be two to a kiss, and there may be a score in a jest ; but wherever there is an element of sacrifice the favour is conferred with pain, and, among generous people, received with confusion. There is no duty we so much underrate as the duty of being happy. By being happy, we sow anonymous benefits upon the world, which remain unknown even to ourselves, or when they are disclosed, surprise nobody so much as the benefactor. The other day, a ragged, barefoot boy ran down the street after a marble, with so jolly an air that he set every one he passed into a good humour ; one of these persons, who had been delivered from more than usually black thoughts, stopped the little fellow and gave him some money with this remark : " You see what sometimes comes of looking pleased." If he had looked pleased before, he had now to look both pleased and mystified. For my part, I justify this encouragement of smiling rather than tearful children ; I do not wish to pay for tears anywhere but upon the stage ; but I am prepared to deal largely in the opposite commodity.

A happy man or woman is a better thing to find than a five-pound note. He or she is a radiating focus of goodwill ; and their entrance into a room is as though another candle had been lighted. We need not care whether they could prove the forty-seventh proposition ; they do a better thing than that, they practically demonstrate the great Theorem of the Liveableness of Life. Consequently, if a person cannot be happy without remaining idle, idle he should remain. It is a revolutionary precept ; but thanks to hunger and the workhouse, one not easily to be abused ; and within practical limits, it is one of the most incontestable truths in the whole Body of Morality. Look at one of your industrious fellows for a moment, I beseech you. He sows hurry and reaps indigestion ; he puts a vast deal of activity out to interest, and receives a large measure of nervous derangement in return. Either he absents himself entirely from all fellowship, and lives a recluse in a garret, with carpet slippers and a leaden inkpot ; or he comes among people swiftly and bitterly, in a contraction of his whole nervous system, to discharge some temper before he returns to work. I do not care how much or how well he works, this fellow is an evil feature in other people's lives. They would be happier if he were dead. They could easier do without his services in the Circumlocution Office, than they can tolerate his fractious spirits. He poisons life at the well-head. It is better to be beggared out of hand by a scapegrace nephew, than daily hag-ridden by a peevish uncle.

And what, in God's name, is all this pother about ? For what cause do they embitter their own and other people's lives ? That a man should publish three or thirty articles a year, that he should finish or not finish his great allegorical picture, are questions of little interest to the world. The ranks of life are full ;

AN APOLOGY FOR IDLERS

and although a thousand fall, there are always some
to go into the breach. When they told Joan of Arc
she should be at home minding women's work, she
answered there were plenty to spin and wash. And so,
even with your own rare gifts ! When nature is " so
careless of the single life," why should we coddle
ourselves into the fancy that our own is of exceptional
importance ? Suppose Shakespeare had been knocked
on the head some dark night in Sir Thomas Lucy's
preserves, the world would have wagged on better or
worse, the pitcher gone to the well, the scythe to the
corn, and the student to his book ; and no one been
any the wiser of the loss. There are not many works
extant, if you look the alternative all over, which are
worth the price of a pound of tobacco to a man of
limited means. This is a sobering reflection for the
proudest of our earthly vanities. Even a tobacconist
may, upon consideration, find no great cause for
personal vain-glory in the phrase ; for although
tobacco is an admirable sedative, the qualities
necessary for retailing it are neither rare nor precious
in themselves. Alas and alas ! you may take it how
you will, but the services of no single individual are
indispensable. Atlas was just a gentleman with a
protracted nightmare ! And yet you see merchants
who go and labour themselves into a great fortune
and thence into the bankruptcy court ; scribblers
who keep scribbling at little articles until their
temper is a cross to all who come about them, as
though Pharaoh should set the Israelites to make a
pin instead of a pyramid : and fine young men who
work themselves into a decline, and are driven off in
a hearse with white plumes upon it. Would you
not suppose these persons had been whispered, by the
Master of the Ceremonies, the promise of some
momentous destiny ? and that this lukewarm bullet
on which they play their farces was the bull's-eye and

centrepoint of all the universe ? And yet it is not so. The ends for which they give away their priceless youth, for all they know, may be chimerical or hurtful ; the glory and riches they expect may never come, or may find them indifferent ; and they and the world they inhabit are so inconsiderable that the mind freezes at the thought.

EL DORADO

It seems as if a great deal were attainable in a world where there are so many marriages and decisive battles, and where we all, at certain hours of the day, and with great gusto and despatch, stow a portion of victuals finally and irretrievably into a bag which contains us. And it would seem also, on a hasty view, that the attainment of as much as possible was the one goal of man's contentious life. And yet, as regards the spirit, this is but a semblance. We live in an ascending scale when we live happily, one thing leading to another in an endless series. There is always a new horizon for onward-looking men, and although we dwell on a small planet, immersed in petty business and not enduring beyond a brief period of years, we are so constituted that our hopes are inaccessible, like stars, and the term of hoping is prolonged until the term of life. To be truly happy is a question of how we begin and not of how we end, of what we want and not of what we have. An aspiration is a joy for ever, a possession as solid as a landed estate, a fortune which we can never exhaust and which gives us year by year a revenue of pleasurable activity. To have many of these is to be spiritually rich. Life is only a very dull and ill-directed theatre unless we have some interests in the piece ; and to those who have neither art nor science, the world is a mere arrangement of colours, or a rough footway where they may very well break their shins. It is in virtue of his own desires and curiosities that any man continues to exist with even patience, that he is charmed by the look of things and people, and that he wakens every morning with a renewed appetite for work and pleasure. Desire and curiosity are the two eyes through which he sees the world in the most enchanted colours : it is they that make women beautiful or fossils interesting : and the man may squander his estate and come to beggary, but if he keeps these two amulets he is still rich in the possibilities of pleasure. Suppose he could take one meal so compact and comprehensive that he should never hunger any more ; suppose him, at a glance, to take in all the features of the world and allay the desire for knowledge ; suppose him to do the like in any province of experience—would not that man be in a poor way for amusement ever after ?

One who goes touring on foot with a single volume in his knapsack reads with circumspection, pausing often to reflect, and often laying the book down to contemplate the landscape or the prints in the inn parlour ; for he fears to come to an end of his entertainment, and be left companionless on the last stages of his journey. A young fellow recently finished the works of Thomas Carlyle, winding up, if we remember aright, with the ten note-books upon Frederick the Great. " What ! " cried the young fellow, in consternation, " is there no more Carlyle ? Am I left to the daily papers ? " A more celebrated instance is that of Alexander, who wept bitterly because he had no more worlds to subdue. And when Gibbon had finished the *Decline and Fall*, he had only a few moments of joy ; and it was with a " sober melancholy " that he parted from his labours.

Happily we all shoot at the moon with ineffectual arrows ; our hopes are set on inaccessible El Dorado ; we come to an end of nothing here below. Interests are only plucked up to sow themselves again, like mustard. You would think, when the child was born, there would be an end to trouble ; and yet it is only the beginning of fresh anxieties ; and when you have seen it through its teething and its education, and at last its marriage, alas ! it is only to have new fears, new quivering sensibilities, with every day ; and the health of your children's children grows as touching a concern as that of your own. Again, when you have married your wife, you would think you were got upon a hilltop, and might begin to go downward by an easy slope. But you have only ended courting to begin marriage. Falling in love and winning love are often difficult tasks to overbearing and rebellious spirits ; but to keep in love is also a business of some importance, to which both man and wife must bring kindness and goodwill. The true love story commences at the altar, where there lies before the married pair a most beautiful contest of wisdom and generosity, and a life-long struggle towards an unattainable ideal. Unattainable ! Ay, surely unattainable, from the very fact that they are two instead of one.

" Of making books there is no end," complained the Preacher ; and did not perceive how highly he was praising letters as an occupation. There is no end, indeed, to make books or experiments, or to travel, or to gathering wealth. Problem gives rise to problem. We may study for ever, and we are never as learned as we would. We have never made a statue worthy of our dreams. And when we have discovered a continent, or crossed a chain of mountains, it is only to find another ocean or another plain upon the further side. In the infinite universe there is room for our swiftest diligence and to spare. It is not like the works of Carlyle, which can be read to an end. Even in a corner of it, in a private park, or in the neighbourhood of a single hamlet, the weather and the seasons keep so deftly changing that although we walk there for a lifetime there will be always something new to startle and delight us.

There is only one wish realisable on the earth; only one thing that can be perfectly attained : Death. And from a variety of circumstances we have no one to tell us whether it be worth attaining.

A strange picture we make on our way to our chimæras, ceaselessly marching, grudging ourselves the time for rest ; indefatigable, adventurous pioneers. It is true that we shall never reach the goal; it is even more than probable that there is no such place ; and if we lived for centuries and were endowed with the powers of a god, we should find ourselves not much nearer what we wanted at the end. O toiling hands of mortals ! O unwearied feet, travelling ye know not whither ! Soon, soon, it seems to you, you must come forth on some conspicuous hilltop, and but a little way further, against the setting sun, descry the spires of El Dorado. Little do ye know your own blessedness ; for to travel hopefully is a better thing than to arrive, and the true success is to labour.

WALKING TOURS

IT must not be imagined that a walking tour, as some would have us fancy, is merely a better or worse way of seeing the country. There are many ways of seeing landscape quite as good ; and none more vivid, in spite of canting dilettantes, than from a railway train. But landscape on a walking tour is quite accessory. He who is indeed of the brotherhood does not voyage in quest of the picturesque, but of certain jolly humours—of the hope and spirit with which the march begins at morning, and the peace and spiritual repletion of the evening's rest. He cannot tell whether he puts his knapsack on, or takes it off, with more delight. The excitement of the departure puts him in key for that of the arrival. Whatever he does is not only a reward in itself, but will be further rewarded in the sequel; and so pleasure leads on to pleasure in an endless chain. It is this that so few can understand; they will either be always lounging or always at five miles an hour; they do not play off the one against the other, prepare all day for the evening, and all evening for the next day. And, above all, it is here that your overwalker fails of comprehension. His heart rises against those who drink their curaçoa in liqueur glasses, when he himself can swill it in a brown John. He will not believe that the flavour is more delicate in the smaller dose. He will not believe that to walk this unconscionable distance is merely to stupefy and brutalise himself, and come to his inn, at night, with a sort of frost on his five wits, and a starless night of darkness in his spirit. Not for him the mild luminous evening of the temperate walker ! He has nothing left of man but a physical need for bedtime and a double night-cap; and even his pipe, if he be a smoker, will be savourless and disenchanted. It is the fate of such an one to take twice as much trouble as is needed to obtain happiness, and miss the happiness in the end; he is the man of the proverb, in short, who goes further and fares worse.

Now, to be properly enjoyed, a walking tour should be gone upon alone. If you go in a company, or even in pairs, it is no longer a walking tour in anything but name; it is something else and more in the nature of a picnic. A walking tour should be gone upon alone, because freedom is of the essence ; because you should be able to stop and go on, and follow this way or that, as the freak takes you ; and because you must have your own pace, and neither trot alongside a champion walker, nor mince in time with a girl. And then you must be open to all impressions and let your thoughts take colour from what you see. You should be as a pipe for any wind to play upon. " I cannot see the wit," says Hazlitt, " of walking and talking at the same time. When I am in the country I wish to vegetate like the country"—which is the gist of all that can be said upon the matter. There should be no cackle of voices at your elbow, to jar on the meditative silence of the morning. And so long as a man is reasoning he cannot surrender himself to that fine intoxication that comes of much motion in the open air, that begins in a sort of dazzle and sluggishness of the brain, and ends in a peace that surpasses comprehension.

During the first day or so of any tour there are moments of bitterness, when the traveller feels more than coldly towards his knapsack, when he is half in a mind to throw it bodily over the hedge, and like Christian on a similar occasion, " give three leaps and go on singing." And yet it soon acquires a property of easiness. It becomes magnetic ; the spirit of the journey enters into it. And no sooner have you passed the straps over your shoulder than the lees of sleep are cleared from you, you pull yourself together with a shake, and fall at once into your stride. And surely, of all possible moods, this, in which a man takes the road, is the best. Of course, if he *will* keep thinking of his anxieties, if he *will* open the merchant Abudah's chest and walk arm-in-arm with the hag— why, wherever he is, and whether he walk fast or slow, the chances are that he will not be happy. And so much the more shame to himself! There are perhaps thirty men setting forth at that same hour, and I would lay a large wager there is not another dull face among the thirty. It would be a fine thing to follow, in a coat of darkness, one after another of these wayfarers, some summer morning, for the first few miles upon the road. This one, who walks fast, with a keen look in his eyes, is all concentrated in his own mind; he is up at his loom, weaving and weaving, to set the landscape to words. This one peers about, as he goes, among the grasses; he waits by the canal to watch the dragon-flies; he leans on the gate of the pasture, and cannot look enough upon the complacent kine. And here comes another, talking, laughing, and gesticulating to himself. His face changes from time to time, as indignation flashes from his eyes or anger clouds his forehead. He is composing articles, delivering orations, and conducting the most impassioned interviews, by the way. A little farther on, and it is as like as not he will begin to sing. And well for him, supposing him to be no great master in that art, if he stumble across no stolid peasant at a corner; for on such an occasion, I scarcely know which is the more troubled, or whether it is worse to suffer the confusion of your troubadour, or the unfeigned alarm of your clown. A sedentary population, accustomed, besides, to the strange mechanical bearing of the common tramp, can in no wise explain to itself the gaiety of these passers-by. I knew one man who was arrested as a runaway lunatic, because, although a full-grown person with a red beard, he skipped as he went like a child. And you would be astonished if I were to tell you all the grave and learned heads who have confessed to me that, when on walking tours, they sang—and sang very ill—and had a pair of red ears when, as described above, the inauspicious peasant plumped into their arms from round a corner. And here, lest you should think I am exaggerating, is Hazlitt's own confession, from his essay *On Going a Journey*, which is so good that there should be a tax levied on all who have not read it :—

" Give me the clear blue sky over my head," says he, " and the green turf beneath my feet, a winding road before me, and a three hours' march to dinner —and then to thinking ! It is hard if I cannot start some game on these lone heaths. I laugh, I run, I leap, I sing for joy."

Bravo ! After that adventure of my friend with the policeman, you would not have cared, would you, to publish that in the first person ? But we have no bravery nowadays, and, even in books, must all pretend to be as dull and foolish as our neighbours. It was not so with Hazlitt. And notice how learned he is (as, indeed, throughout the essay) in the theory of walking tours. He is none of your athletic men in purple stockings, who walk their fifty miles a day : three hours' march is his ideal. And then he must have a winding road, the epicure !

Yet there is one thing I object to in these words of his, one thing in the great master's practice that seems to me not wholly wise. I do not approve of that leaping and running. Both of these hurry the respiration ; they both shake up the brain out of its glorious open-air confusion ; and they both break the pace. Uneven walking is not so agreeable to the body, and it distracts and irritates the mind. Whereas, when once you have fallen into an equable stride, it requires no conscious thought from you to keep it up, and yet it prevents you from thinking earnestly of anything else. Like knitting, like the work of a copying clerk, it gradually neutralises and sets to sleep the serious activity of the mind. We can think of this or that, lightly and laughingly, as a child thinks,

or as we think in a morning doze ; we can make
puns or puzzle out acrostics, and trifle in a thousand
ways with words and rhymes ; but when it comes to
honest work, when we come to gather ourselves together for an effort, we may sound the trumpet as
loud and long as we please ; the great barons of
the mind will not rally to the standard, but sit, each
one, at home, warming his hands over his own fire
and brooding on his own private thought !

In the course of a day's walk, you see, there is
much variance in the mood. From the exhilaration
of the start, to the happy phlegm of the arrival, the
change is certainly great. As the day goes on, the
traveller moves from the one extreme towards the
other. He becomes more and more incorporated
with the material landscape, and the open-air drunken-
ness grows upon him with great strides, until he posts
along the road, and sees everything about him, as in
a cheerful dream. The first is certainly brighter, but
the second stage is the more peaceful. A man does not
make so many articles towards the end, nor does he
laugh aloud ; but the purely animal pleasures, the
sense of physical well-being, the delight of every in-
halation, of every time the muscles tighten down the
thigh, console him for the absence of the others, and
bring him to his destination still content.

Nor must I forget to say a word on bivouacs. You
come to a milestone on a hill, or some place where
deep ways meet under trees ; and off goes the knapsack, and down you sit to smoke a pipe in the shade.
You sink into yourself, and the birds come round and
look at you ; and your smoke dissipates upon the
afternoon under the blue dome of heaven ; and the
sun lies warm upon your feet, and the cool air visits
your neck and turns aside your open shirt. If you
are not happy, you must have an evil conscience.
You may dally as long as you like by the roadside.

It is almost as if the millennium were arrived, when we shall throw our clocks and watches over the house-top, and remember time and seasons no more. Not to keep hours for a lifetime is, I was going to say, to live for ever. You have no idea, unless you have tried it, how endlessly long is a summer's day, that you measure out only by hunger, and bring to an end only when you are drowsy. I know a village where there are hardly any clocks, where no one knows more of the days of the week than by a sort of instinct for the fête on Sundays, and where only one person can tell you the day of the month, and she is generally wrong ; and if people were aware how slow Time journeyed in that village, and what armfuls of spare hours he gives, over and above the bargain, to its wise inhabitants, I believe there would be a stampede out of London, Liverpool, Paris, and a variety of large towns, where the clocks lose their heads, and shake the hours out each one faster than the other, as though they were all in a wager. And all these foolish pilgrims would each bring his own misery along with him, in a watch-pocket ! It is to be noticed, there were no clocks and watches in the much-vaunted days before the flood. It follows, of course, there were no appointments, and punctuality was not yet thought upon. " Though ye take from a covetous man all his treasure," says Milton, " he has yet one jewel left ; ye cannot deprive him of his covetousness." And so I would say of a modern man of business, you may do what you will for him, put him in Eden, give him the elixir of life—he has still a flaw at heart, he still has his business habits. Now, there is no time when business habits are more mitigated than on a walking tour. And so during these halts, as I say, you will feel almost free.

But it is at night, and after dinner, that the best

hour comes. There are no such pipes to be smoked as those that follow a good day's march; the flavour of the tobacco is a thing to be remembered, it is so dry and aromatic, so full and so fine. If you wind up the evening with grog, you will own there was never such grog; at every sip a jocund tranquillity spreads about your limbs, and sits easily in your heart. If you read a book—and you will never do so save by fits and starts—you find the language strangely racy and harmonious; words take a new meaning; single sentences possess the ear for half an hour together; and the writer endears himself to you, at every page, by the nicest coincidence of sentiment. It seems as if it were a book you had written yourself in a dream. To all we have read on such occasions we look back with special favour. " It was on the 10th of April, 1798," says Hazlitt, with amorous precision, " that I sat down to a volume of the new *Héloïse*, at the Inn at Llangollen, over a bottle of sherry and a cold chicken." I should wish to quote more, for though we are mighty fine fellows nowadays, we cannot write like Hazlitt. And, talking of that, a volume of Hazlitt's essays would be a capital pocket-book on such a journey; so would a volume of Heine's songs; and for *Tristram Shandy* I can pledge a fair experience.

If the evening be fine and warm, there is nothing better in life than to lounge before the inn door in the sunset, or lean over the parapet of the bridge, to watch the weeds and quick fishes. It is then, if ever, that you taste Joviality to the full significance of that audacious word. Your muscles are so agreeably slack, you feel so clean and so strong and so idle, that whether you move or sit still, whatever you do is done with pride and a kingly sort of pleasure. You fall in talk with anyone, wise or foolish, drunk or sober. And it seems as if a hot walk purged you, more than of anything else, of all narrowness and pride, and left curiosity to play its part freely, as in a child or a man of science. You lay aside all your own hobbies, to watch provincial humours develop themselves before you, now as a laughable farce, and now grave and beautiful like an old tale.

Or perhaps you are left to your own company for the night, and surly weather imprisons you by the fire. You may remember how Burns, numbering past pleasures, dwells upon the hours when he has been " happy thinking." It is a phrase that may well perplex a poor modern, girt about on every side by clocks and chimes, and haunted, even at night, by flaming dial-plates. For we are all so busy, and have so many far-off projects to realise, and castles in the fire to turn into solid habitable mansions on a gravel soil, that we can find no time for pleasure trips into the Land of Thought and among the Hills of Vanity. Changed times, indeed, when we must sit all night, beside the fire, with folded hands; and a changed world for most of us, when we find we can pass the hours without discontent, and be happy thinking. We are in such haste to be doing, to be writing, to be gathering gear, to make our voice audible a moment in the derisive silence of eternity, that we forget that one thing, of which these are but the parts—namely, to live. We fall in love, we drink hard, we run to and fro upon the earth like frightened sheep. And now you are to ask yourself if, when all is done, you would not have been better to sit by the fire at home, and be happy thinking. To sit still and contemplate, —to remember the faces of women without desire, to be pleased by the great deeds of men without envy, to be everything and everywhere in sympathy, and yet content to remain where and what you are—is not this to know both wisdom and virtue, and to dwell with happiness? After all, it is not they who carry flags, but they who look upon it from a private chamber, who have the fun of the procession. And once you are at that, you are in the very humour of all social heresy. It is no time for shuffling, or for big, empty words. If you ask yourself what you mean by fame, riches, or learning, the answer is far to seek ; and you go back into that kingdom of light imaginations, which seem so vain in the eyes of Philistines perspiring after wealth, and so momentous to those who are stricken with disproportions of the world, and, in the face of the gigantic stars, cannot stop to split differences between two degrees of the infinitesimally small, such as a tobacco pipe or the Roman Empire, a million of money or a fiddle-stick's end.

You lean from the window, your last pipe reeking whitely into the darkness, your body full of delicious pains, your mind enthroned in the seventh circle of content ; when suddenly the mood changes, the weathercock goes about, and you ask yourself one question more : whether, for the interval, you have been the wisest philosopher or the most egregious of donkeys ? Human experience is not yet able to reply ; but at least you have had a fine moment, and looked down upon all the kingdoms of the earth. And whether it was wise or foolish, to-morrow's travel will carry you, body and mind, into some different parish of the infinite.

THE BEGGAR

(1888)

IN a pleasant, airy, uphill country, it was my fortune when I was young to make the acquaintance of a certain beggar. I call him beggar, though he usually allowed his coat and his shoes (which were open-mouthed, indeed) to beg for him. He was the wreck of an athletic man, tall, gaunt, and bronzed ; far gone in consumption, with that disquieting smile of the mortally stricken on his face ; but still active afoot, still with the brisk military carriage, the ready military salute. Three ways led through this piece of country ; and as I was inconstant in my choice, I believe he must have often awaited me in vain. But often enough, he caught me ; often enough, from some place of ambush by the roadside, he would spring suddenly forth in the regulation attitude, and launching at once into his inconsequential talk, fall into step with me upon my farther course. " A fine morning, sir, though perhaps a trifle inclining to rain. I hope I see you well, sir. Why no, sir, I don't feel as hearty myself as I could wish, but I am keeping about my ordinary. I am pleased to meet you on the road, sir. I assure you I quite look forward to one of our little conversations." He loved the sound of his own voice inordinately, and though (with something too off-hand to call servility) he would always hasten to agree with anything you said, yet he could never suffer you to say it to an end. By what transi-tion he slid to his favourite subject I have no memory ; but we had never been long together on the way before he was dealing, in a very military manner, with the English poets. " Shelley was a fine poet, sir, though a trifle atheistical in his opinions. His ' Queen Mab,' sir, is quite an atheistical work. Scott, sir, is not so poetical a writer. With the works of Shakespeare I am not so well acquainted, but he was a fine poet. Keats—John Keats, sir—he was a very fine poet." With such references, such trivial criticism, such loving parade of his own knowledge, he would beguile the road, striding forward uphill, his staff now clapped to the ribs of his deep, resonant chest, now swinging in the air with the remembered jauntiness of the private soldier ; and all the while his toes looking out of his boots, and his shirt looking out of his elbows, and death looking out of his smile, and his big, crazy frame shaken by accesses of cough.

He would often go the whole way home with me : often to borrow a book, and that book always a poet. Off he would march, to continue his mendicant rounds, with the volume slipped into the pocket of his ragged coat ; and although he would sometimes keep it quite a while, yet it came always back again at last, not much the worse for its travels into beggardom. And in this way, doubtless, his knowledge grew and his glib, random criticism took a wider range. But my library was not the first he had drawn upon : at our first encounter, he was already brimful of Shelley and the atheistical " Queen Mab," and "Keats —John Keats, sir." And I have often wondered how he came by the acquirements ; just as I often wondered how he fell to be a beggar. He had served through the Mutiny—of which (like so many people) he could tell practically nothing beyond the names of places, and that it was " difficult work, sir," and very hot, or that so-and-so was " a very fine commander, sir." He was far too smart a man to have remained a private ; in the nature of things, he must have won his stripes. And yet here he was without a pension. When I touched on this problem, he would content himself with diffidently offering me advice. " A man should be very careful when he is young, sir. If you'll excuse me saying so, a spirited young gentleman like yourself, sir, should be very careful. I was perhaps a trifle inclined to atheistical opinions myself." For (perhaps with a deeper wisdom than we are inclined in these days to admit) he plainly bracketed agnosticism with beer and skittles.

Keats—John Keats, sir—and Shelley were his favourite bards. I cannot remember if I tried him with Rossetti ; but I know his taste to a hair, and if ever I did, he must have doted on that author. What took him was a richness in the speech ; he loved the exotic, the unexpected word ; the moving cadence of a phrase ; a vague sense of emotion (about nothing) in the very letters of the alphabet : the romance of language. His honest head was very nearly empty, his intellect like a child's ; and when he read his favourite authors, he can almost never have understood what he was reading. Yet the taste was not only genuine, it was exclusive ; I tried in vain to offer him novels ; he would none of them ; he cared for nothing but romantic language that he could not understand. The case may be commoner than we suppose. I am reminded of a lad who was laid in the next cot to a friend of mine in a public hospital, and who was no sooner installed than he sent out (perhaps with his last pence) for a cheap Shakespeare. My friend pricked up his ears ; fell at once in talk with his new neighbour, and was ready, when the book arrived, to make a singular discovery. For this lover of great literature understood not one sentence out of twelve, and his favourite part was that of which he understood the least—the inimitable, mouth-filling rodomontade of the ghost in *Hamlet*. It was a bright day in hospital when my friend expounded the sense of this beloved jargon : a task for which I am willing to believe my friend was very fit, though I can never regard it as an easy one. I know indeed a point or two, on which I would gladly question Mr. Shakespeare, that lover of big words, could he revisit the glimpses of the moon, or could I myself climb backward to the spacious days of Elizabeth. But in the second case, I should most likely pretermit these questionings, and take my place instead in the pit at the Blackfriars, to hear the actor in his favourite part, playing up to Mr. Burbage, and rolling out—as I seem to hear him—with a ponderous gusto—

" Unhousel'd, disappointed, unanel'd."

What a pleasant chance, if we could go there in a party ! and what a surprise for Mr. Burbage, when the ghost received the honours of the evening !

As for my old soldier, like Mr. Burbage and Mr. Shakespeare, he is long since dead ; and now lies buried, I suppose, and nameless and quite forgotten, in some poor city graveyard.—But not for me, you brave heart, have you been buried ! For me, you are still afoot, tasting the sun and air, and striding southward. By the groves of Comiston and beside the Hermitage of Braid, by the Hunters' Tryst, and where the curlews and plovers cry around Fairmilehead, I see and hear you, stalwartly carrying your deadly sickness, cheerfully discoursing of uncomprehended poets.

G. K. CHESTERTON

ON LYING IN BED

LYING in bed would be an altogether perfect and supreme experience if only one had a coloured pencil long enough to draw on the ceiling. This, however, is not generally a part of the domestic apparatus on the premises. I think myself that the thing might be managed with several pails of Aspinall and a broom. Only if one worked in a really sweeping and masterly way, and laid on the colour in great washes, it might drip down again on one's face in floods of rich and mingled colour like some strange fairy rain; and that would have its disadvantages. I am afraid it would be necessary to stick to black and white in this form of artistic composition. To that purpose, indeed, the white ceiling would be of the greatest possible use; in fact it is the only use I think of a white ceiling being put to.

But for the beautiful experiment of lying in bed I might never have discovered it. For years I have been looking for some blank spaces in a modern house to draw on. Paper is much too small for any really allegorical design : as Cyrano de Bergerac says : " Il me faut des géants." But when I tried to find these fine clear spaces in the modern rooms such as we all live in I was continually disappointed. I found an endless pattern and complication of small objects hung like a curtain of fine links between me and my desire. I examined the walls; I found them to my surprise to be already covered with wall-paper, and I found the wall-paper to be already covered

209

with very uninteresting images, all bearing a ridiculous resemblance to each other. I could not understand why one arbitrary symbol (a symbol apparently entirely devoid of any religious or philosophical significance) should thus be sprinkled all over my nice walls like a sort of small-pox. The Bible must be referring to wall-papers, I think, when it says "Use not vain repetitions, as the Gentiles do." I found the Turkey carpet a mass of unmeaning colours, rather like the Turkish Empire, or like the sweetmeat called Turkish Delight. I do not exactly know what Turkish Delight really is; but I suppose it is Macedonian Massacres. Everywhere that I went forlornly with my pencil or my paint brush, I found that others had unaccountably been before me, spoiling the walls, the curtains, and the furniture with their childish and barbaric designs.

.   .   .   .   .   .

Nowhere did I find a really clear space for sketching until this occasion when I prolonged beyond the proper limit the process of lying on my back in bed. Then the light of that white heaven broke upon my vision, that breadth of mere white which is indeed almost the definition of Paradise, since it means purity and also means freedom. But alas! like all heavens, now that it is seen it is found to be unattainable; it looks more austere and more distant than the blue sky outside the window. For my proposal to paint on it with the bristly end of a broom has been discouraged—never mind by whom; by a person debarred from all political rights—and even my minor proposal to put the other end of the broom into the kitchen fire and turn it into charcoal has not been conceded. Yet I am certain that it was from persons in my position that all the original inspiration came for covering the ceilings of palaces and cathedrals with a riot of fallen angels or victorious gods. I am sure that it was only because Michaelangelo was engaged in the ancient and honourable occupation of lying in bed that he ever realised how the roof of the Sistine Chapel might be made into an awful imitation of a divine drama that could only be acted in the heavens.

The tone now commonly taken towards the practice of lying in bed is hypocritical and unhealthy. Of all the marks of modernity that seem to mean a kind of decadence, there is none more menacing and dangerous than the exaltation of very small and secondary matters of conduct at the expense of very great and primary ones, at the expense of eternal ties and tragic human morality. If there is one thing worse than the modern weakening of major morals it is the modern strengthening of minor morals. Thus it is considered more withering to accuse a man of bad taste than of bad ethics. Cleanliness is not next to godliness nowadays, for cleanliness is made an essential and godliness is regarded as an offence. A playwright can attack the institution of marriage so long as he does not misrepresent the manners of society, and I have met Ibsenite pessimists who thought it wrong to take beer but right to take prussic acid. Especially this is so in matters of hygiene; notably such matters as lying in bed. Instead of being regarded, as it ought to be, as a matter of personal convenience and adjustment, it has come to be regarded by many as if it were a part of essential morals to get up early in the morning. It is upon the whole part of practical wisdom; but there is nothing good about it or bad about its opposite.

. . . . . .

Misers get up early in the morning; and burglars, I am informed, get up the night before. It is the great peril of our society that all its mechanism may grow more fixed while its spirit grows more fickle. A man's minor actions and arrangements ought to be free, flexible, creative ; the things that should be un-changeable are his principles, his ideals. But with us the reverse is true ; our views change constantly ; but our lunch does not change. Now, I should like men to have strong and rooted conceptions, but as for their lunch, let them have it sometimes in the garden, sometimes in bed, sometimes on the roof, sometimes in the top of a tree. Let them argue from the same first principles, but let them do it in a bed, or a boat, or a balloon. This alarming growth of good habits really means a too great emphasis on those virtues which mere custom can ensure ; it means too little emphasis on those virtues which custom can never quite ensure, sudden and splendid virtues of inspired pity or of inspired candour. If ever that abrupt appeal is made to us we may fail. A man can get used to getting up at five o'clock in the morning. A man cannot very well get used to being burnt for his opinions ; the first experiment is commonly fatal. Let us pay a little more attention to these possibilities of the heroic and the unexpected. I dare say that when I get out of this bed I shall do some deed of an almost terrible virtue.

For those who study the great art of lying in bed there is one emphatic caution to be added. Even for those who can do their work in bed (like journalists), still more for those whose work cannot be done in bed (as, for example, the professional harpooners of whales), it is obvious that the indulgence must be very occasional. But that is not the caution I mean. The caution is this : if you do lie in bed, be sure you do it without any reason or justification at all. I do not speak, of course, of the seriously sick. But if a healthy man lies in bed, let him do it without a rag of excuse ; then he will get up a healthy man. If he does it for some secondary hygienic reason, if he has some scientific explanation, he may get up a hypochondriac.

THE ARCHITECT OF SPEARS

THE other day, in the town of Lincoln, I suffered an optical illusion which accidentally revealed to me the strange greatness of the Gothic architecture. Its secret is not, I think, satisfactorily explained in most of the discussions on the subject. It is said that the Gothic eclipses the classical by a certain richness and complexity, at once lively and mysterious. This is true ; but Oriental decoration is equally rich and complex, yet it awakens a widely different sentiment. No man ever got out of a Turkey carpet the emotions that he got from a cathedral tower. Over all the exquisite ornament of Arabia and India there is the presence of something stiff and heartless, of something tortured and silent. Dwarfed trees and crooked serpents, heavy flowers and hunchbacked birds accentuate by the very splendour and contrast of their colour the servility and monotony of their shapes. It is like the vision of a sneering sage, who sees the whole universe as a pattern. Certainly no one ever felt like this about Gothic, even if he happens to dislike it. Or, again, some will say that it is the liberty of the Middle Ages in the use of the comic or even the coarse that makes the Gothic more interesting than the Greek. There is more truth in this ; indeed, there is real truth in it. Few of the old Christian cathedrals would have passed the Censor of Plays. We talk of the inimitable grandeur of the old cathedrals ; but indeed it is rather their gaiety that we

G. K. CHESTERTON

do not dare to imitate. We should be rather surprised
if a chorister suddenly began singing " Bill Bailey "
in church. Yet that would be only doing in music
what the mediævals did in sculpture. They put into
a Miserere seat the very scenes that we put into a
music-hall song : comic domestic scenes similar to
the spilling of the beer and the hanging out of the
washing. But though the gaiety of Gothic is one of
its features, it also is not the secret of its unique
effect. We see a domestic topsy-turvydom in many
Japanese sketches. But delightful as these are, with
their fairy tree-tops, paper houses, and toddling,
infantile inhabitants, the pleasure they give is of a
kind quite different from the joy and energy of the
gargoyles. Some have even been so shallow and
illiterate as to maintain that our pleasure in mediæval
building is a mere pleasure in what is barbaric, in
what is rough, shapeless, or crumbling like the rocks.
This can be dismissed after the same fashion ; South
Sea idols, with painted eyes and radiating bristles,
are a delight to the eye ; but they do not affect it in
at all the same way as Westminster Abbey. Some
again (going to another and almost equally foolish
extreme) ignore the coarse and comic in mediævalism,
and praise the pointed arch only for its utter purity
and simplicity, as of a saint with his hands joined in
prayer. Here, again, the uniqueness is missed. There
are Renaissance things (such as the ethereal silvery
drawings of Raphael), there are even pagan things
(such as the Praying Boy), which express as fresh and
austere a piety. None of these explanations explain.
And I never saw what was the real point about Gothic
till I came into the town of Lincoln, and saw it
behind a row of furniture-vans.

I did not know they were furniture-vans ; at the
first glance and in the smoky distance I thought they
were a row of cottages. A low stone wall cut off the

214

wheels, and the vans were somewhat of the same colour as the yellowish clay or stone of the buildings around them. I had come across that interminable Eastern plain which is like the open sea, and all the more so because the one small hill and tower of Lincoln stands up in it like a lighthouse. I had climbed the sharp, crooked streets up to this ecclesiastical citadel ; just in front of me was a flourishing and richly coloured kitchen garden ; beyond that was the low stone wall ; beyond that the row of vans that looked like houses ; and beyond and above that, straight and swift and dark, light as a flight of birds, and terrible as the Tower of Babel, Lincoln Cathedral seemed to rise out of human sight.

As I looked at it I asked myself the questions that I have asked here : What was the soul in all those stones ? They were varied, but it was not variety ; they were solemn, but it was not solemnity ; they were farcical, but it was not farce. What is it in them that thrills and soothes a man of our blood and history, that is not there in an Egyptian pyramid or an Indian temple or a Chinese pagoda ? All of a sudden the vans I had mistaken for cottages began to move away to the left. In the start this gave to my eye and mind I really fancied that the Cathedral was moving towards the right. The two huge towers seemed to start striding across the plain like the two legs of some giant whose body was covered with the clouds. Then I saw what it was.

The truth about Gothic is, first, that it is alive, and second, that it is on the march. It is the Church Militant ; it is the only fighting architecture. All its spires are spears at rest ; and all its stones are stones asleep in a catapult. In that instant of illusion, I could hear the arches clash like swords as they crossed each other. The mighty and numberless columns seemed to go swinging by like the huge feet of imperial elephants. The graven foliage wreathed and blew like banners going into battle ; the silence was deafening with all the mingled noises of a military march ; the great bell shook down, as the organ shook up, its thunder. The thirsty-throated gargoyles shouted like trumpets from all the roofs and pinnacles as they passed ; and from the lectern in the core of the cathedral the eagle of the awful evangelist clashed his wings of brass.

And amid all the noises I seemed to hear the voice of a man shouting in the midst like one ordering regiments hither and thither in the fight ; the voice of the great half-military master-builder ; the architect of spears. I could almost fancy he wore armour while he made that church ; and I knew indeed that, under a scriptural figure, he had borne in either hand the trowel and the sword.

I could imagine for the moment that the whole of that house of life had marched out of the sacred East, alive and interlocked, like an army. Some Eastern nomad had found it solid and silent in the red circle of the desert. He had slept by it as by a world-forgotten pyramid ; and been woke at midnight by the wings of stone and brass, the tramping of the tall pillars, the trumpets of the waterspouts. On such a night every snake or sea-beast must have turned and twisted in every crypt or corner of the architecture. And the fiercely coloured saints marching eternally in the flamboyant windows would have carried their glorioles like torches across dark lands and distant seas ; till the whole mountain of music and darkness and lights descended roaring on the lonely Lincoln hill. So for some hundred and sixty seconds I saw the battle-beauty of the Gothic ; then the last furniture-van shifted itself away ; and I saw only a church tower in a quiet English town, round which the English birds were floating.

ON THE CRYPTIC AND THE ELLIPTIC

SURELY the art of reporting speeches is in a strange state of degeneration. We should not object, perhaps, to the reporter's making the speeches much shorter than they are; but we do object to his making all the speeches much worse than they are. And the method which he employs is one which is dangerously unjust. When a statesman or philosopher makes an important speech, there are several courses which the reporter might take without being unreasonable. Perhaps the most reasonable course of all would be not to report the speech at all. Let the world live and love, marry and give in marriage, without that particular speech, as they did (in some desperate way) in the days when there were no newspapers. A second course would be to report a small part of it; but to get that right. A third course, far better if you can do it, is to understand the main purpose and argument of the speech, and report that in clear and logical language of your own. In short, the three possible methods are, first, to leave the man's speech alone; second, to report what he says or some complete part of what he says; and third, to report what he means. But the present way of reporting speeches (mainly created, I think, by the scrappy methods of the *Daily Mail*) is something utterly different from both these ways, and quite useless and misleading.

The present method is this: the reporter sits listening to a tide of words which he does not try to understand, and does not, generally speaking, even try to take down; he waits until something occurs in the speech which for some reason sounds funny, or memorable, or very exaggerated, or, perhaps, merely concrete; then he writes it down and waits for the next one. If the orator says that the Premier is like a porpoise in the sea under some special circumstances, the reporter gets in the porpoise even if he leaves out the Premier. If the orator begins by saying that Mr. Chamberlain is rather like a violoncello, the reporter does not even wait to hear why he is like a violoncello. He has got hold of something material, and so he is quite happy. The strong words are all put in ; the chain of thought is left out. If the orator uses the word " donkey," down goes the word " donkey." If the orator uses the word " damnable," down goes the word " damnable." They follow each other so abruptly in the report that it is often hard to discover the fascinating fact as to what was damnable or who was being compared with a donkey. And the whole line of argument in which these things occurred is entirely lost. I have before me a newspaper report of a speech by Mr. Bernard Shaw, of which one complete and separate paragraph runs like this :—

" Capital meant spare money over and above one's needs. Their country was not really their country at all except in patriotic songs."

I am well enough acquainted with the whole map of Mr. Bernard Shaw's philosophy to know that those two statements might have been related to each other in a hundred ways. But I think that if they were read by an ordinary intelligent man, who happened not to know Mr. Shaw's views, he would form no impression at all except that Mr. Shaw was a lunatic of more than usually abrupt conversation and disconnected mind. The other two methods would certainly have done Mr. Shaw more justice : the reporter should either have taken down verbatim what the speaker really said about Capital, or have given an outline of the way in which this idea was connected with the idea about patriotic songs.

218

But we have not the advantage of knowing what Mr. Shaw really did say, so we had better illustrate the different methods from something that we do know. Most of us, I suppose, know Mark Antony's Funeral Speech in *Julius Cæsar*. Now Mark Antony would have no reason to complain if he were not reported at all ; if the *Daily Pilum* or the *Morning Fasces*, or whatever it was, confined itself to saying, " Mr. Mark Antony also spoke," or " Mr. Mark Antony, having addressed the audience, the meeting broke up in some confusion." The next honest method, worthy of a noble Roman reporter, would be, that since he could not report the whole of the speech, he should report some of the speech. He might say—" Mr. Mark Antony, in the course of his speech, said :—

" ' When that the poor have cried Cæsar hath wept : Ambition should be made of sterner stuff.' "

In that case one good, solid argument of Mark Antony would be correctly reported. The third and far higher course for the Roman reporter would be to give a philosophical statement of the purport of the speech. As thus :—" Mr. Mark Antony, in the course of a powerful speech, conceded the high motives of the Republican leaders, and disclaimed any intention of raising the people against them ; he thought, however, that many instances could be quoted against the theory of Cæsar's ambition, and he concluded by reading, at the request of the audience, the will of Cæsar, which proved that he had the most benevolent designs towards the Roman people." That is (I admit) not quite so fine as Shakespeare, but it is a statement of the man's political position. But if a *Daily Mail* reporter were sent to take down Antony's oration, he would simply wait for any expressions that struck him as odd and put them down one after another without any logical connection at all. It would turn out something like this : " Mr. Mark Antony wished for his audience's ears. He had thrice offered Cæsar a crown. Cæsar was like a deer. If he were Brutus he would put a wound in every tongue. The stones of Rome would mutiny. See what a rent the envious Casca paid. Brutus was Cæsar's angel. The right honourable gentleman concluded by saying that he and the audience had all fallen down." That is the report of a political speech in a modern, progressive, or American manner, and I wonder whether the Romans would have put up with it.

The reports of the debates in the Houses of Parliament are constantly growing smaller and smaller in our newspapers. Perhaps this is partly because the speeches are growing duller and duller. I think in some degree the two things act and re-act on each other. For fear of the newspapers politicians are dull, and at last they are too dull even for the newspapers. The speeches in our time are more careful and elaborate, because they are meant to be read, and not to be heard. And exactly because they are more careful and elaborate, they are not so likely to be worthy of a careful and elaborate report. They are not interesting enough. So the moral cowardice of modern politicians has, after all, some punishment attached to it by the silent anger of heaven. Precisely because our political speeches are meant to be reported, they are not worth reporting. Precisely because they are carefully designed to be read, nobody reads them.

Thus we may concede that politicians have done something towards degrading journalism. It was not entirely done by us, the journalists. But most of it was. It was mostly the fruit of our first and most natural sin—the habit of regarding ourselves as conjurers rather than priests, for the definition is that a

conjurer is apart from his audience, while a priest
is a part of his. The conjurer despises his congregation ; if the priest despises any one, it must be himself. The curse of all journalism, but especially of
that yellow journalism which is the shame of our
profession, is that we think ourselves cleverer than the
people for whom we write, whereas, in fact, we are
generally even stupider. But this insolence has its
Nemesis ; and that Nemesis is well illustrated in this
matter of reporting.

For the journalist, having grown accustomed to
talking down to the public, commonly talks too low
at last, and becomes merely barbaric and unintelli-
gible. By his very efforts to be obvious he becomes
obscure. This just punishment may specially be
noticed in the case of those staggering and staring
headlines which American journalism introduced and
which some English journalism imitates. I once saw
a headline in a London paper which ran simply thus :
" Dobbin's Little Mary." This was intended to be
familiar and popular, and therefore, presumably,
lucid. But it was some time before I realised, after
reading about half the printed matter underneath,
that it had something to do with the proper feeding
of horses. At first sight, I took it, as the historical
leader of the future will certainly take it, as con-
taining some allusion to the little daughter who so
monopolised the affections of the Major at the end
of *Vanity Fair*. The Americans carry to an even
wilder extreme this darkness by excess of light. You
may find a column in an American paper headed
" Poet Brown Off Orange-flowers," or " Senator
Robinson Shoehorns Hats Now," and it may be quite
a long time before the full meaning breaks upon you :
it has not broken upon me yet.

And something of this intellectual vengeance
pursues also those who adopt the modern method

of reporting speeches. They also become mystical,
simply by trying to be vulgar. They also are con-
demned to be always trying to write like George R.
Sims, and succeeding, in spite of themselves, in
writing like Maeterlinck. That combination of words
which I have quoted from an alleged speech of Mr.
Bernard Shaw's was written down by the reporter
with the idea that he was being particularly plain
and democratic. But, as a matter of fact, if there
is any connection between the two sentences, it must
be something as dark as the deepest roots of Browning,
or something as invisible as the most airy filaments of
Meredith. To be simple and to be democratic are
two very honourable and austere achievements ;
and it is not given to all the snobs and self-seekers to
achieve them. High above even Maeterlinck or
Meredith stand those, like Homer and Milton, whom
no one can misunderstand. And Homer and Milton
are not only better poets than Browning (great as he
was), but they would also have been very much
better journalists than the young men on the *Daily
Mail*.

As it is, however, this misrepresentation of speeches
is only a part of a vast journalistic misrepresentation
of all life as it is. Journalism is popular, but it is
popular mainly as fiction. Life is one world, and
life seen in the newspapers another ; the public
enjoys both, but it is more or less conscious of the
difference. People do not believe, for instance, that
the debates in the House of Commons are as dramatic
as they appear in the daily papers. If they did they
would go, not to the daily paper, but to the House of
Commons. The galleries would be crowded every
night as they were in the French Revolution ; for
instead of seeing a printed story for a penny they would
be seeing an acted drama for nothing. But the people
know in their hearts that journalism is a conventional

art like any other, that it selects, heightens, and falsifies. Only its Nemesis is the same as that of other arts : if it loses all care for truth it loses all form likewise. The modern who paints too cleverly produces a picture of a cow which might be the earthquake at San Francisco. And the journalist who reports a speech too cleverly makes it mean nothing at all.

THE WORSHIP OF THE WEALTHY

THERE has crept, I notice, into our literature and journalism a new way of flattering the wealthy and the great. In more straightforward times flattery itself was more straightforward ; falsehood itself was more true. A poor man wishing to please a rich man simply said that he was the wisest, bravest, tallest, strongest, most benevolent and most beautiful of mankind ; and as even the rich man probably knew that he wasn't that, the thing did the less harm. When courtiers sang the praises of a king they attributed to him things that were entirely improbable as that he resembled the sun at noonday, that they had to shade their eyes when he entered the room, that his people could not breathe without him, or that he had with his single sword conquered Europe, Asia, Africa, and America. The safety of this method was its artificiality ; between the king and his public image there was really no relation. But the moderns have invented a much subtler and more poisonous kind of eulogy. The modern method is to take the prince or rich man, to give a credible picture of his type of personality, as that he is businesslike, or a sportsman, or fond of art, or convivial, or reserved ; and then enormously exaggerate the value and importance of these natural qualities. Those who praise Mr. Carnegie do not say that he is as wise as Solomon and as brave as Mars ; I wish they did. It would be the next most honest thing to giving their real reason for praising him, which is simply that he has money. The journalists who write about Mr. Pierpont Morgan do not say that he is as beautiful as Apollo ; I wish they did. What they do is to take the rich man's superficial life and manner, clothes, hobbies, love of cats, dislike of doctors, or what not ; and then with the assistance of this realism make the man out to be a prophet and a saviour of his kind, whereas he is merely a private and stupid man who happens to like cats or to dislike doctors. The old flatterer took for granted that the king was an ordinary man, and set to work to make him out extraordinary. The newer and cleverer flatterer takes for granted that he is extraordinary, and that therefore even ordinary things about him will be of interest.

I have noticed one very amusing way in which this is done. I notice the method applied to about six of the wealthiest men in England in a book of interviews published by an able and well-known journalist. The flatterer contrives to combine strict truth of fact with a vast atmosphere of awe and mystery by the simple operation of dealing almost entirely in negatives. Suppose you are writing a sympathetic study of Mr. Pierpont Morgan. Perhaps there is not much to say about what he does think, or like, or admire ; but you can suggest whole vistas of his taste and philosophy by talking a great deal about what he does not think, or like, or admire. You say of him— " But little attracted to the most recent schools of German philosophy, he stands almost as resolutely aloof from the tendencies of transcendental Pantheism as from the narrower ecstasies of Neo-Catholicism." Or suppose I am called upon to praise the charwoman who has just come into my house, and who certainly deserves it much more. I say :—" It would be a mistake to class Mrs. Higgs among the followers of Loisy ; her position is in many ways different ; nor is she wholly to be identified with the concrete Hebraism of Harnack." It is a splendid method as it gives the flatterer an opportunity of talking about something else besides the subject of the flattery, and it gives the subject of the flattery a rich, if somewhat bewildered, mental glow, as of one who has somehow gone through agonies of philosophical choice of which he was previously unaware. It is a splendid method ; but I wish it were applied sometimes to charwomen rather than only to millionaires.

There is another way of flattering important people which has become very common, I notice, among writers in the newspapers and elsewhere. It consists in applying to them the phrases " simple," or " quiet," or " modest," without any sort of meaning or rela-tion to the person to whom they are applied. To be simple is the best thing in the world ; to be modest is the next best thing. I am not so sure about being quiet. I am rather inclined to think that really modest people make a great deal of noise. It is quite self-evident that really simple people make a great deal of noise. But simplicity and modesty, at least, are very rare and royal human virtues, not to be lightly talked about. Few human beings, and at rare intervals, have really risen into being modest ; not one man in ten or in twenty has by long wars become simple, as an actual old soldier does by long wars become simple. These virtues are not things to fling about as mere flattery ; many prophets and righteous men have desired to see these things and have not seen them. But in the description of the births, lives, and deaths of very luxurious men they are used incessantly and quite without thought. If a journalist has to describe a great politician or financier (the things are substantially the same) entering a room or walking down a thoroughfare, he always says, " Mr. Midas was quietly dressed in a black frock coat, a white waistcoat, and light grey trousers, with a plain green tie and simple flower in his button-hole." As if any one would expect him to have a crimson frock coat or spangled trousers. As if any one would expect him to have a burning Catherine wheel in his button-hole.

But this process, which is absurd enough when applied to the ordinary and external lives of worldly people, becomes perfectly intolerable when it is applied, as it always is applied, to the one episode which is serious even in the lives of politicians. I mean their death. When we have been sufficiently bored with the account of the simple costume of the millionaire, which is generally about as complicated as any that he could assume without being simply thought mad ; when we have been told about the modest home of the millionaire, a home which is generally much too immodest to be called a home at all ; when we have followed him through all these un-meaning eulogies, we are always asked last of all to admire his quiet funeral. I do not know what else people think a funeral should be except quiet. Yet again and again, over the grave of every one of those sad rich men, for whom one should surely feel, first and last, a speechless pity—over the grave of Beit, over the grave of Whiteley—this sickening nonsense about modesty and simplicity has been poured out. I well remember that when Beit was buried, the papers said that the mourning-coaches contained everybody of importance, that the floral tributes were sumptuous, splendid, intoxicating ; but, for all that, it was a simple and quiet funeral. What, in the name of Acheron, did they expect it to be ? Did they think

there would be human sacrifice—the immolation of
Oriental slaves upon the tomb ? Did they think that
long rows of Oriental dancing-girls would sway
hither and thither in an ecstasy of lament ? Did they
look for the funeral games of Patroclus ? I fear they
had no such splendid and pagan meaning. I fear
they were only using the words " quiet " and
" modest " as words to fill up a page—a mere piece
of the automatic hypocrisy which does become too
common among those who have to write rapidly and
often. The word " modest " will soon become like
the word " honourable," which is said to be employed
by the Japanese before any word that occurs in a
polite sentence, as " Put honourable umbrella in
honourable umbrella-stand " ; or " condescend to
clean honourable boots." We shall read in the future
that the modest king went out in his modest crown,
clad from head to foot in modest gold and attended
with his ten thousand modest earls, their swords
modestly drawn. No ! if we have to pay for splendour let us praise it as splendour, not as simplicity.
When next I meet a rich man I intend to walk up
to him in the street and address him with Oriental
hyperbole. He will probably run away.

THE WHEEL

In a quiet and rustic though fairly famous church
in my neighbourhood there is a window supposed
to represent an Angel on a Bicycle. It does definitely
and indisputably represent a nude youth sitting on
a wheel ; but there is enough complication in the
wheel and sanctity (I suppose) in the youth to warrant
this working description. It is a thing of florid

Renascence outline, and belongs to the highly pagan period which introduced all sorts of objects into ornament : personally I can believe in the bicycle more than in the angel. Men, they say, are now imitating angels ; in their flying-machines, that is : not in any other respect that I have heard of. So perhaps the angel on the bicycle (if he is an angel and if it is a bicycle) was avenging himself by imitating man. If so, he showed that high order of intellect which is attributed to angels in the mediæval books, though not always (perhaps) in the mediæval pictures.

For wheels are the mark of a man quite as much as wings are the mark of an angel. Wheels are the things that are as old as mankind and yet are strictly peculiar to man ; that are prehistoric but not pre-human.

A distinguished psychologist, who is well acquainted with physiology, has told me that parts of himself are certainly levers, while other parts are probably pulleys, but that after feeling himself carefully all over, he cannot find a wheel anywhere. The wheel, as a mode of movement, is a purely human thing. On the ancient escutcheon of Adam (which, like much of the rest of his costume, has not yet been discovered) the heraldic emblem was a wheel—*passant*. As a mode of progress, I say, it is unique. Many modern philosophers, like my friend before mentioned, are ready to find links between man and beast, and to show that man has been in all things the blind slave of his mother earth. Some, of a very different kind, are even eager to show it ; especially if it can be twisted to the discredit of religion. But even the most eager scientists have often admitted in my hearing that they would be surprised if some kind of cow approached them moving solemnly on four wheels. Wings, fins, flappers, claws, hoofs, webs, trotters, with all these the fantastic families of the earth come against us and close around us, fluttering and flapping and rustling and galloping and lumbering and thundering ; but there is no sound of wheels.

I remember dimly, if, indeed, I remember aright, that in some of those dark prophetic pages of Scripture, that seem of cloudy purple and dusky gold, there is a passage in which the seer beholds a violent dream of wheels. Perhaps this was indeed the symbolic declaration of the spiritual supremacy of man. Whatever the birds may do above or the fishes beneath his ship, man is the only thing to steer ; the only thing to be conceived as steering. He may make the birds his friends, if he can. He may make the fishes his gods, if he chooses. But most certainly he will not believe a bird at the masthead ; and it is hardly likely that he will even permit a fish at the helm. He is, as Swinburne says, helmsman and chief : he is literally the Man at the Wheel.

The wheel is an animal that is always standing on its head ; only it does it so rapidly that no philosopher has ever found out which is its head. Or if the phrase be felt as more exact, it is an animal that is always turning head over heels and progressing by this principle. Some fish, I think, turn head over heels (supposing them, for the sake of argument, to have heels) ; I have a dog who nearly did it ; and I did it once myself when I was very small. It was an accident ; and, as that delightful novelist, Mr. de Morgan, would say, it never can happen again. Since then no one has accused me of being upside down except mentally : and I rather think that there is something to be said for that ; especially as typified by the rotary symbol. A wheel is the sublime paradox ; one part of it is always going forward and the other part always going back. Now this, as it happens, is highly similar to the proper condition of any human soul or any political state. Every sane soul or state looks at once backwards and forwards ; and even goes backwards to come on.

For those interested in revolt (as I am) I only say meekly that one cannot have a Revolution without revolving. The wheel, being a logical thing, has reference to what is behind as well as what is before. It has (as every society should have) a part that perpetually leaps helplessly at the sky ; and a part that perpetually bows down its head into the dust. Why should people be so scornful of us who stand on our heads ? Bowing down one's head in the dust is a very good thing, the humble beginning of all happiness. When we have bowed our heads in the dust for a little time, the happiness comes ; and then (leaving our heads in the humble and reverent position) we kick up our heels behind in the air. That is the true origin of standing on one's head ; and the ultimate defence of paradox. The wheel humbles itself to be exalted ; only it does it a little quicker than I do.

NOTES

FRANCIS BACON

Francis Bacon (1561–1626) was the greatest intellect of
the Elizabethan age. By his ability, applied to law
and politics, he became successively Queen's Counsel,
Attorney-General, and Lord Chancellor. By the dry
light of reason he conceived, and in " The Advance-
ment of Learning " (1605) and the " Novum Organum "
(1620) partly carried out, a far-reaching revolution in
philosophy and scientific method. Unfortunately he
subordinated morals to intellect, and, while Lord
Chancellor, was charged with bribery, found guilty,
fined, and deprived of his position.

Bacon's " Essays " differ from others in that they
were written to be of special use to " princes," or kings,
not for the man in the street. They are only occasionally familiar or on trivial subjects. They excel rather in
dignity of tone, soundness of practical wisdom, and the
terseness of the disjointed aphorisms of which they
mainly consist. They are, as has been justly remarked,
" the first true English prose-classic."

Of Studies.

P. 3, l. 5.   *Expert :* experienced.
 l. 6.   *Particulars :* particular circumstances and events.
 l. 14.   *Provning :* pruning.
 l. 27.   *Curiously :* in great detail ; with great care.
P. 4, l. 2.   *Argument :* a subject for consideration.
 l. 3.   *Distilled Bookes :* epitomes ; summaries.
 l. 5.   *Conference :* consultation ; conversation.
    Full : well-informed.
 l. 8.   *Present Wit :* quick intelligence ; presence of mind.
 l. 12.   *Naturall Philosophy :* science.
 l. 13.   *Abeunt studia in Mores :* " Studies affect character."
    Ovid, " Heroides," xv. 83.
 l. 14.   *Stond :* stop ; hindrance.
 l. 17.   *Reines :* kidneys.

ll. 21–22. *Wit be called away :* if his mind wander from the subject.

l. 24. *Schoole-men :* philosophers and theologians of the Middle Ages, noted for their hair-splitting logical distinctions.

ll. 24–25. *Cymini sectores :* Antoninus Pius " was called Cymini Sector, a carver, or divider of Comine seede, which is one of the least seedes"; hence the phrase is equivalent to " hair-splitters."

l. 25. *Not Apt . . . Matters :* slow in the motion of his mind to and fro.

Of Travaile.

P. 5, l. 20. *Consistories Ecclesiasticke :* Church Courts.

ll. 24–25. *Disputations :* debates.

l. 28. *Magazens :* magazines ; arsenals.

Burse : the Exchange.

l. 32. *Cabinets :* curiosities.

l. 36. *Triumphs ; Masques :* see the following essay.

P. 6, l. 3. *Roome :* space, compass.

l. 16. *Adamant :* magnet.

l. 32. *Fame :* report.

l. 35. *Place :* precedence.

Words : insults ; high words.

P. 7, l. 8. *Advised :* deliberate.

ll. 9–10. *His country manners :* the manners of his country.

l. 11. *Prick in :* intermingle, plant among.

Of Masques and Triumphs.

Masque : a sort of dramatic spectacle, in which the characters personified mythological deities, etc.

Triumph : a festival show, pageant.

P. 7, l. 18. *Quire :* choir.

l. 19. *Broken Musicke :* music for various instruments playing together.

l. 20. *Ditty :* the words of a song, the song itself.

Device : setting, situation.

l. 26. *Nice :* scrupulous, fastidious.

l. 27. *Catches :* themes or phrases ; parts.

l. 31. *Take :* capture, captivate.

P. 8, l. 7. *To come down from the Scene :* after the Masque, the actors commonly came down from the stage into the audience, and all joined in a dance.

l. 8. *Motions :* movements, probably in dumb-show.

l. 16. *Oes :* round bright spots.

Spangs : spangles.

l. 20.   *Vizars :* visors, masks.
l. 22.   *Antimasque :*   a grotesque interlude introduced
   between the acts of the masque, to which it served as
   a foil and contrast.
l. 24.   *Antiques :* buffoons.
l. 25.   *Ethiopes :* Ethiopians.
     Turquet : perhaps a player dressed as a Turk.
l. 26.   *Statua :* statue.
P. 9, l. 1.   *Just :* tournament, tilt.
     Barriers : the lists in which a tournament was fought.
l. 6.   *Bravery :* finery.
l. 7.   *Furniture :* trappings, harness.

Of Discourse.

P. 9, l. 10.   *Hold all Arguments :*   argue in favour of any
   proposition.
l. 18.   *Give the Occasion :* introduce a topic of conversation.
P. 10, l. 2.   *Vaine :* vein, kind of conversation.
l. 3.   *Parce . . . Loris :*   Ovid, " Metamorphoses," ii.
   127.   " Spare the spur, young man, and use the reins
   more firmly."
l. 14.   *Poser :* one who " poses " or puts questions.
l. 19.   *Galliard :*   a spirited or gay dance for two.
l. 30.   *Speech of Touch :*   speech that touches or affects
   other people personally.
l. 32.   *Comming home to :*   having special reference to,
   especially in a harmful way.
P. 11, l. 1.   *Drie Blow :*   joke ;   smart hit—opposed to a
   wound that draws blood.
ll. 7–8.   *Speech of Interlocution :*   the replies made to the
   continuous remarks of another person.
l. 9.   *Setled Speech :*   a deliberate speech of some length.
l. 11.   *Course :* race ; running.
l. 13.   *Circumstances :* introductory details.

Of Youth and Age.

P. 11, l. 20.   *Invention :* imagination.
l. 26.   *Julius Cæsar :*   Cæsar's great achievements   in
   government and war belong to his maturity, not to his
   youth.
ll. 26–27.   *Septimius Severus :*   Roman Emperor, A.D. 193–
   211, at the age of forty-seven.
ll. 27–28.   *Iuventutem . . . plenam :*   Spartianus, *Vita Sep-
   timi Severi.*   " He spent a youth full of error, indeed of
   madness."

l. 31. *Augustus Cæsar :* the first Roman Emperor (63 B.C.–A.D. 14).

Cosmus : (1389–1464) one of the greatest of the Medici family, and governor of Florence.

P. 12, l. 1. *Gaston de Fois :* one of Charlemagne's knights.

l. 4. *Execution :* action ; carrying out instructions.

l. 15. *Degrees :* steps, stages.

l. 16. *Care not :* are not careful or cautious.

l. 20. *Unready :* ill-trained.

l. 23. *Period :* termination, completion.

l. 28. *For Succession :* for the future.

l. 29. *Are Actours :* govern.

l. 30. *Externe :* external.

l. 34. *Rabbine :* Rabbi.

The Text : Joel ii. 28.

P. 13, l. 8. *Hermogenes :* a famous Greek rhetorician, *c.* A.D. 170.

l. 14. *Tully :* Cicero.

Hortensius : a Roman orator, 114–50 B.C., who rose to fame at the age of nineteen.

ll. 14–15. *Idem . . . decebat :* " He did not change, but a change would have become him." Cicero, *Brutus*, 95.

l. 17. *Tract of yeares :* length of years ; more advanced age.

l. 18. *Scipio Affricanus :* 234–183 B.C., distinguished himself as a youth in the Punic Wars, and held several public offices in Rome before the legal age.

Livy : the Roman historian. The reference to Scipio Africanus is to his " History of Rome," xxxviii. 53.

l. 19. *Ultima . . . :* Ovid, " Heroides," ix. 23-24. " The end was inferior to the beginning."

RICHARD STEELE

Sir Richard Steele (1672–1729) was born in Dublin, and educated at the Charterhouse and Merton College, Oxford. He was a survival of the dashing Cavalier type, with the addition of a tender conscience. His adventurous spirit carried him from Oxford into the Life Guards, and afterwards founded " The Tatler " (1709), and created the Spectator Club. His chivalrous morality produced " The Christian Hero " (1701), and several comedies in which he broke with the Restoration tradition by ranging wit on the side of virtue. His essays in " The Tatler " and " The Spectator " (1711) show the same preoccupation with " the reformation of the world " by means of good-humoured raillery and satire on all departures from good sense and toleration.

Mr. Bickerstaff on Himself.

> *Mr. Bickerstaff :* Steele's pen-name. It was invented by Swift for his ironical pamphlets on the astrologer, Partridge.

P. 17, l. 9. *Bills of mortality :* official returns of the births and deaths occurring in a certain district within a given time.

> l. 21. *Tom's, Will's . . . :* well-known London coffee-houses of the time.

> l. 23. *Dates :* letters.

P. 18, l. 5. *Decipher :* identify.

> l. 10. *Lucubrations :* compositions produced by candle-light, *i.e.* with toil and study.

> l. 16. *Pastoral letter :* an address to the clergy of a diocese by their bishop ; a letter written from the country.

P. 19, l. 25. *Taw :* a game at marbles.

> l. 26. *Gaming :* gambling ; playing at games.

> l. 28. *False concords :* probably mistakes in Latin syntax, such as the agreement of subject and verb.

> l. 34. *Occult sciences :* alchemy, astrology, magic, etc.

Fashionable Affectations.

P. 20, l. 14. *Sanguine :* abounding with blood, ruddy (the original meaning of the word).

> l. 18. *Humour :* disposition, caprice, fancy.

> l. 27. *Closet :* a small private room.

> l. 31. *Glass :* telescope ; opera-glass.

P. 21, l. 11. *Gascon :* of Gascony, a province in S.W. France.

> l. 15. *Without :* unless.

> l. 31. *Alexander the Great :* (356–323 B.C.) King of Macedonia, and famous as the conqueror of the East as far as India.

P. 22, l. 9. *The noose :* or knot, of marriage.

> " *For ever and aye* " : in the marriage oath.

> l. 20. *Complexion :* nature, character.

P. 23, l. 9. *Roasting :* making fun of.

> *Smoking :* ridiculing.

> l. 15. *Beaux esprits :* fine wits ; fine spirits.

On Long-winded People.

P. 23, l. 25. *Boccalini* (bokkalee'nee) : an Italian satirist (1556–1613).

l. 28. *Guicciardini* (gueechyardee′nee) : a famous Italian historian and statesman (1483–1540), chiefly known by his vast history of Italy between 1494 and 1532.

l. 31. *Donne :* a great divine and poet (1573–1631), famous for his sermons, and his " metaphysical " poetry.

P. 24, l. 1. *Moses :* in the first chapter of Genesis.

l. 19. *Baker's Chronicle :* " Chronicle of the Kings of England " (1643), by Sir Richard Baker.

P. 25, l. 20. *Methusalem :* the character in the Old Testament supposed to have lived longest.

l. 21. *Postdiluvians :* people who have lived since the Flood.

P. 26, l. 28. *Automaton :* a self-moving machine.

l. 36. *Tatler :* the newspaper in which this essay appeared (1709).

The Art of Story-telling.

P. 27, l. 10. *Templar :* a member of the Inner, or of the Middle Temple, two of the London Inns of Court— the four societies which have the right of calling persons to the English bar.

P. 28, l. 23. *Conceits :* humorous or far-fetched ideas.

l. 37. *Parts :* good qualities, talents.

P. 29, l. 36. *Impertinent :* not pertinent ; not to the point.

P. 30, l. 6. *Stone-horse :* stallion.

l. 19. *Sir William Temple :* a statesman and author (1628–1699), chiefly remembered by the fact that Swift was his secretary.

P. 31, l. 12. *The Revolution :* the flight of James II and the succession of William and Mary, in 1688.

On Judicious Flattery.

P. 33, l. 13. *Listed :* enlisted.

l. 17. *There are :* there are some men.

l. 21. *The spleen :* an attack of melancholy or bad temper.

P. 34, l. 24. *Parts :* good qualities.

P. 35, l. 8. *Terence :* the great Latin comic writer, 195–159 B.C.

P. 36, l. 7. *Of parts :* accomplished ; clever.

A Coffee-house and its Frequenters.

P. 37, l. 16. *Levee :* a reception or assembly held by a king.

l. 24. *Inns of Court :* see note to P. 27, l. 10.

l. 28. *Westminster : i.e.* the law-courts in Westminster Hall.

NOTES

P. 38, l. 1. *Virtuoso :* one who is skilled in the fine arts—music, painting, etc.

l. 13. *Deshabille :* undress ; careless or incomplete dress.

P. 39, ll. 16–17. *At legal value :* without interest.

l. 18. *The public stocks :* the National Debt ; Government securities.

P. 40, l. 1. *First minister :* prime minister.

The Spectator Club.

P. 40, l. 11. *Parts :* talents, accomplishments.

l. 16. *Humour :* caprice, fancy, whim, disposition.

l. 26. *Lord Rochester :* John Wilmot, Earl of Rochester (1647–1680), was one of the friends of Charles II, and distinguished himself in the Dutch wars. He was noted for his wit.

Sir George Etherege : (1635?–1691) one of the great comic writers of the Restoration stage.

Both Rochester and Etherege were " fine gentlemen " of the Restoration Court.

P. 41, l. 16. *Quorum :* the Justices present at the court, of whom there had to be at least a certain number.

l. 17. *Quarter-session :* a criminal court held quarterly by Justices of the Peace.

ll. 21–22. *Inner Temple :* one of the Inns of Court. See note to P. 27, l. 10.

l. 24. *Humorsome :* eccentric ; capricious.

l. 28. *Aristotle :* one of the greatest Greek philosophers (384–322 B.C.). The reference here is to his " Poetics."

Longinus : a Greek philosopher and grammarian of the third century A.D. He is best known for his treatise " On the Sublime."

l. 29. *Littleton, Coke :* two famous lawyers of the early seventeenth century. Their works or reports formed part of a student's reading in law.

l. 30. *Marriage-articles :* a legal agreement regarding the property of the persons about to marry.

l. 31. *Leases :* contracts letting a farm, house, etc., for a number of years.

Tenures : the conditions on which land is held by its occupier.

ll. 36–37. *Demosthenes :* the greatest ancient Greek orator.

l. 37. *Tully :* Cicero, the greatest of Roman orators.

P. 42, l. 14. *Will's :* the coffee-house in Russell Street, Covent Garden, frequented by men of letters.

l. 16. *The Rose :* a tavern frequented by actors.

P. 44, l. 16. *Humorists :* eccentric people.
l. 26. *Habits :* clothes ; fashions.
P. 45, l. 1. *Monmouth :* son of Charles II. He rebelled against James II in 1685, was defeated at Sedgemoor, and executed.
l. 3. *The Park :* Hyde Park, London.
l. 24. *Chamber-counsellor :* a lawyer who gives his advice privately, but does not plead in court.

JOSEPH ADDISON

Joseph Addison (1672–1719) was a contemporary of Steele at the Charterhouse and Oxford. He was educated for the diplomatic service, and was appointed Under-Secretary of State, and, in 1709, Secretary for Ireland ; but on the fall of the Whigs in 1711 he was put out of office. Addison's main literary work was comprised in the essays he contributed to " The Tatler " and " The Spectator." If not so robust or original as Steele, he is more elegant and restrained, and less sentimental ; and he developed, with a surer eye for character, the Spectator Club, and in particular the Sir Roger we know. Of his prose, Johnson said, " Whoever wishes to attain an English style, familiar but not coarse, and elegant but not ostentatious, must give his days and nights to the volumes of Addison."

Sir Roger at Home.

P. 49, l. 7. *Humour :* likes and dislikes ; disposition.
l. 15. *For that :* because.
P. 50, l. 32. *Conversation :* behaviour, manner of life.
P. 51, l. 1. *Humorist :* a man given to caprice or eccentricity.
P. 52, l. 3. *Digested :* arranged.
l. 11. *Dr. South :* Robert South (1634–1716), a court preacher with a homely style.
l. 14. *Tillotson :* (1630–1694) archbishop of Canterbury. He cultivated a clear, concise style, and a moderation characteristic of his age.
Saunderson : (1587–1663) bishop of Lincoln, and professor of divinity at Oxford.
Barrow : (1630–1677) a Cambridge professor, of high standing as a mathematician, a divine, and a classical scholar.
l. 15. *Calamy :* (1642–1686) a Cambridge divine.

NOTES

Sir Roger at Church.

P. 53, l. 20.   *Change :* the Stock Exchange.
P. 54, l. 11.   *Particularities :* peculiarities.
P. 55, l. 8.   *Catechising day :* a day on which children, in the English Church, are examined on their catechism.
l. 13.   *Clerk :* church officer.
l. 16.   *Incumbent :* occupant.

Sir Roger at the Assizes.

P. 56, l. 26.   *County assizes :* the sittings of a court held at intervals in English counties, at which causes are tried by judges of the High Court of Justice on circuit and a jury.
P. 57, ll. 8–9.   *Shoots flying :* shoots birds on the wing—regarded as something of a feat in those days.
l. 10.   *Petty jury :* a jury which tries the final issue of fact in a case.
l. 14.   *Quarter-sessions :* a criminal court held quarterly by Justices of the Peace.
l. 21.   *Cast :* defeated in a law-suit.
P. 59, l. 24.   *Aggravation :* exaggeration.
P. 60, l. 4.   *Conjuring :* entreating.

Sir Roger in London.

P. 60, l. 21.   *Gray's Inn :* one of the Inns of Court. See note to P. 27, l. 10.
l. 25.   *Eugene :* Prince of Savoy, a dashing general in the War of the Spanish Succession, to the military success of which he contributed with Marlborough.
l. 32.   *Scanderbeg :* a name given by the Turks to George Castriota, the patriot chief of Epirus, in Greece (1414–1467).
P. 61, l. 21.   *Dr. Barrow :* see note to P. 52, l. 14.
l. 24.   *Mark :* a coin worth 13s. 4d.
P. 62, l. 2.   *Moll White :* an old woman supposed by the countryfolk to be a witch.
l. 35.   *The late act :* the Act against Occasional Conformity rejected in 1704, but passed in 1711. It was intended to exclude from office Nonconformists who " occasionally conformed " to the rites of the Anglican church in order to qualify for municipal and other offices.
P. 63, l. 1.   *Dissenter :* a member of a church other than the Church of England. Many dissenters did not observe Christmas Day.
l. 14.   *The pope's procession :* an annual Whig procession.

239

l. 26.   *Baker's Chronicle :* see note to P. 24, l. 19.
l. 35.   *Waited on :* accompanied.
P. 64, l. 4.   *Boys :* waiters.

The Dream.

P. 64, l. 10.   *Socrates :* the great Greek philosopher of the fifth century B.C. Many of his wise reflections are recorded in the writings of Plato.
l. 16.   *Horace :* the Roman satirical poet (65–8 B.C.).
l. 24.   *Jupiter :* chief of the Roman gods.
P. 65, l. 18.   *Fardel :* burden.
P. 66, l. 11.   *Spleen :* the organ supposed to be the seat of melancholy and bad temper—hence spite ; melancholy; ill-humour.
P. 67, l. 30.   *The colic :* severe indigestion.
l. 37.   *The gripes :* severe pain in the intestines.
P. 69, l. 7.   *Trapsticks :* sticks used in the game of trap-ball.

Remarks on the English by the Indian Kings.

P. 72, l. 12.   *In black :* the black Geneva gown formerly worn in the pulpit.
P. 73, l. 14.   *Covered rooms :* sedan-chairs.
P. 74, l. 8.   *Black spots :* small patches of black silk worn on the face to bring out the complexion by contrast.

Mischiefs of Party Spirit.

P. 75, l. 10.   *Prick-eared cur :* from "Henry V," Act II, Sc. 1, l. 44 ; here applied to the Puritans, whose ears stood out more prominently because they wore their hair short.
ll. 23–24.   *To the prejudice of the land-tax :* the land-tax, paid by the Tory land-owners, had recently been increased by more accurate valuation of estates. Sir Roger attributes this to the party spirit of the Whigs.
P. 76, l. 9.   *Plutarch :* the Greek biographer and philosopher, best known for his " Parallel Lives " of Greeks and Romans.
l. 19.   *That great rule :* St. Luke vi. 27–37.
P. 77, l. 23.   *Postulatums :* postulates, assumptions.
l. 34.   *Guelfes and Gibelines :* or Guelphs and Ghibellines : the papal and imperial factions which were constantly at strife in Italy from the twelfth century to the fifteenth.
l. 35.   *The League :* the Catholic League formed by Henry, Duke of Guise, in 1576, against the Huguenots or Protestants in France.

NOTES

OLIVER GOLDSMITH

Oliver Goldsmith (1728–1774) was the son of an Irish clergyman—the kindly Mr. Primrose of " The Vicar of Wakefield." After desultory studies at Dublin, Edinburgh, and Leyden, he travelled on foot over France, Switzerland, and Italy, earning his living by his flute. On his return to London, he produced various types of work : essays, collected in " The Citizen of the World " ; a novel, " The Vicar of Wakefield " ; two plays, " The Good-natured Man " and " She Stoops to Conquer " ; and a few poems, including " The Traveller " and " The Deserted Village." His kindly humour and universal good-nature shine through all he wrote, and a natural and limpid style of exquisite charm has placed his work among the classics.

War.

P. 82, l. 25. *To grant :* the Hudson Bay Company, founded in 1670, by Royal Charter.

P. 83, l. 14. *Dispossessed them :* in the Seven Years' War (1756–1763).

P. 84, l. 25. *Daures :* the people of Dauria, a district just north of Manchuria, and on the southern shores of Lake Baikal.

Doctors.

P. 85, l. 33. *Confucius :* the great Chinese moralist and philosopher (550–478 B.C.). His maxims, which are widely known and quoted among the Chinese, have played an important part in forming the national character.

P. 86, l. 15. *Electuary :* a composition of medicinal powders with honey or sugar.

The Story of the Man in Black.

P. 88, l. 30. *Amphitheatre :* circus, arena.

P. 89, l. 30. *Bonze :* a Buddhist priest.

P. 91, l. 10. *Sensibility :* emotion.

P. 92, l. 26. *Cribbage :* a game of cards.

P. 93, l. 11. *Tacitus :* the Roman historian (*c.* A.D. 55–*c.* 117), and the son-in-law of Agricola.

l. 29. *Ovation :* a triumphal procession, such as was granted by the Romans to their most successful generals.

l. 33. *Hunks :* miser.

Parliamentary Elections.

P. 94, l. 20. *Feast of the Lanterns :* " Tradition says that the daughter of a famous mandarin, walking on the edge of a lake one evening, fell in and was drowning. The father, with all his neighbours, went with lanterns to look for her, and happily she was rescued. In commemoration thereof an annual festival was held on the spot, and grew in time to the celebrated ' Feast of Lanterns' " (Brewer).

P. 95, l. 24. *Culverin :* a type of cannon formerly used.

P. 96, l. 26. *Levee :* an assembly received by some great man.

A Reverie.

P. 99, l. 14. *Landau :* a carriage with a top that might be opened centrally and thrown back.

l. 18. *Berlin :* a covered carriage, with a seat behind, protected by a hood.

l. 27. *Colley Cibber :* a lesser dramatist (1671–1757). He had a quarrel with Pope, who made him the hero of his " Dunciad."

P. 100, l. 8. *The Bee :* a periodical edited by Goldsmith. It ran from October 6 till November 24, 1759.

l. 22. *Whimsical figure :* John Hill, M.D., a prolific miscellaneous writer on a great variety of subjects, mostly in a scurrilous and satirical style. His papers, " The Inspector," were published in the London " Daily Advertiser " in March 1751. The nosegay refers to his writings on botany.

P. 101, l. 5. *Jehu :* a furious driver ; a coachman. There is a humorous allusion to 2 Kings ix. 20.

l. 10. *Harlequin :* the chief character in a pantomime. He wears a tight spangled dress, and carries a wand by means of which he is supposed to remain invisible and to play tricks.

l. 20. *Proteus :* an old man of the sea, and Neptune's herdsman. He was remarkable for his power of changing into any shape or form he chose.

l. 21. *Rigadoon :* a lively dance.

l. 23. *The person . . . :* Arthur Murphy (1727–1805), author of a tragedy, the " Orphan of China," several comedies, and other miscellaneous works. All his plots were taken from previous writers.

P. 102, l. 22. *One dictionary :* perhaps that of the French Academy, published in 1694.

NOTES

l. 26. *Rambler :* a periodical edited by Dr. Johnson, 1750–1752.
l. 29. *Apollo :* the god of poetry.
l. 30. *Clio :* the muse of history.
P. 103, l. 13. *An historian :* David Hume (1711–1776), philosopher and historian, and author of " Essays Moral and Political " and " History of England." The first volume of the " History " was published in 1754.
l. 29. *A romance :* " Roderick Random " (1748), by Smollett, who also wrote a " History of England from the Revolution " (1757).
l. 33. *Cervantes :* the great Spanish novelist (1547–1616), best known by his " Don Quixote."
   Segrais : a French poet and wit (1624–1701).

CHARLES LAMB

Charles Lamb (1775–1834) was educated at Christ's Hospital, London, where he formed a friendship with Coleridge. He was employed as a clerk, first at South Sea House, and later at the India House. He is best known as the author of the " Essays of Elia," which express freely his whimsical personality and humour, his love of London and of the antique and peculiar in literature, in furniture, books, and customs. With his sister, Mary, he also published " Tales from Shakespeare." His " Adventures of Ulysses," a simple version of the " Odyssey," is still popular.

The Londoner.

P. 107, l. 5. *Day :* November 9th. Lamb's own birthday was February 10th.
l. 15. *Spital Sermon :* one of the sermons formerly preached on Easter Monday and Tuesday from a special pulpit at St. Mary Spital, outside Bishopsgate.
ll. 16–17. *Whittington . . . :* a reference to the legend, according to which Dick Whittington rose, with the help of his cat, from an apprentice to Lord Mayor of London.
ll. 26–27. *A charming young woman :* probably a reference to Lamb's passion for the young lady called in his essays Alice Winterton.
P. 108, l. 10. *Silly :* in the old sense of " simple."

243

Arcadia : a pastoral region in southern Greece, represented as an ideal of rustic simplicity and contentment.

l. 11. *Epsom Downs :* in Surrey.

P. 109, l. 4. *Polity :* political philosophy.

ll. 11–12. *" Found tongues . . .": * "As You Like It," Act II, Sc. i, ll. 16–17.

All Fools' Day.

P. 109, l. 26. *The motley :* the parti-coloured dress worn by professional fools : hence, folly.

ll. 28–29. *Free of the corporation :* a member of the guild of fools, with all its privileges.

ll. 29–30. *Meets . . . forest :* from "As You Like It," Act II, Sc. vii, l. 12.

P. 110, l. 1. *Stultus sum :* I am a fool (*Latin*).

l. 5. *Gooseberry : sc.* wine. The drink is appropriate from its association of its name with the foolish goose.

l. 6. *Politic :* prudent : associated with prudent men.

l. 7. *Troll :* to sing the parts in succession, as in a round or catch.

The catch of Amiens : or rather, the parody of it, from "As You Like It," Act II, Sc. v, l. 50.

l. 13. *Give him :* drink his health.

l. 15. *The party :* the person, *i.e.* the greatest fool.

l. 18. *Hobby :* hobby-horse, *i.e.* particular whim or weakness (of mind).

Dust away : shake.

ll. 20–21. *The crazy . . . chimes :* Wordsworth, "The Fountain."

l. 23. *A salamander-gathering :* Empedocles, a Greek philosopher of the fifth century B.C., is said to have thrown himself down the crater of Etna. Salamanders were lizards supposed able to live in fire.

l. 24. *Samphire :* a herb that grows chiefly on cliffs along the coast. Cf. "Lear," Act IV, Sc. vi, l. 15.

l. 27. *Cleombrotus :* a youth who drowned himself after reading Plato on Immortality.

l. 30. *Calenturists :* the calenture, or hot fever, is a kind of delirium that occurs on board ship in the tropics. It sometimes causes sailors to leap into the sea, imagining they see green fields and trees there.

l. 31. *Gebir :* actually an Arabian alchemist of the eighth century A.D., and not connected with the tower of Babel.

P. 111, l. 1.   *Grand :* Grand Master, or president of a lodge of freemasons.

l. 3.   *Stammerers :* an allusion to the confusion of tongues (Genesis xi. 6–10), and to Lamb's own stammer.

l. 4.   *Herodotus :* the first great Greek historian. He does not refer to the tower of Babel.

l. 5.   *Toise :* a French measure, almost equal to $6\frac{1}{2}$ feet.

l. 7.   *Nuncheon :* luncheon.

l. 8.   *Shinar :* or Senaar : the Jewish name for Babylonia.

l. 10.   *Monument :* a column, over 200 feet high, built by Sir Christopher Wren, and erected as a memorial of the Great Fire.

ll. 13–14.   *Another globe :* Alexander the Great is said to have wept for more worlds to conquer.

l. 15.   *Adams :* Parson Adams, a character in Fielding's " Joseph Andrews."   " 'Odso " was a favourite oath of his.

l. 17.   *Slipslop :* a character in " Joseph Andrews."

ll. 21, 23.   *Raymund Lully, Duns :* thirteenth-century philosophers.

ll. 25–26.   *Logical forms :* a pun on the use of " form " to mean (*a*) the forms of syllogistic reasoning, and (*b*) long wooden benches.

l. 28.   *Stephen :* a simpleton in Ben Jonson's " Every Man in his Humour."

   Cokes : a simpleton in Jonson's " Bartholomew Fair."

l. 29.   *Aguecheek :* a foolish character in " Twelfth Night."

l. 30.   *Devoir :* duty, respects.

   Shallow : a foolish country justice in " The Merry Wives of Windsor," and " 2 Henry IV."

l. 31.   *Silence :* a country justice in " 2 Henry IV."

l. 32.   *Slender :* Shallow's cousin.

l. 35.   *R— — :* Ramsay, of the " London Library " in Ludgate Street.

P. 112, l. 7.   *Granville S—— :* Sharp, an advocate of the abolition of slavery.

ll. 9–10.   *King . . . :* from the poem on a nightingale, by the Elizabethan poet Barnfield.

l. 12.   *Armado :* a pompous Spaniard in " Love's Labour's Lost."

   Quisada : Don Quixote.

l. 14.   *Ornature :* adornment.

I   245

l. 19. *Macheath :* a highwayman in Gay's " Beggar's
Opera," who sings :—
> " How happy could I be with either,
> Were t'other dear charmer away ! "

l. 23. *Malvolian :* like that of Malvolio, in " Twelfth
Night," smugly complacent.

l. 27. *Goodly-propertied :* endowed with such charms.

P. 113, l. 1. *Architect . . . :* St. Matthew vii. 24.

l. 5. *Talent :* St. Luke xix. 12–28.

l. 8. *Tendre :* tenderness.

l. 9. *Virgins :* St. Matthew xxv. 1–13.

l. 11. *Answered :* proved satisfactory.

l. 23. *Dotterel :* a kind of plover.

l. 25. *Received :* accepted.

ll. 25–26. *Whereof . . . worthy :* Hebrews xi. 38.

l. 28. *White boys :* favourites.

Modern Gallantry.

P. 114, l. 5. *Civility :* civilisation.

l. 14. *Dorimant :* a gallant in Etherege's comedy " The
Man of Mode."

ll. 14–15. *Fish-wife :* a woman who sells fish. Fish-wives
were noted for coarseness.

l. 15. *Kennel :* gutter.

l. 23. *Box-coat :* thick overcoat for wear on the box-seat
of a coach beside the driver.

l. 34. *Rider :* commercial traveller.

l. 37. *Lothbury :* the business quarter of London.

P. 115, l. 9. *Account :* advantage.

l. 21. *" Overstood her market " :* set too high a price on
herself in the " marriage market," by rejecting suitors,
and lost the chance of marriage.

P. 116, l. 2. *Casualties :* what is due to accident or chance,
e.g. in one's social position.

l. 16. *Eld :* old age.

l. 17. *Yield the wall :* allow a woman to take the inside
of the pavement.

l. 19. *Grandam :* grandmother.

ll. 19–20. *Preux Chevalier :* valiant knight (French).

l. 20. *Sir Calidore :* a knight typifying courtesy in
Spenser's " Faerie Queene."
Sir Tristan : one of the most courteous knights of the
Round Table.

P. 118, l. 15. *Of :* part of.

l. 22. *Additaments :* additions.

My First Play.

P. 118, l. 31. *Drury:* Drury Lane Theatre, with which David Garrick was associated both as a leading actor and as part proprietor.

P. 119, l. 11. *Orders:* tickets for free admission.

l. 20. *Sheridan:* Richard Brinsley Sheridan, the famous orator and dramatist (1751–1816), best known as the author of " The Rivals " and " The School for Scandal."

l. 24. *Quadrille:* a game of cards played by four persons.

l. 25. *Harmonious:* she was a famous singer.

l. 29. *Billets:* tickets.

P. 120, l. 2. *Ciceronian:* dignified or lofty in the style of the greatest Roman orator, Cicero.

l. 9. *Seneca:* a Roman stoic philosopher (A.D. 2–65).
Varro: a Roman writer on antiquities and agriculture.

ll. 13–14. *Climbed . . . honours:* became a churchwarden.

l. 14. *St. Andrew's:* a parish in Holborn, London.

l. 18. *Arabian paradises:* supreme delights in paradise were promised by Mahomet to the faithful.

l. 29. *Centre:* *sc.* of the earth.

ll. 32–33. *Uncomfortable:* causing discomfort.

l. 37. *Nonpareil:* a kind of apple.

P. 121, l. 5. *Pro:* for, instead of (Latin).

l. 9. *Plate:* engraving.

l. 10. *Rowe:* poet, dramatist, and editor of Shakespeare (1674–1718).

ll. 10–11. *The tent scene:* Act V, Scene II.

l. 15. *Pilasters:* small pillars on which the boxes rested.

l. 18. *Raised:* exalted.

l. 21. *Rose:* were turned up.
" *Fair Aurorus* " : from the first line of the first song in " Artaxerxes "—" Fair Aurora, prithee stay."

l. 26. *Artaxerxes:* an opera by Arne which first appeared in 1762.

l. 32. *Darius:* King of Persia, 521–485 B.C. He began a war with Greece, in which he was defeated at Marathon.
In the midst of Daniel: see Daniel vi.

l. 35. *Persepolis:* the ancient capital of Persia.

l. 36. *The burning idol:* the sun, which they worshipped.

P. 122, l. 1. *Significations:* emblems.

ll. 1–2. *Elemental fire:* ordinary fire, regarded by the ancients as one of the elements.

l. 4. *Harlequin :* the clown.

l. 8. *St. Denys :* a French saint who, according to the legend, walked four miles after he was beheaded (A.D. 251).

l. 13. *Rich :* a comic writer (1681–1761) who used the pseudonym of Lun.

l. 16. *Lud :* a legendary King of Britain, from whom London is supposed to derive its name.

l. 23. *The Way of the World :* a comedy by Congreve, 1700.

l. 29. *Pantaloonery :* buffoonery, clowning.

l. 33. *Gothic heads :* gargoyles.

l. 35. *Church :* St. Mary's, or the Temple Church, built by the Knights Templars, 1241.

P. 123, l. 37. *Mrs. Siddons :* one of the greatest English actresses. She first became famous in the part of Isabella in " The Fatal Marriage," by Thomas Southerne.

The Superannuated Man.

Sera tamen . . . : " Liberty has remembered me though late " (Virgil, " Eclogues," i. 28).

A Clerk . . . : Colman, " Inkle and Yarico," iii. 1. (" O'Keefe " is an error of Lamb's).

P. 124, l. 13. *Appreciate :* estimate.

l. 16. *Mincing Lane :* the East India Company's office was actually in Leadenhall Street. The change is intentional.

P. 125, l. 17. *Livelily :* clearly ; to the life.

P. 127, l. 27. *Boldero . . . :* fictitious names.

l. 28. *Esto perpetua ! :* " Last for ever " (Latin).

l. 34. *Bastille :* the State prison in Paris, destroyed by the people in the French Revolution.

P. 128, ll. 13–14. *I have a . . . home-feeling of :* I feel at home in.

ll. 26–27. *That's born . . . :* Middleton, " The Mayor of Queensborough," I, i, 120 :—

" . . . he that's born and has his years come to him In a rough desert."

P. 129, l. 5. *Rule-of-three :* proportion.

l. 16. *A Tragedy :* " The Vestal Virgin," Act V, Sc. 1.

l. 17. *Howard :* a seventeenth-century historian and poet. He collaborated with Dryden in " The Indian Queen."

l. 26. *In the state militant :* still fighting, *i.e.* working.

NOTES

P. 130, l. 15. *Gresham :* the founder of the Royal Exchange (1519–1579), and a great financier and merchant.

  Whittington : thrice Lord Mayor of London (about 1360–1425).

l. 24. *Aquinas :* St. Thomas Aquinas (1227–1274), an Italian divine of profound learning.

l. 25. *My mantle . . . . :* as Elijah bequeathed his mantle to Elisha, 1 Kings xix. 19.

l. 34. *Carthusian :* one of the Carthusian order of monks, founded A.D. 1086 at Chartreuse, in France.

P. 131, l. 2. *Bond Street :* to suggest the fashionable quarter of London, in contrast to the streets associated with the company's offices.

l. 12. *Everlasting flint :* " Romeo and Juliet," Act II, Sc. vi, l. 17.

  Vocal : resounding.

l. 13. *'Change time :* business hours at the Royal Exchange.

l. 14. *Elgin marbles :* fragments of Greek sculpture, chiefly from the Parthenon, at Athens. They were collected and brought to England by Lord Elgin in 1802, and bought by the British Museum in 1816.

l. 23. *Genius :* spirit peculiar to the day.

ll. 27–28. *Washed the Ethiop white :* "made Black Monday a pleasant day." For the allusion see Jeremiah xiii. 23.

l. 28. *Black :* dismal, because it meant returning to work.

  Is gone of : has become of.

l. 34. *Cantle :* fragment, piece.

P. 132, l. 3. *Lucretian :* like the spectator's pleasure described by the Latin poet Lucretius : " It is a pleasure to stand upon the shore and to see ships tossed upon the sea ; a pleasure to stand in the window of a castle and to see a battle and the adventures thereof below. . . ."

l. 11. *Operative :* working.

ll. 14–15. *Bowl . . . fiends :* " Hamlet," II, ii, 490–491 :—

  " And bowl the round nave down the hill of heaven
  As low as to the fiends ! "

ll. 17–18. *Retired Leisure . . . trim gardens :* Milton, " Il Penseroso " :—

  " Retired Leisure,
  That in trim gardens takes his pleasure."

l. 19. *Vacant :* free from care, on holiday.

l. 22.   *Cum dignitate :* an abbreviation of Cicero's *otium cum dignitate,* dignified leisure.

l. 26.   *Opus operatum est :* the work is finished (Latin).

l. 28.   *The day :* my life.

Rejoicings upon the New Year's Coming of Age.

Coming of Age : reaching his majority, the age of twenty-one.

P. 133, l. 4.   *The Festivals :* Christmas Day, The Circumcision, Epiphany, Candlemas Day, Lady Day, All Saints, All Souls, and The Apostles' Days.

l. 10.   *The Fasts :* days, such as Ash Wednesday and Good Friday, on which the church enjoins fasting.

l. 14.   *Ash Wednesday :* the first day of Lent.

l. 16.   *Domine :* schoolmaster—from the discipline required in Lent.

l. 17.   *Vigil :* the day and night immediately preceding a festival.

l. 19.   *To their day :* punctually.
          Covers : places at table.

l. 28.   *Shrove Tuesday :* the last day before Lent.
          Moveables : festivals, the date of which varies from year to year.

l. 33.   *Lady Day :* March 25th.

ll. 33–34. *Kept . . . aloof : i.e.* acted like a Lady.

l. 35.   *Twelfth Day :* January 6th, also called Epiphany.

l. 37.   *Frost-cake :* a cake with icing like hoar frost.
          Epiphanous : a word coined for the sake of the pun, and probably equivalent to " diaphanous," transparent.

P. 134, l. 1.   *Green . . . white :* according as they occurred in summer or winter.

l. 2.   *Lent and his family :* the forty fast days of Lent.

l. 8.   *April Fool :* April 1st.

l. 10.   *Erra Pater :* an eminent Jewish astrologer.

l. 12.   *A scheme :* an astrological forecast, a horoscope.

l. 14.   *Twenty-First of June :* usually considered the longest day.

l. 15.   *Twenty-Second . . . :* the shortest day.

l. 18.   *Lord Mayor's Day :* November 9th.

l. 19.   *Barons :* sides ; joints of beef.

l. 21.   *Sackcloth :* the sign of penitence.
          Bib . . . : required because he was not accustomed to feasting.

l. 24.   *Dried ling :* salted fish such as was largely used during Lent instead of meat, which was forbidden.

NOTES

l. 28.   *Custard :* a feature of Lord Mayors' banquets.
l. 33.   *Cock broth :* cock-fighting was commonly associated with Shrove Tuesday.
l. 35.   *Pheasant :* shot on the previous day, on the opening of the season.
ll. 35–36.   *No love lost :* no loss of good-feeling. The phrase usually implies an unfriendly relation.
l. 36.   *The Last of Lent :* Good Friday.
l. 36–37.   *Spunging upon . . . :* staving off the fasts of Lent with the fried pancakes associated with Shrove Tuesday.
P. 135, ll. 3–4.   *Thirtieth of January :* the day of Charles I's execution, 1649.
l. 7.   *Calf's head :* a symbol of the execution. After the Restoration, Puritans often celebrated this event, in secret, by feasts including such dishes.
ll. 8–9.   *Incontinently :* immediately.
ll. 9–10.   *March Manyweathers :* perhaps the last three days of March, associated with variable weather.
l. 12.   *Herodias' daughter :* the dancer who obtained from King Herod the head of John the Baptist on a platter. St. Matthew xiv. 6–12.
l. 14.   *Stomach :* appetite.
l. 15.   *Restorative :* a pun on " Restoration Day."
ll. 15–16.   *Oak Apple :* worn by the Royalists on Restoration Day—May 29th—in memory of Charles I's escape from the Roundheads after the battle of Worcester by hiding in an oak. May 29th was the day of Charles II's birth and of his Restoration.
l. 19.   *Twelfth of August . . . :* the birthday of George IV, who was a Whig in politics.
ll. 20–21.   *Twenty-Third of April :* St. George's Day, which had begun to be celebrated by Tories as the king's birthday.
l. 27.   *Fine clothes :* symbols of the festivities.
l. 33.   *Rounded :* whispered.
l. 34.   *Bi-geny :* having two birthdays ; being born on two different days.
l. 35.   *Candlemas :* February 2nd. In the Roman Catholic Church the priests at this festival bless the candles, which are afterwards carried in procession.
P. 136, l. 3.   *The same lady :* Candlemas Day is the feast of the Purification of the Virgin Mary.
l. 7.   *Founder :* of the feast, *i.e.* New Year's Day.
l. 15.   *Quarter Days :* the four days on which rent is paid for the preceding quarter of the year.

l. 17. *"New Brooms"* : which "sweep clean."
l. 19. *Fifth of November:* Guy Fawkes' Day.
l. 26. *Boutefeu:* incendiary; firebrand (French).
l. 29. *Put beside . . . :* put out in . . .
l. 33. *Mumchance:* silent.
P. 137, ll. 4–5. *Greek Calends, Latter Lammas:* non-existent days. The Calends was the first day of the month in the Roman system; it does not appear in the Greek.
l. 10. *for the nonce:* for the occasion.
l. 11. *"Miserere":* the penitential Psalm li., which begins "Miserere mei, Domine."
l. 12. *Mumping:* mumbling.
ll. 12–13. *Old Mortification:* Ash Wednesday.
l. 20. *Burden:* chorus.
l. 28. *Kept Lent:* kept what had been lent to them.
l. 29. *Valentine's Day:* February 14th.
l. 31. *Dog Days:* the hottest days in summer, associated with the rising of the Dog-Star, Sirius.
P. 138, l. 2. *Ember Days:* twelve fast days, kept on the first Wednesday, Friday, and Saturday after the first Sunday in Lent, Whitsunday, Holyrood Day (September 14th), and St. Lucy's Day (December 13th).
l. 4. *Septuagesima:* the third Sunday before Lent.
l. 7. *Rogation Days:* the three days preceding Ascension Day.
l. 8. *Putting the question:* a pun on *rogatio* (Latin), "asking"; making a proposal of marriage.
l. 9. *At a distance:* by the interval between the days.
l. 14. *Doited:* in her dotage.
ll. 22–23. *Eve of St. Christopher:* July 24th, the Day itself being July 25th.
l. 27. *On the bat's back . . . :* "The Tempest," Act V, Sc. i, l. 91.
l. 29. *Aves, Penitentiaries:* prayers, and penitential psalms.

Old China.

P. 139, l. 18. *Terra firma:* solid earth.
l. 24. *Mandarin:* a Chinese nobleman or official.
l. 29. *Hither:* nearest the spectator.
P. 140, l. 2. *Hay:* an old English country dance.
l. 3. *Couchant:* lying down.
l. 5. *Cathay:* China.
l. 6. *Cousin:* actually his sister, Mary Lamb.

l. 7. *Hyson :* strong green tea.

l. 9. *Speciosa miracula :* beautiful marvels.

l. 35. *Folio Beaumont and Fletcher :* the first collected edition of the plays of Beaumont and Fletcher, published in 1647.

P. 141, l. 19. *Corbeau :* black suit.

l. 28. *Print :* engraving.

l. 29. *Lionardo :* Leonardo da Vinci (1452-1519), the great Italian artist.

l. 34. *Colnaghi's :* a well-known firm of printsellers.

l. 35. *a wilderness of :* "The Merchant of Venice," Act III, Sc 1, l. 106.

l. 37. *Enfield, Potter's Bar :* in Middlesex, just north of London.

Waltham : in Essex.

P. 142, l. 10. *Izaak Walton :* author of "The Compleat Angler " (1593-1683).

l. 11. *The Lea :* a tributary of the Thames at London.

l. 16. *Piscator :* a well-to-do angler in Walton's book.

ll. 25-26. *The battle of Hexham, the Surrender of Calais :* historical plays by George Colman, written in 1789 and 1791 respectively.

l. 36. *Rosalind, Viola :* the heroines of "As You Like It" and "Twelfth Night."

P. 144, l. 21. *Cotton :* Charles Cotton (1630-1687), of Beresford Hall, Staffordshire. He was author of one of the dialogues in the fifth edition of "The Compleat Angler," and of the "New Year Poem" from which Lamb here quotes.

P. 145, l. 28. *Crœsus :* King of Lydia, in Asia Minor, in the sixth century B.C. He was believed to be the wealthiest man in the world.

l. 29. *R—— :* Baron Nathan Meyer de Rothschild (1777-1896), a great Jewish banker and financier.

l. 92. *Bed-tester :* the canopy over the head of a bed.

l. 33. *Madonna-ish :* with something of the look attributed by painters to the Virgin Mary, or Madonna.

WILLIAM HAZLITT

William Hazlitt (1778-1830), born at Maidstone, was the son of a Unitarian minister. His early inclination for painting, which he soon abandoned, appears indirectly in many of his essays. In literature he excelled in

intellectual and imaginative criticism, especially of the
Elizabethan age, as in " Characters of Shakespeare's
Plays " (1817–1818), " Lectures on the English Poets "
(1818–1819), and " The English Comic Writers "
(1819). His appreciation of his contemporaries, in
" The Spirit of the Age " (1825), while generally just
and penetrating, is sometimes warped by his revolutionary opinions and the animosities of a passionate nature
with a touch of misanthropy. His familiar essays in
" Table Talk " (1821–1822), and the posthumous
" Sketches and Essays," which contain some of his best
work, have less charm than " The Essays of Elia," but
the tone is more virile and the style more brilliant and
robust.

On a Sun-dial.

To carve . . . : from " 3 Henry VI," Act II, Sc. v, l.
24.
P. 149, l. 4. *Conceit :* a striking thought.
   l. 18. *Brenta :* a river flowing into the Gulf of Venice
to the north of the Po and the Adige.
P. 150, ll. 16–17. *" Morals on the time " :* from " As You
Like It," Act II, Sc. vii, l. 29.
P. 152, l. 7. *Memento mori :* " Remember that you must
die " (Latin) ; a reminder that death is inevitable.
   l. 15. *L'Amour . . . :* " Love makes the time pass "
(French).
   ll. 16–17. *Le Temps . . . :* " Time makes love pass."
   l. 21. *Pour passer le temps :* " to pass the time."
   l. 24. *In transitu :* " in transition " (Latin) ; in a state of
perpetual movement or flux.
P. 153, l. 5. *Caput mortuum :* worthless residue (Latin). In
alchemy, the term was applied to the residuum left after
distillation of any substance.
P. 154, l. 7. *Rousseau :* a great French writer (1712–1778)
on social and political theory, and on education. His
greatest works are his novel, " La Nouvelle Héloïse,"
the " Contrat Social," the educational treatise,
" Emile," and his " Confessions."
   The account referred to occurs in Part II, Book xi
of " La Nouvelle Héloïse."
   l. 12. *Allons . . . :* " Come, boy ; I am more of a child
than you " (" La Nouvelle Héloïse," Part I, Book i).
   l. 27. *" Lend it both . . ." :* " Hamlet," Act I, Sc. ii,
l. 249.

NOTES

P. 155, ll. 13-15. *"With its brazen throat . . ."*: an inaccurate quotation of "King John," III. iii. 37-
39 :—

"... the midnight bell
Did, with his iron tongue and brazen mouth,
Sound on into the drowsy ear of night."

ll. 15-16. *"Swinging slow . . ."*: Milton, "Il Penseroso," 76.

P. 156, l. 3-4. *De non . . .*: "The same reasoning applies
to things that don't appear as to things that don't
exist" (Latin).

l. 6. *In vacuo:* in a vacuum (Latin) ; in the void.

l. 9. *Bona fide:* trustworthy.

l. 28. *Death-watch:* a popular name for certain insects
which produce a ticking noise.

P. 157, ll. 4-5. *"The poor man's only music"*: "Frost at
Midnight," 29.

ll. 32-34. *"Goes to church . . ."*: "Twelfth Night,"
Act I, Sc. iii, ll. 119-122.

l. 33. *Coranto:* a quick, lively dance, distinguished by a
running or gliding step.

ll. 33-34. *Cinquepace:* a dance, the steps of which were
regulated by the number five.

P. 158, ll. 9-11. *"Sing . . ."*: Wordsworth, "The Fountain," 13-15.

ll. 16-17. *Beggar's Opera:* a musical play by John Gay
(1728). Macheath, the highwayman, is arrested and
sent to Newgate, but escapes through the agency of the
warder's daughter, Lucy.

ll. 17-18. *Venice Preserved:* a tragedy in blank verse
(1682) by Otway (1652-1685). The alternative title is
"A Plot Discovered."

l. 20. *Sterne:* a reference to "Tristram Shandy," by
Laurence Sterne (1713-1768), in which Toby is the
hero's uncle.

l. 24. *"Why dance ye . . ."*: source unidentified.

P. 159. l. 4. *"As in a map . . ."*: Cowper, "The Task,"
vi. 17.

ll. 35-36. *"With light-winged toys . . ."*: "Othello," I.
iii. 268-269.

"... light wing'd toys
Of feather'd Cupid. . . ."

P. 160, ll. 3-4. *"Diana . . ."*: Diana, or Artemis, was the
goddess of hunting, and her attributes were usually the
bow, arrow, and quiver, or the spear, stags, and dogs.

255

Hazlitt here refers, presumably, to the statue of Artemis, with a fawn, preserved in the Louvre, in Paris.

ll. 16–17. " *With lack-lustre eye* " : " As You Like It," Act II, Sc. vII, l. 21.

l. 19. *Mr. Shandy* : in Sterne's " Tristram Shandy." He paid special attention to winding up the clock at regular intervals.

On Nicknames.

Hæ nugæ . . . : " These trifles lead to serious things " (Horace, " Ars Poetica," 451–452).

P. 161, l. 9. *Vitelli, Orsini* : rival families or parties in Rome. The Orsini were prominent supporters of the Guelph, the Vitelli of the Ghibelline, faction.

ll. 9–10. *Guelph, Ghibellines* : parties in mediæval Italy, supporting respectively the Pope and the Emperor.

l. 10. *The civil wars* : the Wars of the Roses, 1455–1485, and the Civil War, 1642–1646.

l. 11. *The League* : the Holy League (1571), founded in France by the family of Guise, for the maintenance of the Roman Catholic religion and the exclusion of Protestant princes from the throne.

l. 18. *Foxe's Book of Martyrs* : John Foxe (1516–1587) was a Presbyterian churchman. The first English edition of his " Actes and Monuments," popularly known as " The Book of Martyrs," was published in 1563.

l. 19. *Neale's History of the Puritans* : Daniel Neal (1678–1743) was a London clergyman whose best work was a history of the Puritans down to 1689.

l. 20. *The fires in Smithfield* : in the sixteenth century, heretics were burnt in Smithfield, an open space, situated outside the north-west walls of the city of London, and commonly used for horse and cattle markets.

l. 22. *Inquisition* : in the Roman Catholic Church, a tribunal for the suppression and punishment of heretics.

P. 162, ll. 3–4. " *The priest . . .* " : " The Beggar's Opera," i. 1.

l. 18. *Barbare* : a barbarian, as opposed to a civilised man.

l. 20. *Anti-Jacobin* : opposed to the Jacobins, an extreme section of the revolutionary party in France, in 1789, and to their opinions. They advocated reason as against authority in politics, and applied the ideal of equality to an impracticable degree in social life. Their most famous members were Marat, Danton, and Robespierre.

ll. 33–34. *"Malignants"* : a nickname applied by the Roundheads to the Royalists in the Civil War, 1642–1648.

l. 35. *Noms-de-guerre* : " war-names " (French) ; names assumed by persons engaged in some enterprise.

P. 163, ll. 5–7. *"Sound them . , "*. a version of " Julius Caesar," I. II. 145–147 :—

" Sound them, it doth become the mouth as well ;
Weigh them, it is as heavy ; conjure with 'em,
Brutus will start a spirit as soon as Caesar."

l. 12. *Buonaparte* : Napoleon was born in Corsica. The eminent character was Coleridge.

l. 14. *Mr. Southey* : Robert Southey (1774–1843), the friend of Wordsworth and Coleridge, was by this time extremely conservative, and Poet Laureate. He was thus obnoxious to Hazlitt.

l. 24. *Hath Britain . . .* : " Cymbeline," Act III, Sc. IV, ll. 135–139.

P. 165, l. 8. *"Brevity . . . wit"* : " Hamlet," Act II, Sc. II, l. 90.

l. 11. *Carte-blanche* : full scope.

ll. 20–21. *"The unbought grace of life . . ."* : Burke, " Reflections on the Revolution."

ll. 22–24. *"Leave the will puzzled . . ."* : from the same source.

ll. 24–25. *"No Popery" cry* : the outcry and rioting, generally known as the Gordon Riots, in June 1780, at the culmination of the agitation, under the leadership of Lord George Gordon, against the Roman Catholics.

P. 166, l. 27. *In vacuo* : " in a vacuum " (Latin).

P. 167, ll. 9–10. *"As rage . ."* : " Troilus and Cressida," I. III. 51–52 ·

". . . why then the thing of courage
As roused with rage with rage doth sympathize."

ll. 13–14. *"A nickname . . ."* : Sir Thomas Browne, " Hydriotaphia," iv. 23.

l. 33. *"The Talents"* : the ministry of Lord Grenville (1806–1807), which included Fox and Addington.

P. 168, l. 5. *Canning . . . a noble lord* : Canning so ridiculed Henry Addington, afterwards Lord Sidmouth.

ll. 10–11. *With so small a web . . . :* " Othello," II. 1. 167–168 :—

> " With as little a web as this will I ensnare as great a fly as Cassio."

l. 22. *Called out of their names :* addressed by a wrong or inaccurate name.

l. 29. *" Causa . . ." :* " The cause of the cause is the cause of the effect " (Latin).

l. 37. *Hotspur :* Henry Percy, son of the Earl of Northumberland, in " 1 Henry IV." He says to Mortimer (I. III. 224–225) :—

> " I'll have a starling shall be taught to speak Nothing but ' Mortimer'."

P. 170, l. 8. *Junius :* the anonymous author of the " Letters of Junius " (1769–1771), which bore on the title-page the motto, " Stat nominis umbra " (There remains the shadow of a name) from Lucan, " Pharsalia," i. 135.

ll. 11–12. *Michael Angelo :* one of the greatest Italian sculptors, painters, and architects (1475–1564).

John Cavanagh.

This is an extract, complete in itself, from Hazlitt's essay " The Indian Jugglers."

P. 170, l. 24. *Has not left his peer :* " Lycidas," l. 9.

P. 171, l. 2. *The Roman poet :* Horace, in his " Odes," III. i. 40.

ll. 6–7. *" In the instant " :* " Macbeth," Act I, Sc. v, l. 55.

ll. 7–8. *Domestic treason . . . :* " Macbeth," III. II. 24–26 :—

> Treason has done his worst : nor steel, nor poison, Malice domestic, foreign levy, nothing, Can touch him further.

l. 11. *Making it :* gaining the point by his stroke.

P. 172, l. 7. *Brougham :* (1778–1868) Lord Chancellor, writer, and one of the founders of the " Edinburgh Review."

l. 8. *Canning :* Foreign Minister (1822–1827), Prime Minister (1827), and founder of " The Anti-Jacobin." His politics were thus opposed to Hazlitt's.

l. 9. *The Quarterly :* the " Quarterly Review " was founded in 1809 by John Murray as a Tory rival to the " Edinburgh Review." It made virulent attacks on Lamb, Keats, Leigh Hunt, and Hazlitt himself.

Let ball : a ball which touches the net or an opponent but is otherwise good is called a let ball and is considered out of play.

ll. 9–10. *The Edinburgh Review :* the Whig review founded in 1802, and edited at this time by Francis Jeffrey. It was notable for its attacks on the Lake poets.

l. 10. *Cobbett :* (1766–1835) the son of a farm-labourer, and by turns soldier, journalist, and politician. He wrote a simple, vigorous style, and is best remembered for his " Rural Rides."

Junius : see note to P. 170, l. 8.

l. 12. *Fourteen :* fifteen points were required to make the game.

l. 25. *Ace :* a point in the game.

l. 33. *Rosemary Branch :* a pleasure resort.

P. 173, l. 1. *All :* each.

l. 18. *Clenched fist :* the ball was normally struck with the open hand.

l. 19. *Copenhagen House :* a pleasure resort.

l. 35. *The balance :* the balance of power.

l. 36. *Castlereagh :* Foreign Secretary, 1812–1822.

P. 174, l. 1. *Mr. Croker :* (1780–1857) a prominent Tory politician, Secretary to the Admiralty, and a contributor to the " Quarterly Review."

l. 5. *Mr. Murray :* John Murray (1778–1843), son of the founder of the publishing house.

ll. 7–8. *Hungerford Stairs :* on the Thames near Charing Cross.

l. 17. *Racket-player :* a player at rackets, a game played with ball and rackets in a four-walled court.

l. 29. *The Fleet, King's Bench :* debtors' prisons, where the prisoners were allowed to play games.

P. 175, l. 6. *Mr. Peel :* later Sir Robert Peel (1700–1850).

l. 7. *Speaker :* the chairman of the House of Commons.

ll. 12–13. *Let no rude hand . . . :* from Wordsworth, " Ellen Irwin."

l. 13. *Hic Jacet :* " Here lies " ; *i.e.* epitaph.

R. L. STEVENSON

Robert Louis Stevenson (1850–1894) was born and educated in Edinburgh. In 1875 he was called to the Bar, but never practised. He was forced to travel for his health, and finally settled in Samoa. His fame rests chiefly on " Treasure Island," " Kidnapped," " The

Black Arrow," and similar tales of adventure, and on collections of essays, such as " Virginibus Puerisque," in all of which he employs a brilliant style carefully polished to a French clearness and precision.

An Apology for Idlers.

P. 179, ll. 2–3. *Lèse-respectability :* a crime against respect-ability—a word coined on the analogy of " lèse-majesty."

ll. 23, 24. *Alexander . . . Diogenes :* Diogenes was a Greek philosopher of austere life. When Alexander the Great, meeting him in Corinth, asked if he could oblige him in any way, he answered, " Yes, by standing out of my sunshine." Alexander admired his independence.

P. 180, l. 1. *Barbarians :* the Goths, under Alaric, who captured and sacked Rome in A.D. 410.

l. 2. *Fathers :* the Roman Senators.

l. 22. *Montenegro :* a small country included, since 1918, in Yugoslavia.

ll. 23–24. *Richmond :* a park near the Thames as it enters London.

l. 27. *Macaulay :* the essayist and historian (1800–1859), who was remarkable for his precocity as a schoolboy.

l. 34. *Johnson :* Samuel Johnson (1709–1784), author of the famous Dictionary, and the subject of Boswell's " Life." He was at Oxford for fourteen months, but left without a degree.

P. 181, l. 7. *The Lady of Shalott :* in Tennyson's well-known poem of that name.

l. 19. *Emphyteusis :* in Roman law, a perpetual right in a piece of land, for which a yearly rent was paid to the proprietor.

l. 20. *Stillicide :* a restraint preventing a Roman pro-prietor from building to the extremity of his estate.

l. 26. *Dickens :* the Victorian novelist (1812–1870), whose parents were extremely poor, and who therefore received little regular education.

Balzac : Honoré de Balzac (1799–1850), perhaps the greatest of French novelists, and author of the collection of romances, called " La Comédie Humaine," in which he deals with all aspects of French society. Most of his life he was very poor.

l. 33. *Burn :* small stream (Scots).

P. 182, l. 1. *Mr. Worldly Wiseman :* in Bunyan's " Pilgrim's Progress," an inhabitant of the town of Carnal Policy, who tries to dissuade Christian from going on his journey.

l. 23. *Sloughs, Thickets :* difficulties, like the Slough of Despond, such as met Christian on his journey.

ll. 25-26. *By root-of-heart :* by rote, by heart.

P. 183, l. 4. *Workhouse :* poorhouse.

ll. 6-7. *Sainte-Beuve :* the greatest of French critics (1804-1869), chiefly famous for his periodical essays " Causeries du Lundi."

P. 184, l. 18. *Belvedere :* an open turret on the top of a house, commanding a good view.

l. 23. *Sublunary :* beneath the moon, *i.e.* earthly.

l. 33. *Shepherd . . . hawthorn :* Milton, " L'Allegro," ll. 67-68.

P. 185, l. 34. *Breeched :* put into trousers.

P. 186, l. 28. *Colonel Newcome :* a character in Thackeray's novel, " The Newcomes." He is a simple-minded and honourable gentleman.

l. 29. *Fred Bayham :* a jolly character in " The New-comes."

l. 31. *Mr. Barnes :* Barnes Newcome, a mean villain in " The Newcomes."

Falstaff : the fat knight and " boastful soldier " in Shakespeare's " Henry IV."

l. 33. *Barabbas :* the Jew, similar in character to Shylock, in Marlowe's play, " The Jew of Malta."

l. 35. *Northcote :* (1746-1831), a portrait-painter and author, who was assistant to Sir Joshua Reynolds. Hazlitt published some of his " Conversations."

P. 188, ll. 13-14. *Body of Morality :* the whole set of rules governing human conduct.

l. 27. *Circumlocution Office :* a satirical name for a Govern-ment department in Dickens's " Little Dorrit."

P. 189, ll. 5-6. *So careless . . . life :* " In Memoriam," liv.

l. 9. *Sir Thomas Lucy :* There was a tradition, now dis-proved, that Shakespeare's poaching of deer in the park of Sir Thomas Lucy, near Stratford, was the cause of his going to London.

El Dorado.

El Dorado : " the land of gold " (Spanish). The name was generally applied, in the sixteenth century, to the land between the Orinoco and the Amazon.

P. 191, l. 13. *Amulets :* any object, such as a gem, carried on the person as a charm against harm.

EIGHT ESSAYISTS

l. 28. *Carlyle :* the essayist and historian (1795–1881), whose " History of Frederick the Great " is among his best works.

l. 33. *Alexander :* Alexander the Great, King of Macedon (356–323 B.C.).

l. 35. *Gibbon :* in his Autobiography, Gibbon (1737–1794) thus describes the completion of his great work, " The History of the Decline and Fall of the Roman Empire " : " It was on the . . . 27th of June, 1787, between the hours of eleven and twelve, that I wrote the last lines of the last page, in a summer-house in my garden. . . . I will not dissemble the first emotions of joy on recovery of my freedom, and, perhaps, the establishment of my fame. But my pride was soon humbled, and a sober melancholy was spread over my mind, by the idea that I had taken an everlasting leave of an old and agreeable companion, and that, whatsoever might be the future date of my *History,* the life of the historian must be short and precarious."

P. 192, l. 27. *The Preacher :* a translation of the title " Ecclesiastes." For the quotation see Ecclesiastes xii. 12.

P. 193, l. 12. *Chimæra :* an extravagant fancy : originally, a fabulous monster, with a lion's head, a goat's body, and a serpent's tail.

Walking Tours.

P. 194, l. 3. *Humours :* moods, states of mind.

l. 18. *Curaçoa :* a liqueur first made at Curaçoa, in the West Indies.

l. 19. *Brown John :* an earthenware vessel or bottle.

l. 27. *Night-cap :* a dram taken before going to bed.

P. 195, l. 25. *Christian :* the hero of Bunyan's " Pilgrim's Progress." After Christian reached the Cross and the Sepulchre, his burden, of sin, fell from his back, and he " gave three leaps for joy, and went on singing."

l. 29. *Lees :* dregs, what is left over.

l. 35. *Abudah :* a merchant of Bagdad, haunted every night by an old hag.

P. 196, l. 26. *Troubadour :* minstrel.

P. 199, ll. 26–29. *" Though ye take . . ." :* a quotation from Milton's " Areopagitica."

l. 32. *The elixir of life :* a liquor supposed to have the power of indefinitely prolonging life.

P. 200, ll. 18–19. *The new Héloïse :* a romance by Rousseau, " La Nouvelle Héloïse " (1761).

l. 19. *Llangollen :* a town on the Dee, in N.E. Wales. The Vale of Llangollen is famous for its scenery, and much visited by tourists.

l. 25. *Heine :* one of the greatest of German lyric poets (1797–1856).

Tristram Shandy : the best-known work of Laurence Sterne (1713–1768).

P. 201, l. 4. *Humours :* oddities.

l. 11. *" Happy thinking" :* a phrase from " The Rigs of Barley."

l. 24. *Gear :* property, possessions.

P. 202, l. 8. *Philistines :* a term used by Matthew Arnold to describe people deficient in culture and enlightenment.

The Beggar.

P. 203, l. 31. *Queen Mab :* a poem published by Shelley in 1813, when he was eighteen.

P. 204, l. 22. *The Mutiny :* the Indian Mutiny, 1857–1858.

l. 37. *Agnosticism :* a word coined in 1869 by Professor Huxley : the belief that anything beyond material objects and the human mind is unknowable.

Beer and skittles : Bohemian pleasures.

P. 205, l. 3. *Rossetti :* Dante Gabriel Rossetti (1828–1882), one of the Pre-Raphaelites, and author of " The Blessed Damozel," and translations from Dante. He has all the qualities that Stevenson mentions in the next few lines.

l. 27. *Rodomontade :* a boastful speech.

l. 33. *Revisit . . . :* from " Hamlet," I. iv. 51–54 :—
" What may this mean,
That thou, dead corse, again, in complete steel,
Revisit'st thus the glimpses of the moon,
Making night hideous?"

l. 35. *The spacious days :* from Tennyson's " Dream of Fair Women " :—
" Dan Chaucer, the first warbler, whose sweet breath
Preluded those melodious bursts, that fill
The spacious times of great Elizabeth
With sounds that echo still."

P. 206, l. 1. *The Blackfriars :* an apartment in the dissolved monastery of the Black Friars, adapted for a play-house, and purchased by James Burbage in 1596.

l. 2. *Mr. Burbage :* Richard Burbage, son of James, and

an actor of leading parts, such as Hamlet, on the Elizabethan stage.

l. 4. *Unhousel'd . . . :* "Hamlet," Act I. Sc. v, l. 77.
Unhousel'd : not having received the sacrament.
Disappointed : not appointed or prepared.
Unanel'd : not having received extreme unction.

ll. 14–17. *Comiston, Hermitage of Braid, Hunters' Tryst, Fairmilehead :* in the Braid Hills, just south of Edinburgh.

G. K. CHESTERTON

Gilbert Keith Chesterton (1874–1936) was born in Kensington and studied at St. Paul's School and the Slade School of Art. He gives the impression of abounding energy and spontaneity, and there is usually sound sense beneath the glitter of his paradox. His work is mainly directed against the narrowness of Puritanism, and finds expression through such various channels as the Father Brown detective stories, historical works, novels, poems, and essays. He also wrote lively studies of Dickens, Browning, and Chaucer.

On Lying in Bed.

P. 209, l. 6. *Aspinall :* a brand of enamel.

l. 21. *Cyrano de Bergerac :* the hero of the play of that name, by the French dramatist Edmond Rostand (1868–1920).

l. 22. *" Il me faut . . . " :* " I must have giants."

P. 210, ll. 7–8. *" Use not . . . do " :* St. Matthew vi. 7.

ll. 12–13. *Macedonian Massacres :* the massacres of Bulgarians by Turkish irregular troops in 1876. Similar massacres of Armenians occurred in Asia Minor and in Constantinople in 1896.

ll. 29–30. *Debarred from . . . rights :* when this essay was written, women had not yet been given the vote.

P. 211, l. 2. *Michaelangelo :* one of the greatest Italian sculptors, painters, and architects (1475–1564).

l. 5. *Sistine Chapel :* a chapel in the Vatican, at Rome, built in the fifteenth century, and notable for the number of great artists employed in decorating the walls.

l. 24. *Ibsenite :* Henrik Ibsen (1828–1906), a Norwegian, and one of the greatest modern dramatists, was fond of portraying the self-righteous and narrow-minded type of character here alluded to.

NOTES

The Architect of Spears.

P. 213, l. 7. *Gothic :* a style of architecture prevalent in Western Europe from the twelfth century to the sixteenth. Its most prominent characteristic is the pointed arch.

l. 10. *Classical :* belonging to Greece and Rome.

l. 30. *The Censor of Plays :* the Lord Chamberlain.

P. 214, l. 2. *Bill Bailey :* a popular song about the time this essay was written, *i.e.* about thirty years ago.

l. 5. *Miserere seat :* a hinged folding-seat in a church stall. When turned up it shows a bracket on which a standing person can lean back. It is made out of pity for the aged or infirm.

l. 29. *Raphael :* the great Italian painter (1483–1520).

P. 215, l. 22. *Pagoda :* idol-house : temple.

P. 216, l. 8. *The awful evangelist :* Ezekiel xvii.

l. 17. *Trowel and . . . sword :* Nehemiah iv. 17.

l. 27. *Crypt :* underground cell or chapel.

l. 30. *Gloriole :* halo.

On the Cryptic and the Elliptic.

P. 219, ll. 4–5. *Funeral Speech :* " Julius Caesar," III. п.

P. 221, l. 5. *Yellow journalism :* the sensational journalism which developed in America about 1880.

l. 9. *Nemesis :* retributive punishment.

l. 29. *Vanity Fair :* Thackeray's novel, at the end of which are described Major Dobbin and his daughter Jane.

P. 222, ll. 3–4. *George R. Sims :* a lesser novelist and journalist of the late nineteenth century.

l. 5. *Maeterlinck :* a Belgian mystical poet and dramatist (1862–1949), best known in England as author of " L'Oiseau Bleu " (1909).

l. 11. *Browning :* his poetry is remarkable for its frequent depth and obscurity.

l. 13. *Meredith :* the great Victorian novelist, noted for his fine imagination.

The Worship of the Wealthy.

P. 224, l. 2. *Mr. Carnegie :* the Scottish-American millionaire and philanthropist.

l. 3. *Mars :* the Roman god of war.

l. 7. *Pierpont Morgan :* a well-known American banker and millionaire.

l. 8. *Apollo :* the Greek god of music and poetry, and the type of manly youth and beauty.

l. 35. *Transcendental :* concerned with what is independent of experience in human knowledge.

Pantheism : a form of philosophy which considers everything as a manifestation of God, or one absolute being.

l. 36. *Neo-Catholicism :* the liberal Catholicism of Lammenais about 1830 ; also that of a party in the Church of England which imitates Roman Catholic doctrine and ritual, and desires reunion with the Church of Rome.

P. 225, l. 4. *Loisy :* a French theologian.

l. 6. *Harnack :* a great German theologian (1851–1930) who laid great stress on practical Christianity.

P. 226, l. 4. *Midas :* the Phrygian king with the golden touch.

l. 10. *Catherine wheel :* an ornamented circular window, with radiating divisions of various colours.

l. 29. *Beit :* Sir Otto Beit (1865–1930), a great financier and art collector.

l. 30. *Whiteley :* William Whiteley (1831–1907), born at Wakefield, came to London as a shopman, and in a short time established a gigantic establishment, which, with its branches, became known as " The Universal Provider."

l. 37. *Acheron :* a river of Hades or the lower world of the Greeks ; here used for Hades itself.

P. 227, l. 5. *Patroclus :* the friend of Achilles in Homer's " Iliad." The elaborate funeral ceremonies are described in Book XXIII.

The Wheel.

P. 228, l. 24. *Escutcheon :* coat of arms.

l. 27. *Passant :* walking.

P. 229, l. 9. *Dream of wheels :* Ezekiel i. 15–21.

ll. 18–19. *Helmsman and chief :* " Atalanta in Calydon " (Swinburne's " Coll. Poetical Works," Heinemann, 1927, vol. ii. p. 328.)

ll. 29–30. *Mr. de Morgan :* a realistic novelist who wrote " It Never Can Happen Again " (1909).

ESSAY QUESTIONS

FRANCIS BACON

1. Illustrate from the essays (*a*) Bacon's desire to be of special service to princes, (*b*) his occasional adoption of the familiar tone.
2. Discuss Bacon's prose and its qualities.
3. Contrast the essays of Bacon with those of any other essayist represented in this volume. Illustrate by quotation, and reference to particular essays.
4. Write an essay (if possible, in the manner of Bacon) on : (*a*) Diaries ; (*b*) Foreign Travel ; (*c*) Hiking ; (*d*) Reading for Use and Reading for Pleasure.

RICHARD STEELE

1. Illustrate from his essays (*a*) Steele's moral purpose in writing ; (*b*) his chivalry. Consider what light your illustrations throw on their historical background.
2. Collect Steele's maxims on behaviour in social life. How far do they still apply ?
3. Write a note on Steele's (*a*) humour, (*b*) satire, (*c*) sentiment. Illustrate by quotation.
4. From the remarks of Bacon and Steele, write an essay on Conversation, adding advice or remarks of your own.
5. Write an essay on . (*a*) School Fashions ; (*b*) Bores ; (*c*) A Defence of Ugliness ; (*d*) Modern Affectations ; (*e*) Short-winded People.

JOSEPH ADDISON

1. Write a note on Addison's (*a*) humour, (*b*) satire.
2. From the essays of Addison and Steele, write a note on the social and political life of the Age of Anne.
3. Write an essay on : (*a*) The Modern Party System ; (*b*) The functions of the Newspaper ; (*c*) Remarks on the English by a Chinese Visitor ; (*d*) Contentment.

EIGHT ESSAYISTS

OLIVER GOLDSMITH

1. " No man ever put so much of himself into his books as Goldsmith." Discuss with reference to his essays ; and compare with his self-revelation in " The Vicar of Wakefield " and " The Deserted Village."

2. Write a note on Goldsmith's (a) use of irony ; (b) satire of clergy, doctors, and soldiers.

3. Compare the use of anecdote made by Steele and Goldsmith in their essays.

4. Write an essay on : (a) Quacks (cf. " Tono-Bungay ") ; (b) War—the Great Illusion ; (c) Philanthropy ; (d) A Modern Election.

CHARLES LAMB

1. State and discuss Lamb's defence of the town, and contrast with the views of Wordsworth.

2. Describe Lamb's character as revealed in his essays.

3. Discuss the appropriateness of Lamb's (a) personifications, (b) puns, (c) use of archaic English, (d) allusions.

4. In the manner of Lamb, or from suggestions of his, write an essay on : (a) The Charm of Old Things compared with the Charm of New ; (b) Disillusionments of Growing Up ; (c) The Good Old Days ; (d) My First Play ; (e) Relations ; (f) New Year's Day ; (g) Leisure.

5. Write an essay discussing one of the following topics : (a) The age of chivalry is gone ; (b) " Had I a son . . . he should do nothing." (c) " A thing was worth buying then, when we felt the money that we paid for it." (d) The wisdom of folly. (e) The folly of wisdom. (f) Sunday. (g) Inferiority Complexes.

WILLIAM HAZLITT

1. Illustrate from his essays Hazlitt's knowledge of (a) Shakespeare, (b) English literature, (c) the Bible. Compare him in these respects with Lamb, and account for their knowledge.

2. What do you gather from his essays as to Hazlitt's (a) relations with his contemporaries ; (b) character and tastes ; (c) political views.

3. Write a note on Hazlitt's (a) satire ; (b) use of quotations ; (c) insight into the mind ; (d) style.

ESSAY QUESTIONS

4. How are Lamb and Hazlitt characteristic writers of the Romantic Revival ?

5. Extend the essay on Nicknames.

6. Write an essay on : A great sportsman.

7. " Nicknames govern the world." " What's in a name ? " Discuss.

R. L. STEVENSON

1. Illustrate from his essays Stevenson's knowledge of the Bible and " The Pilgrim's Progress."

2. How is Stevenson's scheme of values opposed to that widely held nowadays ?

3. Write a letter to a friend giving advice for a walking tour on which he is to set out.

4. Write an essay on one of the following subjects : (a) " To travel hopefully is better than to arrive " ; (b) " The true success is to labour " ; (c) The Education of the Streets.

G. K. CHESTERTON

1. Write a note on Chesterton's use of paradox. What light does it throw on his work and character ?

2. What is the meaning of the title, " On the Cryptic and the Elliptic ? "

3. Write a note on the character of (a) Greek, (b) Norman, architecture.

4. Write an essay on one of the following subjects : (a) Widows ; (b) Blondes ; (c) Traffic ; (d) " Shockers " ; (e) The Telephone ; (f) Impenitence ; (g) The Films.

PRINTED BY R. & R. CLARK, LTD., EDINBURGH

THE SCHOLAR'S LIBRARY

Select List

DR. JOHNSON: A Selection from Boswell's Biography. Edited by M. Alderton Pink, M.A.

SHELLEY: SELECTIONS FROM HIS POETRY. Edited by F. B. Pinion.

HOMER: The Iliad and the Odyssey. Extracts from the Translations by Lang, Leaf and Myers, and Butcher and Lang. Edited by H. M. King and H. Spooner.

GREECE AND ROME: A Selection from the Works of Sir James George Frazer. Chosen by S. G. Owen.

MODERN ENGLISH PROSE. First Series. Selected and Edited by Guy Boas, M.A.

MODERN ENGLISH PROSE. Second Series. Selected and Edited by Guy Boas, M.A.

MODERN ENGLISH PROSE. Third Series. Selected and Edited by Guy Boas, M.A.

MODERN ENGLISH PROSE. Fourth Series. Selected and Edited by Guy Boas, M.A.

WORLDS TO CONQUER. Edited by P. D. Cummins.

ADVENTURE SOUGHT AND UNSOUGHT. Selected and Edited by P. D. Cummins.

SEA VOYAGES OF EXPLORATION. Selected and Edited by G. A. Sambrook, M.A.

MODERN TRAVEL: An Anthology. Selected and Edited by Frederick T. Wood, B.A., Ph.D.

MODERN AUTOBIOGRAPHY: An Anthology. Edited by Frederick T. Wood, B.A., Ph.D.

THE SCHOOLBOY IN FICTION: An Anthology. Selected and Edited by Frederick T. Wood, B.A., Ph.D.

ESSAYS AND SKETCHES. By Charles Dickens. Selected by M. Alderton Pink.

ESSAYS OF ACTION. Selected and Edited by G. F. Lamb.

MODERN PORTRAIT ESSAYS. Edited by M. A. Pink, M.A.

POINTS OF VIEW. Edited by M. A. Pink, M.A.

SCIENCE AND LITERATURE. Edited by W. Eastwood.

TOPICS AND OPINIONS. First Series. Edited by A. F. Scott, M.A.

TOPICS AND OPINIONS. Second Series. Edited by A. F. Scott, M.A.

ARNOLD: ESSAYS IN CRITICISM. Edited by S. R. LITTLEWOOD.

SHORT STORIES BY OSCAR WILDE. Edited by G. C. ANDREWS, M.A.

SHORT HISTORICAL PLAYS. By MODERN AUTHORS. Selected and Edited by E. R. WOOD.

ENGLISH LIFE IN THE EIGHTEENTH CENTURY. Selected and Edited by G. A. SAMBROOK, M.A.

ENGLISH LIFE IN THE NINETEENTH CENTURY. Selected and Edited by G. A. SAMBROOK, M.A.

MODERN POETRY, 1922–1934: AN ANTHOLOGY. Selected and Edited by MAURICE WOLLMAN, M.A.

POEMS OF THE WAR YEARS: AN ANTHOLOGY. Selected and Edited by MAURICE WOLLMAN, M.A.

POEMS OLD AND NEW: AN ANTHOLOGY. Selected and Edited by A. S. CAIRNCROSS, M.A., D.Litt.

MORE POEMS OLD AND NEW: AN ANTHOLOGY. Selected and Edited by A. S. CAIRNCROSS, M.A., D.Litt., and J. K. SCOBBIE, M.A.

LONGER POEMS OLD AND NEW. Selected and Edited by A. S. CAIRNCROSS, M.A., D.Litt.

SELECTIONS FROM SIR W. S. GILBERT. Edited by H. A. TREBLE, M.A.

MODERN SHORT STORIES. First Series. Selected and Edited by A. J. MERSON.

MODERN SHORT STORIES. Second Series. Selected and Edited by A. J. MERSON.

THE POETRY OF HISTORY. Selected and Edited by D. J. PETERS, M.A., and B. E. TOWERS, M.A.

THE SPOKEN WORD. First Series. Selected and Edited by A. F. SCOTT, M.A.

THE SPOKEN WORD. Second Series. Selected and Edited by A. F. SCOTT, M.A.

IN MEMORIAM. Edited by MICHAEL DAVIS, B.A.

THE SCHOLAR'S LIBRARY

Shakespeare

MACMILLAN & CO LTD